T0323241

DIGITAL LUXURY

DIGITAL LUXURY

Transforming Brands & Consumer Experiences

Wided Batat

Los Angeles | London | New Delhi
Singapore | Washington DC | Melbourne

Los Angeles | London | New Delhi
Singapore | Washington DC | Melbourne

SAGE Publications Ltd
1 Oliver's Yard
55 City Road
London EC1Y 1SP

SAGE Publications Inc.
2455 Teller Road
Thousand Oaks, California 91320

SAGE Publications India Pvt Ltd
B 1/I 1 Mohan Cooperative Industrial Area
Mathura Road
New Delhi 110 044

SAGE Publications Asia-Pacific Pte Ltd
3 Church Street
#10-04 Samsung Hub
Singapore 049483

Editor: Matthew Waters
Editorial assistant: Jasleen Kaur
Production editor: Sarah Cooke
Copyeditor: Jane Fricker
Proofreader: Fabienne Pedroletti-Gray
Indexer: Judith Lavender
Marketing manager: Lucia Sweet
Cover design: Francis Kenney
Typeset by: C&M Digitals (P) Ltd, Chennai, India

Library of Congress Control Number: 2019937275

British Library Cataloguing in Publication data

A catalogue record for this book is available from the British Library

ISBN 978-1-5264-5893-3
ISBN 978-1-5264-5894-0 (pbk)

CONTENTS

LIST OF FIGURES

LIST OF TABLES

LIST OF TRENDS

ABOUT THE AUTHOR

Wided Batat is a marketing professor and an internationally renowned expert and speaker on experiential and digital marketing specialized in the fields of retail, luxury, food, well-being, youth cultures, generations Z&Y, millennials and post-millennials, and tourism. She has published dozens of books in English and French, and articles in top-tier academic journals that have received several awards. Professor Batat has introduced an innovative and disruptive approach to global and digital customer experience by providing a strategic framework of the customer experience offline and online and the new experiential marketing mix (7Es). Entrepreneur, Professor Batat is also a bilingual (French and English) international professional trainer and the founder of B&C Consulting Group, an innovative market research and consumer insights company specializing in global and digital customer experience design, buying behavior, and consumer trends. Follow her on LinkedIn and Twitter.

INTRODUCTION

For a long time, traditional luxury brands have been reluctant to accept the opportunities provided by digital technologies. Some of the major concerns have included the increased accessibility of brands online, which might dilute the scarcity and perceived exclusivity of brands; new design technologies that could undermine the heritage, craftsmanship, and sensory experiences that consumers have with brands; and the co-creation and close interaction between the customer and brands that could undermine the aspirational dimension and the distance between the creator and the consumer. In the meantime, anecdotal evidence shows that some luxury brands have already seized the opportunities made possible by digital channels and have integrated them into their strategy without harming the brand's values. For example, Burberry has been recognized as the pioneer of digital collaboration for its work with Snapchat, Google, and YouTube. Because social media increase the visibility of luxury experiences, some research indicates that luxury experiences derived from services may have assumed the role of luxury products in conspicuous consumption. Therefore, the digital context raises two questions: What is the meaning of a digital luxury experience? What are the technologies and devices that luxury companies can use to create pleasurable and profitable digital brand experiences? Therefore, the objective of this book is to explore novel approaches to the study of digital luxury experience as well as to investigate how technologies can enhance or inhibit the luxury industry and consumption experience.

The first part of this book, "The Digital Luxury Experience Revolution," explores the contributions that the concept of customer experience has made to digital luxury marketing in addition to the main challenges that luxury companies are facing when trying to shift or transform their brand experiences. In Chapter 1, I question the meaning of the digital luxury experience and what it represents. I also address why it is so critical for luxury businesses to rethink their digital marketing strategy. In fact, although the implementation of the digital luxury experience is important, most of the digital strategies of luxury companies rely on a product marketing strategy, which is not enough today to offer unique, efficient, and profitable brand experiences. Chapter 1 first explains the transition from luxury as a product to luxury as experience, and then, as an experience within the digital era. Subsequently, I provide an overview of the rise of the luxury experience by offering a new definition of luxury. Finally, I highlight the contributions that the concept of customer experience and its tangible and intangible dimensions has made to digital luxury marketing. In the second chapter, I explain the digital transformation of luxury businesses and describe the evolution of digital marketing in the luxury sector.

Chapter 2 addresses the challenges of this digital transformation in the luxury sector and offers a new digital marketing strategy: "Blue Sunflower Marketing," a disruptive strategy through the use of an innovative tool, and presents the "Digital Luxury Triangle" (DLT), which luxury companies can implement to design successful brand experiences. Chapter 3 examines the way in which luxury companies can connect with digital natives and share luxury experiences with them. Indeed, digital natives are particularly strategic targets for the luxury industry and its services. Not only does this challenge represent a significant task for luxury, but it is also a deeply globalized issue, which is a major asset for these international luxury brands. The objective of this chapter is to identify how digital natives are taking ownership of blogs and developing new relationships with luxury brands. In order to accomplish that, I will begin by presenting the specificities of the digital native generation. I will discuss how the members of this digital generation use social media to develop their online *person-branding*; how they connect with luxury brands as influencers, Instagramers, and bloggers; and how these young people share luxury brand experiences with their followers.

The second part of this book, "Realms of the Digital Luxury Experience," explores, through five chapters, the technologies used by luxury brands to access the five main digital luxury experience realms. In Chapter 4, I present the first realm: the immersive digital luxury experience. In this chapter, I explore the notion of digital immersion and the way luxury companies can use different creative technologies as well as narrative techniques, such as digital storytelling and storydoing, to immerse their customers in pleasurable and emotional customer experiences. In Chapter 5, I introduce the second digital luxury experience realm: the connected digital luxury experience. I explain how connected objects and the Internet of Things (IoT) can be regarded by luxury companies as new databases to be taken into account in order to design highly customized connected luxury experiences. Chapter 6 focuses on the third digital luxury experience realm: the playful digital luxury experience. This chapter introduces the reader to the concept of gamification and its related technologies that luxury businesses can implement to design immersive, emotional, and enjoyable brand experiences. Chapter 7 presents the fourth realm of the digital luxury experience: the humanized digital luxury experience. Artificial intelligence (AI), virtual agents, chatbots, and robots represent some of the future fundamentals of digital luxury experience design. This chapter presents a thoughtful analysis of the technologies related to AI, virtual assistants/agents, chatbots, and robotics in order to understand how luxury professionals in different sectors can use them to design humanized and emotional experiences. Chapter 8, the last chapter in Part II of this book, introduces the fifth realm: the prototyped digital luxury experience. In this chapter, I introduce 3D printing technology and answer the following questions: How is 3D printing used in fashion and luxury today? And, what advantages does it offer when compared to traditional processes?

The third part of this book, "Digital Luxury Experience: What's Next?," explores the future innovations and considerations regarding digital luxury marketing. This part includes three main chapters. In Chapter 9, I introduce the first challenge that luxury companies face when designing the ultimate digital luxury experience and switching to a new experiential marketing mix that goes beyond the traditional use of the mix, by addressing the 7Es: Experience, Exchange, Extension, Emphasis, Empathy capital, Emotional touchpoints, and the Emic/etic process. Chapter 10 will focus on the transition from big data logic to immersive smart data for developing insights into the digital luxury experience by using complementary and alternative market research tools. Finally, in Chapter 11, I conclude by addressing the third challenge, linked to the emergence of a new paradigm: the "phygital" luxury consumption experience. I explore the notion of the phygital context, a new environmental setting combining both physical places and digital spaces in the luxury sector. I also demonstrate how companies can apply it and integrate new and innovative tools and devices in order to create a fluid continuum between the in-store experience and other online platforms.

PART I

THE DIGITAL LUXURY
EXPERIENCE REVOLUTION

1

WHAT DOES DIGITAL LUXURY EXPERIENCE STAND FOR?

INTRODUCTION AND SCOPE

Although the implementation of the digital luxury experience is important, most of the digital strategies of luxury companies rely on a product marketing strategy, which is not enough today to enhance the specificity and the uniqueness of the luxury brand in the eyes of the consumer.

The digital transformation in the luxury sector should be conducted by integrating a customer experience that has been studied and implemented in a physical environment. Its adaptation to a digital context raises many questions about the following aspects: its design and purpose, its perceived value by the customer, its adaptation to e-commerce websites, the translation of its sensory dimensions, its potential to immerse the consumer and make him/her live emotionally rich experiences while providing solutions to his/her problems, and finally the use of immersive technologies in creating unique and memorable digital experiences.

Therefore, prior to defining what digital luxury experience stands for, this chapter will first explain the transition from luxury as a product to luxury as an experience, and then as an experience within the digital era. In this chapter, I trace back the rise of the luxury experience by offering a new definition of luxury that reflects the shift from conspicuous and material luxury consumption to a more experiential and emotional consumption. Then, I will highlight the contributions of the concept of experience to digital luxury to better understand how luxury houses can convert the experiential mindset into strategies, consumer re-enchantment, communication, and techniques of sales to differentiate themselves and develop a strong competitive advantage.

FROM LUXURY EXPERIENCE TO DIGITAL LUXURY EXPERIENCE

Luxury consumption has attracted a lot of interest in the marketing literature in the last 20 years given the reinforcement of luxury as a cultural category in contemporary societies, and the growth of this economic sector since the 1990s (e.g., Okonkwo, 2009, 2010). From investigations of the determinants of legitimate and counterfeit luxury brand purchases to typologies of luxury brands (e.g., Kapferer, 2008; Kapferer and Bastien, 2012) and studies on the consequences of luxurious consumption on societal well-being, luxury has developed into a marketing research domain. Luxury is not an essential quality of a product, service, or lifestyle but rather an experience. It is the combination of a symbolic meaning, subconscious processes, and nonverbal cues resulting from consumption and characterized by fantasies, feelings, and fun. Luxury is a specific type of experience that is desirable, out of the ordinary, and not a necessity. Luxury consumption experiences involve living the consumption activity as the enactment of a lifestyle, personalizing products through rituals, and recognizing brand elements as holy (brand stories are myths, brand visuals are icons, brand shops are temples, brand followers are believers). Various types of luxury brand experiences have been distinguished. For example, Kapferer (2008) distinguished luxury brand experiences as experiences of craftsmanship (e.g., heritage furniture), of modern art (e.g., Yves Saint Laurent clothes), of timeless and internationally recognized quality (e.g., Chanel perfume), and of rarity and exclusiveness (e.g., Ferrari cars).

The digital context creates a unique set of constraints for the development of luxury experiences. The craftsmanship and the artist's "griffe," normally conveyed through all the senses, cannot be experienced given the lack of physical contact with the product or service provider. Fast-paced innovation in digital practices contradicts the notions of traditional craftsmanship and timelessness. Further, digital media are democratic, allowing anybody to engage with the brand from anywhere, lessening the sense of exclusiveness associated with luxury. In spite of those constraints, digital luxury consumption experiences exist. Luxury consumers have embraced the digital environment while many luxury brands have successfully developed social media communication strategies, e-shopping platforms, and digital products in order to be more accessible and create memorable luxury experiences. The constraints of the digital context, however, raise the question of what digital luxury consumption is.

Digital luxury experiences are different from their offline counterparts. In the luxury literature, specific phrases like "luxurious webmosphere" or "luxemosphere" have been coined, indicating the need to adapt traditional conceptualizations to the digital context (e.g., Okonkwo, 2010). Descriptive accounts have highlighted that luxury in a digital environment involves different approaches to storytelling (e.g., Kretz and De Valck, 2010) and consumer–brand relationships. Anecdotal evidence also suggests that luxury in a digital environment places more emphasis on convenience, innovation, and consumer control (e.g., Tran and Voyer, 2013). However, what a digital luxury experience truly is remains unclear. In the digital marketing literature, online consumption experiences have been characterized as "digital virtual," a liminoid experience between the material and the imaginary (e.g., Denegri-Knott and Molesworth, 2010), but what this means for luxury has not been addressed. In order to define what is meant by a digital luxury experience, one needs to know more about the rise of the luxury experience and the way luxury houses can offer a connection and a continuum between the experience in-store and on their websites.

THE RISE OF THE LUXURY EXPERIENCE

Prior to defining the "luxury experience" and what "digital luxury experience" stands for, I first explain what we mean by "luxury," what its origins are, and how the definition of luxury has evolved over time and throughout cultures. In this section, I trace back the rise of luxury and its shift from a traditional perspective to the emergence of a more experiential, subjective, and emotional perspective on luxury consumption within today's contemporary societies. A new definition of the luxury experience that takes into account consumers' emotions and functional needs shaped by both cultural and digital settings will be offered at the end of this section.

Most studies analyzing the luxury sector highlight the difficulty of defining luxury and its typologies. Existing definitions are far from convincing and are limited to certain types of practices, goods, or luxury brands. Definitions also vary amongst luxury market players. For example, Karl Lagerfeld defines luxury in a very subjective way: "my greatest luxury is not having to justify myself to anyone," and in another definition "luxury is the freedom of mind, independence, in short the politically incorrect," or as stated by Coco Chanel, defining "luxury is not the opposite of poverty but that of vulgarity." If we seek a more exhaustive definition of luxury, we can find it in dictionaries that define luxury as a lifestyle characterized by large expenditures devoted to the acquisition of unnecessary goods, for a taste of the world's ostentation, and greater well-being. Therefore, in order to provide a consistent definition of luxury, it is necessary to understand the origins of luxury and the different perspectives related to it.

THE ORIGINS OF LUXURY

According to Batat (2019b), luxury has been studied through two main approaches: conspicuous (American perspective) and distinctive (French perspective). These two approaches explain the motivations that drive individuals to purchase and consume luxury products and services. These two perspectives are built on two main theories: (1) the theory of leisure class or "conspicuous consumption," introduced by the American anthropologist Thorstein Veblen in the United States in 1899; and (2) the "distinction theory" of sociologist Pierre Bourdieu, which was published later in France in 1979. These two theories have dominated studies on the consumption of luxury in many disciplines (e.g., sociology, history, psychology, economics), which then contributed to the definition of luxury marketing and luxury consumption practices.

Conspicuous luxury consumption has contributed much to the understanding of the characteristics of the consumption of luxury products and services. Veblen states that the motivation of the individual to purchase luxury items is to define a social status, which should be recognized by all the other social actors belonging to the same social sphere. This includes understanding luxury consumption practices within the old American aristocracy as well as the adoption of luxury and its codes by new emerging social classes, such as the bourgeoisie and new rich (e.g., wealthy traders from the provinces). Veblen has also identified other forms of waste: "conspicuous/visible leisure," which consists of dedicating time to unproductive tasks, such as reading, learning dead languages (e.g., Latin), music, etc. The conspicuous consumption practices and the desire to show one's wealth can also be expressed through activities that are not related to productive work.

These kinds of practices did not disappear: instead, they still persist in our contemporary consumer societies in which the upper-middle classes, whether they are western, eastern, or from other cultures, are often led to develop and adopt conspicuous consumption lifestyles for several reasons, such as social anxiety, the desire to rise in social status, the search for new consumer experiences, self-esteem enhancement, etc. Therefore, the conspicuous consumption of luxury has a strong link with the individual's emotions and symbolism as well as the meanings individuals assign to their luxury consumption practices, which are anchored within a particular cultural setting and are shaped by certain social norms and codes. Furthermore, Veblen emphasizes the idea that the individual does not consume in order to merely satisfy a tangible need. His/her main expectation is not only related to the utility aspect of the good or service consumed, but it is also related to how individuals consume in order to defend their social status in society and preserve their honor. Thus, conspicuous luxury operates by sending tacit social signs as well as explicit messages, visible or invisible, directly or indirectly, to other social actors who can decode them by referring to the luxury objects and lifestyles displayed by individuals.

Distinctive luxury consumption is based on certain principles of Veblen's approach to conspicuous consumption. In the Bourdieusian perspective, the consumption of luxury is seen as a means that allows individuals to distinguish themselves from the massive trend of consumption prevalent in society. In his theory of distinction, Bourdieu explains that individuals belonging to upper classes who are trying to distinguish themselves construct and affirm an identity of their own. Luxury goods (products and services) are transformed into symbols of power that convey their specific culture and communicate their high social status. The consumption of luxury, therefore, reflects an important social function. It allows the formation of connections and relationships with other social actors belonging to reference groups. In this case, the conspicuous and distinctive consumption of luxury guides the preferences and choices of luxury goods and brands consumed and exhibited in the public sphere. Therefore, to be distinctive, luxury should be inaccessible, exclusive, rare, and new. If luxury becomes widely diffused, it loses its distinctive value and becomes commonplace, mundane, and trivialized. Thus, the distinction theory of the consumption of luxury highlights the importance of status and social life that are structured around codes, symbols, and negotiation strategies. Every consumer plays a specific social role by consuming certain types of luxury goods and brands to affirm his/her social status while differentiating his/her identity. Through the consumption of certain luxury brands, the consumer makes a representation of him/herself and expresses his/her values.

Thus, the two theories refer to a French perspective (distinctive luxury) and an American perspective (conspicuous luxury) that are very complementary and provide a profound comprehension of the social and symbolic dimensions associated with the consumption of luxury and the motivations behind it. This idea supports my proposal for a contemporary definition that views luxury as *"a personal experience that offers a major focus on the intangible dimensions of luxury beyond the functional aspects and incorporates symbolic, social, ideological, subjective, and emotional dimensions."* In this definition, I emphasize the idea that luxury should be defined from the perspective of the consumer and should be applied through a bottom-up approach focusing on how consumers experience luxury and how they interact with the luxury brand and its employees. Therefore, there is not one "luxury" but rather multiple "luxuries," which are all legitimate, interrelated, and which should be considered by luxury businesses when designing their luxury experiences in both digital spaces (e.g., website, blogs, social media) and physical places (in-store experience, hotel, or restaurant).

A HOLISTIC DEFINITION OF LUXURY

In marketing, Kapferer and Bastien explained the difficulty related to the definition of luxury. They indicate a definitional blur of luxury, which in some studies is considered as a "category" and in others as a "field of application" (sector of activity). The two authors associated the notion of the brand with that of luxury to propose an updated definition of luxury: "the concept of luxury is not a category in the absolute, but a relative set that cannot be dissociated from the political and social structure of the century to which it belongs" (2012: 53). By drawing on this definition, Batat (2019b) states that luxury is in each of us and is produced by and for the individuals who practice it. In her book *The New Luxury Experience,* Batat proposed a new holistic definition that integrated seven main perspectives according to which luxury can be defined and expressed:

- The **institutional perspective** refers to the way public organizations define luxury. For example, in France, the Office of the Economic and Social Council commissioned, in 2007, a study on luxury, the production of goods and the rendering of services in the luxury sector. The conclusions show that the French administrative regulations have solved the problem of luxury delimitation by proposing a definition based on the logic of "activity categorization." In France, the luxury sector has always been strictly regulated since the decree of January 29th, 1945, which distinguishes luxury from other segments of the same activity. The decree defines 17 activities related to luxury that include all industries, craftsmanship, and creative activities, ranging from fine art, floral art, and leather to music, publishing, and throughout fashion as well as jewelry.
- The **organizational perspective** states that luxury should be defined from the standpoint of business actors and the luxury industry. In this perspective, luxury groups believe that the definition of luxury should keep its specificity unclear and that the role of advertising and merchandising departments should be to design luxury perceptions based on targets and markets. The objective of advertising and merchandising is, therefore, to convince consumers that these products and brands belong to the field of luxury.
- The **academic perspective** highlights the idea that each discipline approaches luxury according to perspectives and paradigms that are relevant to its field (e.g., defining luxury by the price in economics, luxury as social representations in sociology). In fact, while sociology emphasizes the link between "taste" and "luxury" to underscore the dynamic of social representations that lead to imitation and differentiation, in economics, luxury has been defined in a very pragmatic way, according to the price of goods (products and services). In marketing, authors have attempted to define luxury through the establishment of a categorization of luxury goods.
- The **media perspective** refers to luxury and fashion media that have also contributed to the definition of luxury and its related items. From a media perspective, luxury can also be referred to as refinement, high prices, dreams, preciousness, and celebrity – aspects that are part of extraordinary moments and things that individuals can engage in to please, seduce, and have fun.
- The **craftsmanship perspective** defines luxury as grounded in the work of artisans who are recognized by luxury companies, since they have a creative potential and they have generational stories related to their artisanal craftsmanship. In the common unconscious, craftsmanship is inseparable from luxury in the minds of consumers. In the craftsmanship perspective, luxury is defined by the following aspects: high quality of the goods, ancestral manufacturing methods, transmission of know-how, satisfaction and proximity with customers, and prices defined by the quality of the product and its rarity.
- The **consumer perspective** refers to the definition of luxury from a consumer's standpoint. Thus, defining luxury is related to the perceptions of the consumers and what they consider to be luxury goods. These perceptions are related to consumer profiles

and attitudes towards luxury. Marketing authors Dubois et al. (2001) identified four main attitudes consumers have towards luxury goods:

o   Consumers who perceive luxury as an excessive conspicuous consumption practice;
o   Consumers who equate luxury with a dream and a universe of inaccessible comfort;
o   Consumers who associate dimensions such as passion, fascination, dreams, fanaticism, joy, deep love, and sensitivity to luxury;
o   Consumers who consider that luxury products are an extension of oneself in relation to the personal and social identity of the individual.

Other authors in marketing, such as Vigneron and Johnson (2004), proposed a conceptualization of luxury from the point-of-view of the consumer by constructing a measurement scale composed of five main dimensions: hedonic, self-extended, perceived quality, rarity, and the conspicuous dimension of luxury. For each consumer profile, there is, therefore, a specific attitude towards luxury and its conceptualization that is adapted to each type of consumer.

•   The **historical and cultural perspectives** refer to the cultural diversity and the democratization of access to luxury, especially in emerging countries and amongst the new rich, which generates a great diversity in the definition of what luxury is. Following a historical perspective, the 13th century was marked by the beginning of Italian luxury followed by the rise of French luxury in the 17th century, and the designation in the 18th century of Paris as the world capital of fashion. In the 21st century, we see the emergence of French haute couture and its dissemination into other cultures. The cultural and historical evolution of luxury means luxury brands will have to face major challenges in the future in terms of being able to establish a balance between their historical customers (e.g., French, North American, European) and their new customers (e.g., Chinese, Russian, Indian, African), whose discovery, adoption, and acculturation of luxury is very recent. From this perspective, the definition of luxury is, therefore, primarily cultural. For instance, the French definition of luxury is not similar to North American luxury and even very different when compared to Chinese, Russian, or Arab luxury. Furthermore, authors such as Dubois and Laurent (1996) have compared cultural perceptions of luxury in several countries. A selection of different cultural definitions of luxury based on consumer perceptions is provided in Figure 1.1.

The seven perspectives cited above should be taken into account by luxury businesses and scholars in order to define luxury from the right perspective. Therefore, when exploring how consumers define luxury, we should focus on its evolving and multidimensional aspects. In fact, luxury gathers several meanings that consumers assign to it according to the norms and codes of their consumption cultures. These meanings evolve with time as well as with social and individual changes. Luxury is also closely tied to the culture and practices of the group in which it emerges, shapes, and develops. Therefore, luxury is in all of us. It is produced by and for the individuals and professional, institutional, political, and social actors who practice it. What luxury is for some can, therefore, be mundane for others.

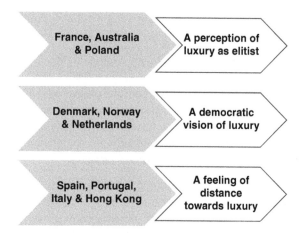

Figure 1.1   Different cultural perceptions of luxury

Thus, the definition of luxury depends on the lens through which it is viewed, something that should be identified prior to designing suitable, emotional, and profitable luxury experiences offline and online. In fact, today's consumers no longer seek to distinguish themselves or to belong to a reference group by consuming luxury goods; they now aspire to live unforgettable and tangible experiences. The rise of the experiential and emotional luxury shows that consumers are now moving from a logic that focused solely on luxury brands to something that values the consumer, makes him/her live memorable experiences, and generates strong emotions. The next section will explain the emergence and the contribution of customer experience to the luxury sector.

WHEN CUSTOMER EXPERIENCE MEETS LUXURY

The aim of this section is to question the concept of "customer experience" and its application in luxury. Indeed, luxury houses should rethink their digital marketing and communication strategies by focusing more on creating unique and profitable luxury experiences with a continuum offline and online. In the luxury sector, the introduction of customer experience responds to major issues related to the change in consumer behavior and the emerging trends generated by the digital transformation of today's societies. Furthermore, customer experience has become an obvious subject in today's businesses, but it is often confused with other concepts, such as customer relationship management, relational marketing, or sensory marketing. There is, thus, a need to clarify the concept of customer experience before examining its implementation in the field of luxury consumption. The key changes in luxury consumer behavior that encouraged the introduction of customer experience in the luxury sector will then be explained.

WHAT IS CUSTOMER EXPERIENCE?

In the last decade, customer experience has taken over relational marketing and its concept of Customer Relationship Management (CRM), which was widely used by companies in the 1990s. The interest of marketing scholars and businesses in the new "customer experience" concept can be explained by the limitations imposed by the use of a CRM approach and its significant shortcomings, such as the idea that CRM and relationship marketing do not adequately address the intangible and symbolic needs and expectations of consumers. Batat (2019a) states that being product-oriented and sales-oriented is, therefore, completely opposed to the idea of a consumer-centric approach used in customer experience, which requires taking into account both consumers' functional and emotional benefits.

According to Batat, the rise of customer experience in marketing highlights the transition from a product-centric logic to an experiential logic that underscores the determining role of customer experience and its legitimacy in both academia and business. Indeed, for marketing scholars and companies, a customer experience framework is holistic by nature and is likely to link a set of variables (functional, emotional, environmental, cultural, etc.) whose analysis is most often conducted separately. The notion of "customer experience" was first introduced in marketing in 1982 by the two pioneering marketing scholars Holbrook and Hirschman. Since Holbrook and Hirschman's seminal work, the concept of experience has been integrated into the field of economics in the book *The Experience Economy*, by Pine and Gilmore, published in 1999, whose contributions have become a central pillar of the foundation of the economy in the current context. Later, other scientific articles and books followed, first in the United States and in Northern Europe, and then in Southern Europe in the late 1990s and early 2000s. According to Lemon and Verhoef (2016), the origins of customer experience can be traced back to the 1960s, when the first influential theories on marketing and consumer behavior were established and disseminated, particularly the work of Philip Kotler (1986) as well as John Howard and Jagdish Sheth (1969).

In their article published in 2016, Lemon and Verhoef presented an analysis of research related to the study of customer experience in marketing. For the two authors, the key question in their research was to explore whether the customer experience, as a subject, is really a new topic. In its current usage, the notion of customer experience integrates several concepts from service marketing (e.g., after-sales service, customer journey, customer satisfaction, loyalty, relationship marketing) and offers a limited view of what the customer experience is, and how can we differentiate it from the user experience. Therefore, to better understand the digital luxury experience, it is important to explore the different facets of the customer experience in the field of marketing according to a chronological approach (Table 1.1) as identified by Lemon and Verhoef (2016), and which highlights the main domains related to the concept of customer experience.

Table 1.1   A chronological approach to customer experience

Year	Domains of customer experience
Between the 1960s and 1970s	The customer buying behavior process: an understanding of the customer experience in decision-making as a process
The 1970s	Consumer satisfaction and loyalty: assessing customers' perceptions and attitudes about a shopping experience
The 1980s	Quality of service: identification of the context and specific elements of the customer experience related to the customer's shopping journey
The 1990s	Relationship marketing: taking into account the customer relationship and adapted responses as part of its customer experience
The 2000s	Customer Relationship Management (CRM): correlation models that identify how specific elements of the customer experience interact with each other. The objective being the optimization of the commercial results
Between the 2000s and 2010s	Customer-centricity and customer orientation: focus on organizational issues for successful customer experience design and management
From 2010 until today	Customer engagement, human, and emotions: recognizing the customer's role in the experience

Therefore, the different definitions of customer experience emphasize the importance of aspects such as subjectivity, intangibility, and symbolism, which are viewed as an integral part of the purchasing and consumption process. Thus, I argue that the transition from "conventional marketing" to "experiential marketing" supports the fundamental role of these dimensions for luxury companies since it creates a durable competitive advantage based on affect, emotion, and empathy connecting the brand with its targets (Batat, 2019a). Therefore, consumption is no longer limited to the functional benefits customers may be looking for, but it is also an "experience" in which the consumer can be involved and immersed. Companies and luxury houses need to rethink their strategies by evolving their traditional marketing tools to better understand the whole customer experience in all luxury sectors through the focus on the relational, emotional, and functional components to offer a memorable and profitable in-store and online experience to their customers.

TREND 1.1

PORSCHE INTEGRATIVE CUSTOMER EXPERIENCE APPROACH

Porsche uses the four-step customer experience approach, which includes listening, providing solutions based on customers' rational and emotional needs, checking if they got things right, and finally, following up customers' issues and resolving them. Porsche measures its performance during critical stages of the customer journey, which is after a deposit, after an experience, and after the customer becomes a Porsche owner. It uses the Net Promoter Score (NPS) since customers are always busy and it is so crucial to provide a way for them to quickly and easily relay their concerns. Customers do not want to spend their valuable time filling out hundreds of questions. In order to offer successful and satisfying experiences to their clients, the integrative Porsche customer experience framework encompasses the following elements:

Customer enthusiasm. Porsche not only cares about satisfying its customers, but it also delights them in order to generate outstanding opportunities for itself. It transforms its customers into fans and secures their long-term loyalty. First, Porsche defines different customer types and categorizes them based on their actions. Then, Porsche designs relevant contact points and processes. Finally, the car brand measures the results and follows its customers in the best possible way – throughout the entire "customer life-cycle," that is, from initial interest to repeat purchase. Porsche makes sure that its customers enjoy the rational appeal of the car and at the same time maximizes the emotional appeal – the perfect combination of both luxury and experience.

Porsche consultants. They recommend comprehensive quality management to satisfy customers, improve cost effectiveness, and minimize risks. This system consists of a strict quality strategy as well as the products, processes, and structures derived from it. The Porsche consultants simplify standard processes, such as the shipment of goods and planning. This enables employees to devote greater attention to their customers. In addition, the consultants and their clients jointly analyze sales areas and create effective planning and market management. This allows Porsche to gain new customers and generate additional revenue.

Porsche Digital GmbH. Porsche has now founded a new company that serves as its digital competence center, which will strengthen the brand, develop innovative customer experiences, and acquire new partners. It combines the traditional Porsche spirit with the power of new technologies. Porsche Digital GmbH also sees itself as an interface between Porsche and innovators worldwide.

Unique and innovative model strategy. Porsche's innovative strategy to expand consists of introducing a combination of non-sports models and sports vehicles. Porsche has expanded the product lineup with vehicles such as SUV and Sedan while launching new sports cars directly aligned with its heritage. Porsche provides an intelligent and effective balance of market expansion for the brand while remaining true to its Porsche heritage, which is especially critical for the loyal Porsche consumers.

Furthermore, the experiential logic suggests that, in comparison with traditional marketing models, the components should be re-examined in the light of the concept of the customer experience. Therefore, luxury companies should not only focus on functional stimuli, but also on emotional ones. The main difference between traditional and experiential marketing is the "goal of luxury consumption." The perceived consumption purpose, as each consumer would define it according to his/her own perspective, goes beyond the "maximization of the utility value" related to goods in search, additionally, of the "maximization of the lived luxury experience" which incorporates not only functional criteria (quality, price, etc.) but also symbolic, emotional, relational, and aesthetic criteria (brand is perceived as an extension of one's identify, well-being, social capital, etc.). Consumers will then seek to maximize their emotional and social benefits and evaluate their customer experience from the "pleasure" they will derive from it. In this perspective, luxury houses should no longer measure customer experience through customer satisfaction, but more through the intensity of both the memory and pleasure the customer luxury experience will generate. It is, therefore, important for luxury companies to set up a new strategy that relies on experiential luxury marketing tools to create and stimulate the customer experience.

TREND 1.2

HOW DOES PRADA CREATE THE IN STORE CUSTOMER EXPERIENCE?

The Prada store has a uniquely ingenious marketing strategy that makes it a difficult competitor in the fashion industry. When it comes to improving its own business, Prada is always in the forefront of using technology to step up its game. Besides having sophisticated Customer Relationship Management (CRM) and Enterprise Resource Planning (ERP) management systems, fascinating dressing rooms made of clear glass that turn opaque as soon as someone steps inside as well as mesmerizing showrooms with video monitors playing clips everywhere, Prada aims to make the purchase process of the customers more efficient and quicker by attaching an electronic tag to each item of the brand. These tags can be read by their smart closets to display information to the customers about the items they have chosen. For example, the smart closets indicate available colors, sizes, similar looking items, and so forth.

Moreover, Prada's customer service is customized: each sales associate handles a specific customer and facilitates his or her purchase to make the experience as refined and exclusive as possible. It is also worth noting that the store itself creates a very personal relationship between the brand and the customer by saving each client's previous purchases as well as favorite salesperson on the customer's loyalty card. This card also allows customers to enter the store through the backdoor and bring their desired items to the store's comfortable lounge.

WHAT ARE THE KEY CHANGES IN LUXURY CONSUMER BEHAVIOR?

Today's luxury consumers are becoming familiar with instant accessibility and will expect their luxury brand experiences to be immediate, personalized, and emotional. Thus, luxury houses need to better understand their customers and the changes in their behaviors in order to design offline and online luxury experiences that customers will really want through meaningful messages that echo throughout different marketplaces and touchpoints. Understanding consumer experiences is an essential mission for luxury businesses and cannot be examined without considering the key changes in consumer behavior that will impact the digital experience or the way customers use technology and technological devices to acquire and experience luxury. This section introduces four significant changes in consumer behavior: emotion, empowerment, postmodernism, and digitization. Luxury companies should take these four factors into consideration when designing online and in-store luxury experiences by focusing on both tangible (e.g., functional, technical) and intangible (e.g., symbolic, social, emotional) needs.

- **The powerful role of emotion in offering memorable luxury experiences**. While authors acknowledge some personal and individual effects on decision-makers, the conventional framework of consumer behavior is mainly cerebral in nature. The new emerging consumption trends have contributed to the shift in the marketing paradigm. Kotler et al. (2010) stated that marketing has moved beyond the age of "messaging" to affecting customers' emotions. Kotler et al. emphasized the key role of emotion in studying consumer decision-making: "The essential difference between emotion and reason is that emotion leads to actions while reason leads to conclusions" (2010: 170).

As society has evolved into digital and experiential consumption, marketing scholars have started to examine the impact of emotions on consumer decision-making. The reason is that the "decision to buy and be loyal to a brand is greatly influenced by emotions" (Kotler et al., 2010: 170). Furthermore, emotions are a powerful resource for capturing experience-driven consumer affection for luxury brands and, consequently, incorporating them into consumers' everyday habits and their identity projects. Thus, creating emotional connections during the shopping process or the luxury experience has a strong impact on the decision-making process and consumer satisfaction. Indeed, consumer emotional involvement increases brand loyalty and sales by improving luxury brand image and positioning. Yet, there are several definitions of "emotion." In 1981, Paul and Anne Kleinginna identified more than 90 definitions of "emotion" that can be found in different disciplines. Following a multidisciplinary and chronological analysis, the two authors proposed a new definition which is more universal and concrete enough to be translated into managerial, marketing, and operational actions. This definition highlights three main characteristics of the notion of "consumer emotion": physiological, behavioral, and the dyad emotion/rationality. The interactions between these three dimensions have a direct impact on the decision-making process in the luxury buying experience. Whether positive or negative, consumer emotion is composed of a mixture of feelings that emerge within luxury consumption experiences and can be primary or secondary.

Primary emotions, such as joy, sadness, disgust, anger, fear, and surprise, are universal and express visible emotions through facial expressions that each individual is capable of recognizing and decoding in different cultures. Secondary emotions are derived from elementary emotions and are influenced by a consumer's personal background, his/her childhood, consumption experiences, and his/her external environment. They often encompass two or a mixture of primary emotions (e.g., contempt is a mixture of two emotions: fear and anger) or from an emotion, such as fear, that creates anxiety. Furthermore, consumer emotion is not static; rather, it evolves through experiences and includes both positive and negative peaks that occur when a consumer is in contact with social actors and other components of his/her immediate environment (e.g., salespeople, brands, services, institutions, other consumers).

In the luxury sector, every purchase is about emotion, but how does emotion contribute to creating a pleasant luxury customer experience? The luxury customer experience is grounded in the idea that the consumer behaves in both a rational and emotional way. For example, a young woman wishing to buy her first luxury brand bag can be divided by opposing rational arguments (I cannot afford it, I do not need this bag, I already have one, it is too expensive, I can wait for sales, etc.) and emotional arguments (it is the same bag as my idol's, I feel confident and beautiful with this bag, I like the brand, etc.).

An emotional experience is, therefore, used to respond to changing consumption patterns as well as to paradoxical aspirations of consumers. Its objective is to privilege pleasure and establish an affective and reassuring relationship while communicating and sharing the values of the luxury brand. By focusing on encouraging emotions, the luxury brand can then reinforce consumer emotions (positive), which accordingly promote action (purchase) and offer a pleasant dimension to the experience in the store (enchantment). Indeed, when customers experience a strong emotion, they tend to act impulsively and spontaneously, without utilizing their cognitive abilities. Based on emotions, luxury houses seek, above all, to reach the heart of consumers, for example, through advertising messages focused on pleasure. Offering emotional luxury experiences is then a very effective tool for creating a strong bond between a luxury brand and its customers.

The role of luxury employees as emotional motivators is critical in creating and offering emotionally charged luxury experiences. Transforming luxury staff into brand ambassadors is a key challenge in the experiential and digital era. Indeed, engaged employees build strong luxury brands and durable emotional connections with customers. Luxury employees act as real emotional stimuli and play a vital role in enhancing positive consumer experiences and attitudes towards the luxury brand. It is important for luxury houses to focus on the "emotional capital" of their employees who are in contact with customers.

TREND 1.3

SONOS FLAGSHIP NEW YORK: THE ART OF CREATING AN EMOTIONAL LUXURY HI-FI EXPERIENCE

Sonos is a high-end brand of audio equipment for the home. Its flagship store in New York at the heart of SoHo is a perfect example of creating powerful emotional in-store customer experiences. In fact, Sonos creates a unique emotional sound experience by doing the opposite of what hi-fi stores are supposed to show to their customers. In its iconic flagship, Sonos does not highlight its product in the store. Instead, when a customer enters the store he/she will see capsules designed to recreate the ambiance of one's home. Sonos offers an immersive emotional experience by allowing its customers to escape the commercial environment of the store and enjoy the product's features in a familiar and relaxed atmosphere that resembles one's home. This will make consumers feel comfortable, as if they are at home, and thus more eager to spend time in the store and/or purchase the product – not because of its premium qualities, but rather because the product reproduces the same feeling experienced at the store, but this time within their own home.

With its emotional and highly experiential concept store, the Californian brand of high-end wireless home entertainment speakers has instantly stood out thanks to an extremely elaborated concept store. From the entrance, one can see that the products are presented all together on the left wall in a way that is instantly more artistic than mercantile and which features items without price tags. In fact, Sonos found that interest in its products came largely from consumers who encountered them at work and played with them at their friends' homes. Thus, the brand has reconstructed seven different environments: seven rooms of a house designed in various styles and represented in seven capsules where clients can test their speakers. No boxes of stacked products or aggressive advertising: the goal here is not to sell everything, but to spread the word about the superior quality of sound, the Sonos brand, and the emotional experience related to it. Each of the seven cabins on the ground floor has the same equipment: speakers, of course, a control tablet, and a TV screen to visually accompany the experience. Totally soundproof once the door is closed, the parts allow pushing the volume thoroughly to test the stereo system to full capacity.

For some years now, Sonos devices have been compatible with most online music catalogs and streaming sources, such as Pandora, Spotify, and others. In the store, too, customers have access to 68 partner services to ensure they always find the music they want to hear on Sonos speakers. Customers can select the proposed content where they find their favorite songs, then compare the three proposed systems, – 3.0, 3.1, and 5.1 – for a totally enveloping sound. The cabins can also be synchronized to test the Sonos multiroom sound system. In order to enhance the emotions generated by the lived experience, in the corridor along the capsules, tablets offer more information about the brand and its products, which can transmit details to consumers by mail. Above, a wall of old music magazines animates the store. This corridor is also the place where customers meet sellers. In order not to confine them to a counter, Sonos has equipped

(Continued)

(Continued)

their sellers with a mobile device that allows them to handle all customer requests wherever they are in the store. Moreover, to enhance customer immersion and emotions, Sonos has built an impressive wall of sound consisting of 297 speakers that are lit by changing colors and visible from outside the shop. Therefore, the customer experience offered by the Sonos flagship store is unique in that it breaks the codes of the classic sale of this type of device, and offers customers an emotional experience of sound that allows them to understand and appreciate the acoustic qualities of Sonos equipment.

Emotional capital refers to the predisposition of employees to show empathy, which is a vital component of the customer experience and has a significant impact on improving the quality of the luxury experience and enhancing the immersion and the well-being of customers in a pleasurable context in which they feel good as well as "understood."

Yet, although the need to hire staff with high emotional capital is evident, it is very complicated to guarantee its durable effect, especially when the physical fatigue and stress of the employees are high due to a lack of sleep or the physical toll of standing for hours. For example, Plaza Athénée Hotel is a symbol of luxury experience and well-being. The Plaza Athénée offers guests a delightful hotel experience and the very best of Paris. It is the element of the emotional hotel experience that quickly provides clients with a unique luxury experience that focuses on consumer pleasure and well-being. The Plaza Athénée has always made every effort to offer the best to its customers: quality services, breathtaking architectural frameworks, attention to the continuous improvement of its services and gastronomy. In fact, it is important to build customer loyalty through an excellent offer and, as much as possible, to encourage customer recommendations at the international level in order to increase its brand image and attractiveness. For this iconic Parisian hotel, awakening the emotions and consumer well-being of the international luxury clientele, therefore, requires a thorough reflection on the adaptation of services to human, cultural, and social sensitivity in a high-end environment. The awakening of emotions impresses itself upon the unconscious that then stimulates desires to continue its way in the process of consumption. Particular attention should, therefore, be paid to the solicitation of the senses. The first contact made with hotel staff are so-called moments of "truth" for those who preside over the interaction between two people: one "in demand for service" and the other "in the service of the customer." In these moments of truth, everything counts, the look, the voice, the flow, the words chosen, and even discretion. Nor do we ignore the importance of implicit cultural expectations.

Depending on the origin of customers, certain attentions and attitudes should be perfectly adapted by hotel staff. The emotional luxury that aims to stimulate, soften, and seduce the highly sensitive luxury clientele has its reason for being in this quest for perfection. Personalization in luxury hotels and palaces will be the only guarantor of customer satisfaction. The ultra-rich guests, for example, tend to raise their level of requirements more and more, and at each level crossed, their tolerance for disappointment diminishes. Only the satisfaction of their emotional desires and their feeling of well-being will make them live a positive and unforgettable experience. To guarantee the emotional luxury experience, luxury houses and hotels should not ignore the fact that the human being is at the heart of every step. Awareness and staff training are, therefore, the only guarantors of this luxury emotional offer. Only the staff will be able to offer, at each stage of the customer's journey in the establishment, the necessary impression of an unforgettable emotional luxury.

• **The advent of an empowered luxury consumer**. The empowered consumer is part of today's digital and experiential consumption settings. Stating that the increasing use of social and mobile technologies is shifting market power from suppliers to consumers and thus creating a new profile of consumer raises significant implications for luxury businesses, and suggests that they should define new strategies to benefit from this trend. According to Hunter and Garnefeld (2008), consumer empowerment can be defined in two ways: as the act of giving consumers power through resources, and as a personal and subjective situation produced by perceptions of collective control. They define consumer empowerment as "a consumer's subjective experience that they have a greater ability than before to intentionally produce desired outcomes and prevent undesired ones and that they are benefiting from the increased ability" (2008: 2). In other words, for consumers, the empowerment experience is two-fold: they request the company to provide them with adequate and transparent information, and a controlled process which is relative.

In the digital era, and in order to become empowered, consumers are expected to develop adequate knowledge and skills to help them understand and select the offers that are suitable for them. Furthermore, marketing scholars state that empowered consumers have a strategic role for brands. They are more likely to drive innovation, productivity, and create a competitive advantage by means of access to relevant information, which is then shared with other consumers. As largely documented by marketing scholars, consumer empowerment is a multidimensional concept that encompasses multiple cognitive, personal, and social elements.

For instance, I identified four pillars of consumer empowerment: (1) consumer competency, which encompasses three key dimensions: cognitive, functional, and social; (2) consumer re(creation), which refers to the capability of consumers to use the actual brand or company product and/or service to create new items by using two approaches: transgression and reappropriation; (3) consciousness of consumer rights related to the awareness of the consumer, which includes three consumption knowledge domains: the ability to understand prices, the ability regarding complaints, and the ability to understand one's rights as a consumer; and (4) consumer resistance, referring to a digital savvy consumer and his/her overexposure to commercial discourses that leads him/her to be more knowledgeable in terms of decoding advertisement messages (Batat, 2019a). Therefore, today's empowered consumers are driving new luxury brand opportunities, as they have access to more information, more choices, and more occasions to globally share and disseminate their opinions and thoughts about brands they value, or hate. Consequently, there has been a radical change in the balance of power between companies and their customers. However, while the rise of the empowered customer undoubtedly signifies a threat to companies who are reluctant to rethink their customer orientation strategies, it also offers a unique opportunity to engage empowered customers and use their creative potential as well as their skills to help build innovative luxury products and design the ultimate luxury experience. Consumer empowerment can then drive luxury brand success and new opportunities. Indeed, brand success does not only depend on a "good idea of products and services" or a "good marketing strategy," but it also needs a "good connection" with the customer. This means that luxury brand loyalty requires respecting the customer and recognizing his/her skills and power, which should not be underestimated. Therefore, empowered consumers need to be stimulated, nurtured, informed, respected, and valued.

- **Keeping up with the new postmodern luxury consumer.** Understanding the changing consumer and the rise of new luxury consumption trends is an essential mission that allows luxury houses to design suitable and profitable experiences. As a consequence of globalization, technology, and sociocultural transformations, new schemes of production and consumption have progressively emerged over the past decade and are replacing the modern approach to the mass production of standardized goods. This new context is also transforming luxury consumption, which is entering a new era of "postmodernism." In order to benefit from these changes, luxury brands should fundamentally transform their thinking processes. They should also re-examine their consumer approaches, offline and online marketing and communication strategies, loyalty programs, customer services, and so forth to offer the ultimate overall luxury customer experience.

Postmodernism, as stated by Venkatesh et al. (1993), is characterized by suspicion towards modern totalitarian thoughts, established rules, standardized knowledge, and the absence of diversity resulting in social chaos and the loss of reference points. Individuals should then redefine their identities and values to achieve their own emancipation, affirm their differences, and thus liberate themselves from modern dominant representations. Therefore, postmodernism rejects the idea of a universal reality by emphasizing its fragmentation, plurality, and diversity, even beyond human understanding. Furthermore, postmodernism offers luxury marketing scholars and luxury businesses a thought-provoking framework for examining or re-examining consumption practices and experiences by shifting the focus from product to consumer. Furthermore, while modern consumer society places the consumer at the end of the process and views him/her as rational, postmodern consumption goes beyond a purely economic vision of the marketplace by focusing on both the emotional and cognitive dimensions of consumer experiences and the meanings the latter gives to his/her consumption practices involving brands, products, services, environment, and social interactions with salespeople, multiple stakeholders, and other consumers.

According to Thomas (1997), the postmodern consumer lives in a society filled with "doubt, ambiguity, and uncertainty." It is this situation that luxury brands should attempt to understand by identifying the macro sociocultural forces influencing consumer behaviors, attitudes, and motivations in order to satisfy the needs and expectations of the consumer in terms of brand experiences if they wish to subsist in the postmodern marketplace. For Batat (2019b), the postmodern luxury consumer demonstrates two key features: multidimensionality (fragmented consumer society) and paradoxical behaviors (juxtaposition and combination of contradictory behaviors). For instance, gender fragmentation and juxtaposition in the market for luxury perfumes is one of the consumption trends that characterize today's postmodern consumer society. Neutral packaging, mixed perfumes, and a growing prevalence of unisex perfumes are but a few signs of the postmodern consumer's impact on the luxury industry. It was in 1995 that Calvin Klein introduced the first ever CK One – a scent that is applicable not only to all sexes, but also to all ages. CK One, a fragrance that has since become a cult favorite, has both female and male characteristics and was the pioneer of a revolution that blurred the lines between genders. Its freshness is aimed at both sexes without discrimination. It was a gamble at the time, a high-risk venture in a world of highly codified perfumery, where cedar and oud dominated men's waters while feminine fragrances were characterized by pink colors and flowers. If the industry remains divided, CK One has the merit of opening up the path to traditional luxury brands, such as Guerlain and Hermes, who have launched a line of mixed fragrances to share. For luxury perfume brands, odors do not have a sex; rather, the perfumes acquire their gender through universes where femininity and masculinity express themselves: through their names, shapes of the bottles, muse, and type of scents.

TREND 1.4

JEAN PAUL GAULTIER AS A POSTMODERN ICON: GENDER NEUTRAL LUXURY

In his fashion designs, Jean Paul Gaultier has always been in search of meetings, exchanges, or even fusion between the sexes. In 1985, he designed an emblematic collection: the wardrobe

(Continued)

(Continued)

for two. For Gaultier, androgyny and gender-mixing are at the heart of his creative process. Far from the unisex trend of the 1970s that tended to annihilate the sexual differences, Jean Paul Gaultier likes to reverse the roles and break established codes that no longer have meaning today. He does not believe that fashion and apparel have a sex or gender. Jean Paul Gaultier is a real postmodern luxury fashion designer, as he likes to reveal the sensitivity of the man and to emphasize feminine power. In 1985, during his memorable parade "And God Created Man," he launched the skirt for men and did not hesitate to play on self-deprecation. Despite its subtle commercial success, this piece has the merit of breaking taboos and generating new questions about sexual identity. For the designer, the answer is simple: a man does not wear his masculinity in his clothes. His masculinity is in his head. Despite the resistance, this favorable climate gradually changes the ambient determinism of gender representation. The designer then imposes a different vision. His collection "A Wardrobe for Two" from the summer of 1985 is the highlight.

- **A digitizing consumption of luxury**. The luxury sector and particularly that of the fashion industry has long hesitated before being tempted by the digital world. Luxury brands, which are elitist, sensed an incompatibility between their values, such as exclusivity and rarity, and the mass market effect symbolized by digitalization that brings gratuitousness and transparency. However, in today's context, digitality is affecting and transforming the entire value chain from Customer Relationship Management (CRM) to in-store experiences and the use of technologies, such as virtual reality and artificial intelligence, to co-create products or to design efficient multichannel luxury experiences. Digital tools give a practical convenience to luxury, which should not be in contradiction with its exceptionalism. Although the use of digital devices is primarily for shopping purchase experiences, the potential of digital is still underestimated when it comes to designing emotional, efficient, and profitable luxury experiences with a fluid continuum from online to in-store experiences. Therefore, understanding the changing consumer, the way he/she uses digital devices to satisfy his/her functional, social, and emotional needs is an essential mission that allows luxury houses to design suitable and profitable business models and positive customer experiences.

Today's luxury businesses are experiencing immediate indicators of the important shift towards a digital reality characterized by multiple transitions: from product to experience, from owning to sharing behaviors, and from brand power to the power of persuasion. These digital trends can be regarded as challenges to or opportunities for luxury companies. Consequently, designing valuable customer experiences has become a top priority for luxury houses today. Gartner says that 89% of businesses anticipate competing principally on the basis of customer experience (Sorofman, 2014). As digital technologies become pervasive, luxury businesses should particularly be interested in understanding the influence of digital technology on customer experience in the luxury sector.

The challenges for luxury businesses are multiple. For one thing, the quality of customer service, which is reflected in the welcome as well as in other considerations, is principal in the world of luxury, but almost inapplicable to the digital world, which is characterized by rather pragmatic, efficient, and fast aspects of the luxury experience. Most of the digital strategies of luxury brands rely on "brand content," which is not enough today to emphasize the specificity and exceptionalism of luxury. That is why luxury brands should go beyond brand content strategies and offer digital experiences rather than digital content.

TREND 1.5

HUBLOT: FROM A DIGITAL CONTENT STRATEGY TO A DIGITAL EXPERIENTIAL BOUTIQUE

Luxury watch brands have been very slow to adapt to the digital age, but many have now begun to focus on e-commerce platforms and experiential retail to pull in consumers. Now LVMH-owned Hublot, a Swiss watch brand that prides itself on being anything but traditional, has developed a new digital technology platform for its Fifth Avenue boutique in New York City, capitalizing on a new customer experience that is emerging in the United States before being rolled out across the entire world in hopes of being a game changer. The new platform allows customers to communicate in real time with Hublot sales managers for a full 360-degree experience without ever having to physically step foot into the boutique. For the customer, it is a FaceTime or Skype call, but the experience is so much richer. Suppose a client is choosing between three different watches and needs a walkthrough of each timepiece. The client can simply schedule an appointment with the Fifth Avenue boutique via Skype or FaceTime, and a salesperson will prepare all of the material in advance. That includes videos that break down the movement piece by piece, technical specs, and more. Clients end up getting a fully immersive overview, and they do not have to spend any extra time researching the product themselves. The high-resolution camera allows the salesperson to show the client all angles of the watch in real time. Whether a client is on a plane, in a lounge, or tied up in the office, the new technology takes digital shopping to the next level and delivers the boutique experience via the digital realm.

Hublot is aware that the key asset of an excellent customer relationship is based on trust, availability, and flexibility, and has thus innovatively imagined a "virtual" digital boutique that perfectly matches the role and presence of its physical boutiques around the world. By remotely offering its customers 3D access to its products, knowledge, and know-how, Hublot is

(Continued)

(Continued)

successfully creating a new bespoke customer service while still preserving the essence of its relationship with the consumer through the element of human connection. This service allows Hublot to get closer to its customers at a distance while helping them discover the Hublot world and watches collection. It is an extra step that Hublot has taken that has placed it amongst luxury brands on the road to an e-commerce platform. Hublot offers its customers the same experience remotely thanks to its Hublot Digital Boutique. By doing this, the watchmaker seems to be attempting a delicate balancing act between tech-enabled convenience and the kind of exclusive, personalized service that still plays an essential role in a luxury brand's appeal.

THE DIGITAL LUXURY EXPERIENCE

The digital luxury experience is related to the integration of technology, big data, artificial intelligence (AI), and other connected objects into online, in-store, and retail luxury offerings. Screens, holograms, video projections, augmented reality, virtual reality, or robots and cyborgs are all digital devices that can be combined to provide enjoyable and effective digital luxury experiences. The logic centered on the digital luxury experience has been developed to complement digital marketing practices based on a product and sales approach that has not allowed luxury companies to take into account intangible and subjective experiential needs of their customers, including emotional, relational, symbolic, and ideological expectations. The concept of digital luxury experience addresses the relationship with the customer from his/her perspective, which evolves and changes according to the stages of the purchase both online and offline (before, during, and after). Thus, the digital luxury experience encompasses both human and technological factors, which are directly or indirectly related to the consumer and the way he/she lives and defines his/her luxury experience. These factors can positively or negatively influence the online and offline consumer and shopping experiences. Furthermore, the digital luxury experience is closely linked to the quality of services as well as to other components, such as well-being, learning, training, digital tools, and marketing techniques. All these elements accompany the customer in his/her luxury experience, and their importance varies according to the experiential stages. Therefore, the main objective of the luxury brand is to guide and assist the customer throughout his/her experiential shopping journey online and in-store by putting him/her at the center of its digital strategy, which requires studying consumer experiential expectations in the digital space as well as within the physical place, prior to setting up the global digital strategy of the company and selecting the technologies that can be used to achieve the company's objectives. The following section will introduce the main drivers of the digital transformation in today's societies. It will then examine in which way the drivers of the digital transformation can affect luxury experiences as well as the main challenges and opportunities that are emerging for luxury companies.

THE DIGITAL TRANSFORMATION OF LUXURY

At first glance, many factors seem opposed to luxury and its digitalization, whether it is the perceived elitism, emotion, and scarcity, or its universality, mass distribution, and mainstream nature. However, digital transformation is everywhere, affecting all sectors, including luxury. This section takes a look at the drivers of the digital transformation of luxury and offers a clear definition of what the digital luxury experience is, and what it is not.

DRIVERS OF THE DIGITAL TRANSFORMATION OF LUXURY

According to Batat (2019a), there are three main drivers of the digital transformation in today's societies: technological, demographic, and socioeconomic. These drivers affect luxury consumption experiences and generate new opportunities and innovation challenges for luxury businesses.

- Technological drivers include four main revolutions: mobile and Internet penetration; the increasing number of connected devices; the intensification of data collection, big data, and the cloud; and user interfaces for more interaction with machines, thanks to artificial intelligence.
- Demographic drivers of the digital transformation refer to two major trends: urbanization and accessibility. Urbanization has contributed to the development of new ways of delivering luxury and approaching supply in order to match consumers' wants and expectations. Mobile phones and Internet access are available even in the most disadvantaged consumption cultures in the world. Making technology accessible to everyone has contributed to enhancing the development of new digital-driver luxury consumption modes.
- Socioeconomic drivers have two aspects that enhance digital transformation in today's societies: the rise of digital native consumption cultures and the alternative sharing economy model. On the one hand, the rise of digital native cultures is a global phenomenon where young people born since 1990 are viewed as digital natives (e.g., Tapscott, 1998) and as a distinct generation with consumption practices that make them different from their prior generations. Nowadays, millennials and post-millennials are the most dominant and largest current generation within the marketplace (e.g., Sweeney, 2005). They are also viewed as empowered and digital experts, who can use their new knowledge to improve their luxury consumption experiences and their social life. On the other hand, the new sharing economy is shifting the logic from a traditional ownership model to a shared consumption of luxury. Also, the necessary technology for introducing a connected peer-to-peer luxury marketplace (e.g., second-hand luxury) has, in recent years, become accessible at a more balanced rate.

TREND 1.6

VESTIAIRE COLLECTIVE: AN E-COMMERCE LEADER FOR LUXURY PRE-OWNED ITEMS

Vestiaire Collective is a leader in the purchase and sale of second-hand luxury goods. Created in 2009, this marketplace connects buyers and sellers of used luxury goods. With more than 6 million members and 800,000 products available for sale, Vestiaire Collective quickly established itself as the European leader in second-hand fashion. Today, present in 57 countries, the marketplace generates 70% of its turnover abroad and will accelerate its development in US and Asian markets.

The strategy of Vestiaire Collective is similar to that of an auction house, where the auctioneer has previously conducted expert appraisals of the products. Vestiaire Collective experts check the quality of the clothes once the sale is guaranteed. It is an expensive service in labor, which lengthens the time of sale since it is necessary to forward the products to the headquarters of the company to store them, but it is justified by the risks incurred by the purchasers, considering the price of products. In addition, the rigorous selection of products on sale allows Vestiaire Collective to focus on the most expensive products, and as the margin is proportional to the selling price (and the inspection and validation costs are not proportional), this way of proceeding is a better source of profitability. The business model is therefore perfectly coherent. Moreover, the initial intuition to favor the community side of Vestiaire Collective gave it a network effect and created a buzz, especially amongst fashion bloggers. Vestiaire Collective can count on loyal and passionate fashion members, who share tips on current trends as well as tips on how to keep the shine of a leather jacket. The website lists 10 million interactions per month. It also offers the opportunity to follow people in the community whose style others like.

Thus, Vestiaire Collective has a business based around three pillars. The first pillar is moderation. When consumers drop a product on the website, a team of over 30 people check the photos and decide if it is likely to sell on the platform. The second pillar is quality control and authenticity. Absolutely 100% of the products sold on the platform will be sent to experts for a quality-authenticity check. Vestiaire Collective has vocation-created insurance in a marketplace where counterfeiting is a major problem. Finally, the third pillar is the community. As mentioned, Vestiaire Collective has 6 million members, who interact through various social features offered by the website. Moreover, to expand its digital experience into reality, Vestiaire Collective has decided to open an ephemeral shop in the heart of Paris in order to provide a completely unified experience to its community. The idea was to offer the community members a space where they can interact, try products, get advice on a sale on the website, interact with website experts, come for coffee, buy flowers, etc., which are all part of creating and offering an exclusive digital and in-store experience to its customers/users.

Digital transformation generates challenges and opportunities for luxury brands. Digital contexts build distinct and unique luxury experiences due to their socio-material characteristics (Batat, 2019a, 2019b). Mobile and social technologies immerse consumers in a world where material functioning is different from physical reality: geographical boundaries are irrelevant, events from the past can be re-enacted by accessing archived data (e.g., Kozinets, 2010), and impossible dreams can become real by creating virtual objects (e.g., Denegri-Knott and Molesworth, 2010). Digital contexts also allow high levels of interactivity with luxury brands so that consumers can play a proactive role in designing valuable experiences (e.g., Hoffman and Novak, 2009). As a result, different consumer luxury cultures specific to the digital environment have emerged giving birth to experiences specific to that environment. As digital technologies become pervasive, luxury brands should be particularly interested in understanding the formation of the new emerging values that consumers assign to their products and services in digitalized settings (e.g., Drell, 2014). Thus, luxury brands are encouraged to supersede the traditional good-centric logic by generating an "online value proposition" to design luxury consumption experiences tailored to the digital context (e.g., Chaffey and Ellis-Chadwick, 2012). Furthermore, the luxury digital element should then allow customers to circulate between different physical (offline) and digital (online) channels so that they can pass from one to the other with ease. This should guarantee consistency in the experiential journey from the physical to the digital context and vice versa. For luxury businesses, it is essential to create effective, high-performance digital customer experiences that are firmly rooted in consumers' daily habits both offline and online.

Yet, designing thematic points of sale equipped with touchpads or other screens giving access to the brand's website, as is available to any other consumer at home, is only a minimalist solution that will barely provide a small, in-store "phygital" purchase experience. The transformation of physical stores involves the use of digital tools to support the customer throughout his/her experiential journey – and it starts well before the customer opens the door of the store. Luxury houses should then combine different tools and strategies to offer the ultimate customer experience and enhance the continuum between the real place and the virtual space, and vice versa.

TREND 1.7

HOW SERGE LUTENS OFFERS NEW WAYS TO DISCOVER ITS PERFUMES: CUSTOMER EXPERIENCE – BETWEEN REAL AND VIRTUAL

In a digital society marked by the mass use of social networks, luxury companies have realized the importance of creating connected points of sale. If showrooming, which consists of

(Continued)

(Continued)

locating an item in the store before buying it online, has become commonplace, the opposite is also true: "webrooming" allows luxury perfume brands, such as Serge Lutens, to identify future online purchases before displaying them in a shop. As for "click-and-collect," if it is not a recent phenomenon, it extends more and more to become one of the main purchasing processes of consumers. Thus, far from the opposition offline/online, Serge Lutens relies on the phygital by bringing the digital experience into the heart of its physical sales places. The goal is to create a sales experience that is both complete and tailor-made. The outlets of Serge Lutens have also used virtual and augmented reality to meet the demands of a connected and pragmatic clientele. The company has embarked on the creation of a customer experience reinvented by digitalization. A mobile application allows the client to experience an augmented reality via a quest for symbols of the house in the virtual gardens of the Royal Palace. By rethinking and innovating its retail experience, Serge Lutens offers a fun and immersive time to its customers while familiarizing them with its codes and history. As the luxury French brand decided to review its marketing strategy in 2016, this will provide customers with a brand image and experience that is more consistent. As perfumery has become an ultra-competitive universe, the Serge Lutens offer should be quickly understandable in order to facilitate a rapid immersion and a continuum of the experience from the digital space to the physical place.

WHAT DIGITAL LUXURY EXPERIENCE IS, AND WHAT IT IS NOT

The confusion and approximations around the complex and multidimensional notion of the digital luxury experience have led me to propose, in this foundational introductory chapter, concepts which have traditionally been associated with digital luxury experiences in order to illustrate the narrow perspective of that scope, its implementation, and its economic stakes in the company's digital strategy in the luxury sector. I will now lay the foundations of a comprehensive definition of what the digital luxury experience is, and what it is not.

DIGITAL LUXURY EXPERIENCE: CUSTOMER EXPERIENCE VS. USER EXPERIENCE.

Digital luxury experience refers to the design of customer experience (CX) in the luxury sector. However, customer experience is not the user experience (UX). While most professionals use the term UX to refer to customer experience, they also need to understand the context and broader applications that CX brings beyond the UX, and at all stages of the customer journey, including when a customer searches for information, compares prices, tries a product, contacts an after-sales service, and so forth. The UX is, therefore, an essential element of the CX and should be considered one of the components of the CX at the same level as other elements, such as CRM, delivery, and loyalty. Luxury businesses interested in the customer experience should first understand the difference between the two notions (UX and CX) as well as identify and analyze in depth the components of the digital luxury experience that are likely to make the design of the UX much stronger, more efficient, and satisfying for the consumer at both functional and emotional levels. Unlike the CX, which has overall implications and a significant impact in terms of offering a suitable luxury experience, UX has a narrow vision, as it is limited to the user's experience and interaction with a specific tool, product, or platform to meet precise needs (e.g., the use of websites, applications, or software). The elements related to the use of these devices, ranging from interface design, ease of use, information architecture, and navigation, to the comprehension of content, learning, and visual hierarchy, come together to create the user experience, whether it is positive or negative. The goal of UX designers is, therefore, to ensure that the company develops technology products and platforms that solve the problem in an efficient and enjoyable way.

The UX is closely tied to the digital luxury experience, and like the other components of the customer experience, UX plays a vital role in customer satisfaction, or dissatisfaction. In order to satisfy their customers, luxury companies should develop an interest in ensuring consistency between UX and CX, as customers do not dissociate the two elements, and tend to interpret all their experiences and exchanges with the luxury brand as a single comprehensive experience without distinction between UX and CX. In fact, in an overall digital luxury experience, the consumer can experience a bad UX and a good CX, and vice versa. Both experiences are taken into account in the evaluation of his/her overall luxury experience that he/she interprets according to his/her own perception and own perceived values. The perception of value is essential to the enjoyment and satisfaction of consumers and is, consequently, of huge significance to luxury companies. The key values (see Table 1.2) luxury businesses should consider when designing luxury digital experiences are reliant on the consumer's personal perceptions: economic, functional, individual, and social outcomes of their customer experiences that are strongly interconnected, but not indistinguishable from each other.

Table 1.2 The key values of consumers

Typology	Characteristic
Value-in-exchange	This refers to the economic aspect of consumer value and includes four main forms of values: low cost; what the consumer needs in a product or a service; the quality a consumer gets for the price he/she pays; and what the consumer gets for what he/she gives
Value-in-marketplace	This describes five forms of consumer values: net value, marketing value, sale value, rational value, and derived value

(Continued)

Table 1.2   (Continued)

Typology	Characteristic
Value-in-time	This is a longitudinal perspective on value providing four temporal and staged forms that correspond with four stages of experience: ex-ante (anticipated) value, transaction (purchase) value, ex-post (consumption) value, and disposition (remembered) value
Value-in-use	This perspective emphasizes customer orientation and the relationships with the service provider, showing profound and more composite relations between sellers and buyers. A service attitude generating qualitative and positive connections allows suppliers to develop a full understanding of co-creating and sharing value with their customers
Value-in-possession	This defines material values as the propensity to place possessions and their purchase as fundamental in a consumer's life. Possessions are then seen as a means to happiness and as an indicator of one's own and others' success
Value-in-experience	Holbrook (1994) proposed a typology of consumer value-in-experience with three dimensions:
	Extrinsic/intrinsic: the consumer perceives value in using or owning a product or service as a means to an end versus an end in itself;
	Self-/other-oriented: the consumer perceives value for the consumer's own benefit versus for the benefit of others;
	Active/reactive: the consumer perceives value through the direct use of an object versus apprehending, appreciating, or otherwise responding to an object.

For example, when someone buys an application that modifies photos on his/her smartphone, the customer bought it because he/she likes software, such as Photoshop, and wanted such detailed, adapted, and accessible features on his/her smartphone. However, when using the application (user experience), he/she will realize that the interface is not easy to understand and that he/she does not have the features that were desired on the phone, which generates a frustration and a negative UX. However, with the online service, the consumer finds that one can call the customer service, who responds in a friendly and quick way to explain, step by step, how to access the desired features. In this case, the customer has just had a positive CX (customer experience): his/her problem is solved; he/she had a good time on the phone with a friendly person who created solutions to the problem. In addition, he/she has been offered a gift or a three-month free subscription to the premium service to discover other features and potentially buy them later (ROI efficiency). In this situation, the customer had a bad UX but a good CX. The same example can work in the opposite direction – in other words, in the case where the UX is good and the CX is bad. Another very common example, in the tourism and travel industry, is when a customer orders his/her plane ticket online, a practice facilitated by the downloading of applications set up by the airlines and available to travelers. In this example, the UX is positive, thanks to the use of an application with an ergonomic interface, which is easy, clear, and has a fast loading time – a process that in total requires no more than 15 minutes for the customer to buy his/her tickets. However, once at the airport, the traveler realizes that the situation is completely different when noticing that long queues have formed and that few wickets are open for the registration or luggage drop.

In this scenario where UX was positive, the traveler has just experienced a very nega-tive CX that will affect his/her tourism experience well beyond the experience of the airport because, in addition to what was already experienced at the airport, the service on board also happens to be of poor quality and the cabin crew is unpleasant with the pas-sengers. Thus, although the use of the application is satisfactory (UX), the other areas of experience (CX) have not been up to the task. UX alone does not satisfy the customer on both functional (ticket price compared to service) and emotional (the feeling of having been disappointed and mistreated by the company and its staff) levels. Figure 1.2 shows the main differences between user experience and customer experience.

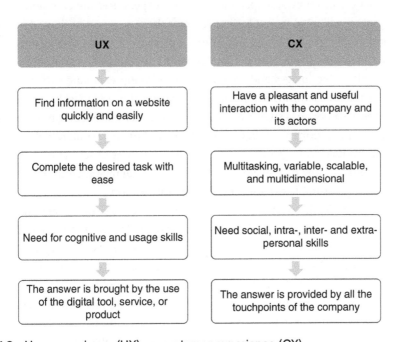

Figure 1.2   User experience (UX) vs. customer experience (CX)

WHAT DOES DIGITAL LUXURY EXPERIENCE MEAN?.

Marketing scholars, such as Punj (2012) and Mathwick et al. (2002), have previously investigated digital experiences, looking at the particular gratifications that consumers gain from using digital technologies. Overall, their works focused on the outcomes of digital consumption that have been found to promote positive utilitarian experiences; enhance socialization and relational experiences; simulate entertainment, hedonic, and playful activities; and focus on aesthetic experiences. Yet, it is not clear in these works how digital experiences differ from their physical counterparts. With regard to utility, Ratchford et al. (2007) indicate that consumers search for products and services and buy them online because it is more convenient. Thus, going online is more effective, more efficient, and less demanding than offline experiences both cognitively and physically, and allows consumers to make better decisions. Consumers feel that they are able to find the product or service that fits their needs or desires best because they have much more information available and access to a wider choice. They also feel that they can obtain the best price for a product thanks to price-comparison tools. Using Holbrook's (1999) terminology of consumer values, we can state that digital technologies enhance experiences of efficiency (convenience) and excellence (better decisions).

The shift from products to digital experiences also underlines the emergence of playful and aesthetic consumption experiences. Playful experiences are common because the interactive nature of digital technologies promotes the emergence of flow when searching for information (e.g., Web surfing) and using a product (e.g., playing video games). For example, Mathwick et al. (2002) state that rich media also allow users to build aesthetically pleasing and attractive images and sounds and to develop elaborate stories transporting consumers to imaginary worlds where they can escape reality and revel in their dreams – all of which, in turn, produce aesthetic consumption experiences. Furthermore, social media are an important component of digital experiences. Mathwick et al. (2008) indicate that social media produce feelings of "we-ness," that is, feelings of fellowship and togetherness in a group that allow the development of strong social relationships that can provide consumers with pleasurable experiences of social integration.

As indicated by Kozinets (2010), communications on social media are digitally mediated; consumers can bond with like-minded individuals whom they could not have reached otherwise because of geographical and time constraints. Altogether, digital technologies, therefore, facilitate the emergence of relational values in digital consumption experiences. Past research indicates that digital technologies produce experiences of enhanced efficiency (convenience) and excellence (best fit), facilitate the emergence of play (flow), create aesthetic experiences (narrative transportation), and allow the development of relationships that would have been otherwise impossible to build (linking value). Such characterizations of digital consumption experiences are very similar to that of offline physical consumption experiences in which these different types of value cohabit. In line with these considerations, digital luxury experience encompasses the UX and all the interactions that an individual is likely to have with a brand/company and across all channels of the brand, including a specific product, such as an application. The digital luxury experience refers to how users make use of the technology and tools available to them and how they view luxury business-related items and services, such as customer service, advertising, reputation of the brand, sales process, price, delivery, and so on. The goal for luxury businesses is to establish a balance between all of these elements in order to satisfy their customers and make them live a pleasant and effective overall luxury experience. All the components associated with the digital luxury experience are presented in Figure 1.3.

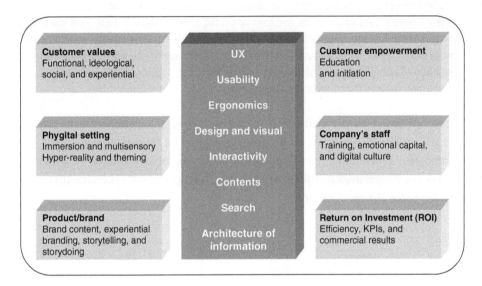

Figure 1.3   The components of the digital luxury experience

In response to the question of the evolution of the digital luxury experience and its continuity from the physical place to the digital space, and vice versa, I can take the example of the retail luxury sector and Burberry, who introduced iPads as part of its in-store experience. At the time, this was viewed as a digital innovation and as a real example of how this device would eventually be integrated into the global digital luxury experience. Devices such as iPads certainly allow a kind of continuum that is a practical and convenient "functional digital luxury experience" continuum; one that is located at one end of the experiential digital sphere and in parallel with the dimension of "emotional digital luxury experience," which is represented by the human aspect and the salesperson–customer interactions. The examination of the Burberry example demonstrates a number of concepts:

- Functional digital luxury experience makes the in-store customer experience as efficient and convenient as possible. This is true as well for the luxury brand's website, which needs to load quickly with available items, immediate shipping information, and more.

However, competitors can copy many elements related to the functional aspects of the digital luxury experience in order to eliminate obstacles to sales and make the purchase easier and more convenient for the customer. Thus, functional digital luxury experience alone is not enough to create a strong and sustainable competitive advantage. But the interesting point about in-store iPads is that, while not bringing many sales for a luxury retailer, this involves an effort to dissolve multiple barriers between internal divisions by providing staff in all Burberry stores with immediate access to information regarding whether products are available in the actual store and elsewhere.

- Emotional digital luxury experience is about creating an immersive, complementary, and unique luxury brand experience, in-store or online, that is totally in tune with the image and positioning of the luxury house's DNA. The distinction and the unique aspects of the luxury brand are created through the overall customer experience and are balanced by a selection of complementary elements, such as technological, practical, symbolic, social, and human factors that characterize the brand.

This rationale based on the distinction of the two types of experiences (emotional and functional) leads me, therefore, to propose, in Figure 1.4, the evolution of the digital luxury experience, which gathers components that are evolving differently according to the kind of the device used by the luxury brand, thus creating several digital luxury experiences (DCX) for the same brand.

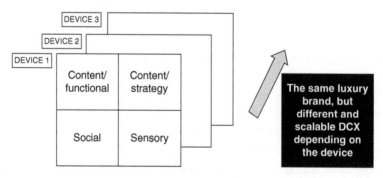

Figure 1.4 The evolution of the digital luxury experience

Furthermore, the digital luxury experience and its content also might differ according to the device used by the consumer (in-store tablet, smartphone, website, etc.). The design and delivery of digital luxury experiences can, therefore, vary in many ways depending on the luxury product, sector, luxury brand value perceived by the consumer, the symbolic and emotional dimensions of the luxury brand, the implication by the location and time that the consumer can dedicate to exchange, and so forth. The consumer can also choose between a functional or an emotional digital luxury experience, or consider both of them as the same experience. For example, a consumer can use his/her computer to access the luxury brand's e-commerce website and potentially choose to access more experiential brand content through videos, magazines, and blogs on another device, such as a tablet or on a smartphone, which is becoming more prevalent.

THE DIGITAL LUXURY EXPERIENCE AND CUSTOMER RE-ENCHANTMENT

In order to achieve an effective as well as a functionally and experientially efficient digital luxury experience while guaranteeing the generation of economic value, luxury companies need to consider a bottom-up, consumer-centric approach in which the starting point would be the user/consumer. By integrating the consumer into their digital and marketing strategies, luxury businesses will have a better chance of understanding the real needs of their customers and, especially, the technology and devices adapted to each expressed need, whether tangible or intangible. This essential step comes well before the conception of the offer (product and service) and the selection of the technological tool. In order to implement all the dimensions of the digital luxury experience at the strategic, marketing, communication, and operational levels, luxury companies should focus on consumer enchantment and how technology and digital devices can be used to succeed in their digital transformation, satisfy and retain their customers, design satisfying and emotional luxury experiences rooted in a phygital (in-store and online) context, and ensure the well-being of their employees while fulfilling a Return on Investment (ROI). In fact, offering a satisfying digital luxury experience means ensuring a consumer's loyalty, positive word-of-mouth, and the creation of a sustainable competitive advantage. However, although the consideration of the new consumer is important for luxury companies who do not have that awareness, most of their digital strategies are based on product marketing, which is not enough today to mark the specificity and the uniqueness of the luxury brand.

Furthermore, customer satisfaction is not enough to retain customers, who need to be enchanted, respected, surprised, and valued by the luxury brand and its staff. The concept of enchantment has been used in the field of marketing and consumer research by Ostergaard et al. (2013), who discussed Ritzer's (2010) enchantment theory and introduced the concept of consumer disenchantment as a critique of modern industrialized society: "societies can be described as disenchanted worlds in that they are characterized as having limited and peripheral space for enchantment, such as magic, religion, mysticism and wonder" (Ostergaard et al., 2013: 337). Amongst the tools and technologies that can help luxury brands create enchanting digital experiences, the following can be considered:

- **Mobile and mobile payment**. The mobile phone has become an essential object in commercial relationships. Firstly, these emergent technologies now allow luxury companies to establish a close connection with their customers and to personalize the messages that are addressed to them. But also, in terms of payment technologies, the phygital concept will revolutionize the act of purchasing goods and services, allowing, for example, customers to pay for their purchases at any time, including as soon as they enter the store.

TREND 1.8

LANCEL OFFERS A NEW MOBILE PAYMENT SYSTEM FOR ITS CHINESE CUSTOMERS

True to its spirit of innovation, Lancel became the first French brand to offer mobile payment methods in stores. By collaborating with a technology payment specialist, Lancel facilitates and enriches the store experience of its Chinese clientele. The luxury leather goods company offers its customers the possibility to use Alipay's mobile applications (owned by Alibaba) and WeChat Pay (owned by Tencent) as a means of payment. In China, these two applications are a real success: Alipay has more than 500 million active users against 600 million subscribers for WeChat. With millions of Chinese tourists visiting European and North American countries each year, the development of mobile payment technologies seems to be essential for international luxury houses.

This is a new system that is primarily aimed at Chinese customers since these two applications are used by hundreds of millions of Chinese consumers. The mobile payment with Alipay and WeChat Pay is now available in most of the brand's shops, such as Paris, New York, and London. Thus, Lancel became one of the first in the luxury sector to use this innovative mode of payment. In Paris, Galeries Lafayette also announced the introduction of mobile payment for its Chinese clientele.

- **Click-and-collect and e-booking**. With click-and-collect, customers can buy online at home or on-the-go and retrieve their items in-store without paying shipping costs. With e-booking, the customer reserves an article before going into the store without obligation of purchase. In the first case, the customer ensures that the product is available before purchasing and retrieving it. In the second, the customer comes into physical contact with the product he/she intends to buy, something that is not possible in e-commerce until the receipt of the product ordered is in the hands of the consumer. For luxury houses, click-and-collect is mainly a way to reduce costs and delivery times because, in order to bring customers into the store and create brand loyalty, it should be a sufficiently positive experience all round. Completely incorporating both into the in-store sales process as well as the customer's journey on the website is a very effective way of creating a positive experience. Luxury companies should propose services that already exist and that should be made omnichannel: the e-reservation; the gift card bought online and usable in-store, which can also be an effective way to bring new customers in-store; the possibility of picking up a gift in-store that rewards you for your online purchases; or an invitation to live a personalized experience in-store. And, if these services are embedded in a mobile application, they can be geolocated and personalized, thereby becoming even more effective.

- **Range extension and the break**. The customer orders an item from the store that is either unavailable on the website or sold out. This new practice can be either in the form of a catalog extension that enriches the still limited supply of the physical store, or in the form of product customization, as is the case in luxury items. However, the most important thing about this approach is that it restores the value of the sellers, who take their place at the heart of the relationship with customers to advise and guide them.
- **Shopper-centric focus**. One of the main differences between traditional marketing, sales, and the phygital is that the company has to think not in "consumer-centric" terms, but in "shopper-centric" terms – that is, to focus not on the customer, but on the buyer. The idea here is that the digital element should put itself in the customer's shoes and offer him/her digital solutions that are useful and enriching while streamlining his/her experience.

Luxury brands can also use numerous technologies, such as iBeacons, quantified-self apps, connected objects, and augmented reality amongst others, to connect real places with virtual space, thus designing suitable personalized phygital customer experiences.

TREND 1.9

ROLEX CREATES PERSONALIZED ONLINE AND OFFLINE CUSTOMER EXPERIENCES

Rolex uses technologies, but also offers innovative and complementary services to provide its customers and website users with a unique, tailor-made customer experience. Amongst these services, Rolex encourages its customers to create their own Rolex watch. A very interesting fact about Rolex is that one can simply visit their website and create his/her own custom-made watch by selecting his/her favorite materials, bezels, and dials that suit his/her personal tastes. Moreover, Rolex wants its customers to reward themselves and to celebrate success. In fact, Rolex customers believe that having a Rolex watch is a reward for themselves upon achieving

(Continued)

(Continued)

a personal success in their career. And, hence, by having the watch on their wrist, they will be undoubtedly interested in showing off their perceived success to others.

In its manufacturing process, Rolex uses a unique and innovative material for better-looking watches. To that effect, Rolex uses a specific type of steel that no one else uses. It requires special tools and skills, and is overall more difficult to work with it. Almost all the customers enjoy the benefit and value once they handle any steel Rolex watch. It is worth mentioning that it takes about a year to make one Rolex watch. On its website, Rolex posts impressive visuals to highlight its appeal and quality. Rolex watch images and videos perfectly capture the value and quality of its products. Rolex's commitment to quality visuals remains consistent on its website where it features extraordinary pictures of the brand's classic timepieces. The continuum in the experience also integrates the new servicing and five-year warranty. Rolex is not only expanding its watch warranty to five years, it is also extending a new service interval recommendation from three years to 10 years. This is a motivating development because it means that Rolex is saying its timepieces can be used for 10 years before they should go in for a cleaning and servicing.

SUMMARY

This chapter has examined the emergence of a new "digital luxury experience" and the key drivers of the digital transformation that affect customer experience online and offline. In this chapter, I have provided a more holistic and contemporary definition of luxury that allows luxury houses and professionals to design experiential offers that include all the dimensions related to luxury as well as emerging changes in the industry and how brands can benefit from them by designing unique luxury experiences that match customer expectations, thereby potentially increasing customer satisfaction, loyalty, and advocacy. In fact, a strong luxury experience can produce significant results, such as more customers, more sales, and more loyalty.

Nevertheless, with the advent of the digital era, many luxury companies are still struggling to identify the necessary action plan and digital strategies to set up. In fact, the luxury experience in the digital age essentially includes interactions of users with a digital interface (computer, tablet, or smartphone) as well as with physical agents in stores. Searching for a product online, using a mobile app to find the closest store location, and searching for technical support information on a smartphone are all digital customer experiences. It is not only a subset of the customer experience, but an integral part of the global experience. However, a good customer experience strategy is not merely a good digital customer experience strategy. Rather, it first requires the integration of the consumer's perspective in order to define the experience before selecting the digital device needed to design a positive and memorable digital luxury experience.

2
A NEW DIGITAL MARKETING STRATEGY FOR LUXURY EXPERIENCE DESIGN

INTRODUCTION AND SCOPE

Customer experience is a major element of the digital transformation in the luxury sector. Today, luxury brands are entering an experiential era that encourages them to set up new digital strategies as well as innovative marketing and communication actions involving profound changes that affect all of the company's functions. Indeed, luxury businesses can create a competitive advantage as well as attract and retain customers by shifting to a new digital marketing strategy focused on the implementation of the digital luxury experience. Prior to mastering the technology at the heart of the digital experience, luxury companies should adopt a bottom-up approach in order to fully understand the emotional, experiential, social, and functional needs of their actual and potential customers. However, extending customer experience in the digital sphere involves multiple challenges for luxury brands. By changing their practices, they will, therefore, have a better chance of understanding customers' digital experience needs before implementing a technological device.

Chapter 2 highlights the digital transformation of luxury houses and explains the evolution of digital marketing in the luxury sector. In this chapter, I examine the challenges and contributions of the customer experience as they apply to the design of memorable, efficient, and profitable digital luxury experiences. This chapter also introduces a new digital marketing strategy, "Blue Sunflower Marketing," which provides a disruptive approach to digital luxury, and other innovative tools, such as the Digital Luxury Triangle (DLT), that luxury companies can use to design successful and satisfying digital experiences.

THE EVOLUTION OF DIGITAL MARKETING IN LUXURY

The properties of technological tools and digital channels change and evolve as the Web evolves. The shift from Web 1.0 to Web 3.0 has strongly marked the changes related to the use of technologies in the digital strategy of luxury companies. Today, Web 3.0 is an obvious factor that luxury brands should take into account in their digital marketing strategies by incorporating three main specificities:

- The use of digital tools with high interactivity through exchange platforms and social networks, such as Facebook and YouTube;
- The proliferation of technological platforms and devices;
- The speed and immediacy of exchanges, thanks to high-speed Internet.

Figure 2.1 outlines the key features that emphasize the shift from the static and functional digital luxury era characterized by Web 1.0, to an experiential and immersive digital luxury marketing that is part of the Web 3.0 era. The transition from Web 1.0 to Web 3.0 or even Web 4.0 encourages luxury businesses to implement digital marketing tools that are compatible with designing efficient, profitable, and ultimate luxury experiences by setting up interactive, sensory, and immersive digital strategies. The shift from static to experiential digital luxury can be achieved by placing the customer at the heart of the company's strategy. The evolution of digital marketing in the luxury sector highlights three main periods that reflect the changes in the objectives of the digital strategy as well as the technologies and platforms used by marketing and communication professionals to make them succeed and meet the expectations of the targets.

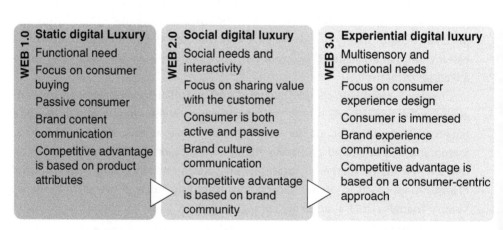

Figure 2.1   The shift from Web 1.0 to 3.0

FUNCTIONAL DIGITAL LUXURY (2003–2007)

The first years of the digital era in the field of luxury were marked by the Web 1.0, and its use as a top-down distribution channel by luxury companies in different sectors. In the era of static digital luxury, the two main elements of the Web were technology and content, which were used to facilitate the dissemination of information enabling offline and online transactions as well as the delivery of content or tangible products. Digital marketing and branding in the static digital marketing context included various aspects:

- Delivery of goods purchased on the website of the luxury brand;
- The downloading speed of content on the website (details, etc.);
- Online reward offers, such as vouchers or points;
- The location of a luxury brand store by search engines;
- Visual interface of the contents;
- Ease of navigation and good ergonomics of the brand's website;
- Personal offline assistance.

For luxury brands, it was, therefore, essential to remain attentive to the appearance of a new technology, a new tool, or a new use that could generate new behaviors. The Internet, by its size and its anchoring in the daily life of individuals, constitutes an opportunity for luxury brands' development and dynamism. Yet, when the Internet appeared in the 1990s, luxury brands were cautious about its use. They feared a loss of control, a destruction of their exclusivity, and rarity values. Marketing actions related to static digital luxury in the era of Web 1.0 were limited and included aspects such as the replication of offline luxury marketing strategies by using websites to disseminate content in the form of static brochures or adding conversational content. Luxury companies had the power to delete, control, or disclose information that they deemed in the best interest of the brand image or the sale. Figure 2.2 shows marketing actions and the tools used in this static digital luxury era.

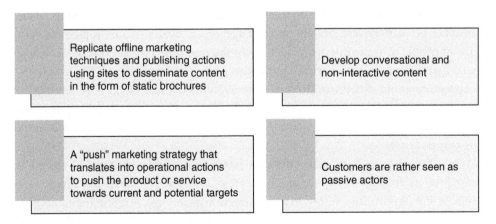

Figure 2.2 Marketing actions in static digital luxury

In this first phase, e-commerce was at its very beginning. Many luxury businesses were skeptical, but some of them have embarked upon the adventure without being sure of the outcome and the compatibility of e-commerce and luxury. The uncertainty related to the use of the Internet is linked to the risks associated with this tool, although it acknowledged multiple advantages for luxury brands. From the luxury brands' perspective, the Internet is an economic tool in terms of communication because the costs are lower than for other channels. In addition, luxury companies believe that the Internet is favorable because it allows the provision of a maximum of information simultaneously to many people. It is an almost unlimited medium where it is possible to show consumers what the DNA of a luxury brand is, through photos, videos, and product presentations.

For consumers, the Internet is perceived as a dynamic and innovative tool through which they can easily access brand information at any time of the day or night, without even moving around. However, at that time, users were unable to find what they were looking for and the Internet was used as a complementary tool to other media. Compared to a classic brochure, the Internet helps build a more personal and intimate relationship between the luxury brand and the consumer. Consumers particularly appreciate the websites of luxury brands with perfect aesthetics and which communicate in an understandable way. Yet, at the beginning of the static digital period, there were some limits related to the use of the Internet. It was perceived by luxury brands as a risky communication tool because consumers can take control of it (e.g., Okonkwo, 2009). By creating forums or blogs, Internet users are not only passive actors, but they can produce content about the brands as well. Luxury consumers, on the other hand, perceive the Internet as an interface that can be impersonal and complex. They do not appreciate a tool where everyone seems to be treated in the same way. These rather negative impressions are to be relativized according to the luxury brands' product categories. The Internet would not be suitable for conveying the image of luxury products whose dream content is their raison d'être (as for cosmetics and perfumes). Watches and accessories, on the other hand, can allow the integration of the Internet, while still offering a more prestigious catalog. Consumer perceptions also depend on their age: older consumers might perceive luxury as incompatible with the Internet, which is not the case with younger consumers who are digital natives and ultra-connected. During this period, e-commerce was regarded both as an opportunity and as a threat. Hermes, Tiffany, Burberry, and Gucci were amongst the first luxury fashion brands to focus on digital development and to start selling their products online. Indeed, the luxury sector is constantly evolving by innovating and seeking new growth factors.

While luxury brands typically develop selective networks of physical stores, the Internet offers consumers who do not have close access to one of the few luxury stores available the opportunity to buy their products and services (e.g., Seringhaus, 2005). These virtual shops may also be suitable for consumers who feel intimidated when entering luxury brand stores. Furthermore, the Internet offers many consumer services, such as product customization, online payment, and delivery. Also, an e-commerce website provides information in a new way, with photos, and videos, to help compensate for the lack of physical contact. Luxury brands, however, should be careful to maintain their essence and remain consistent with their identity (e.g., Geerts and Veg-Sala, 2011). With these many benefits, the demand for online luxury goods worldwide is growing (e.g., Okonkwo, 2010). However, at that time and according to Dall'Olmo Riley and Lacroix (2003), only 5% of consumers visited luxury brand websites to purchase a luxury product. This can be explained by the major potential risks perceived by consumers and which are related to the online purchase of luxury items:

- As the Internet is a large distribution channel, luxury brands using it might face an increased risk of spreading counterfeits (Kapferer and Bastien, 2012). Furthermore, luxury brands also fear a potential cannibalization of e-commerce compared to their traditional stores (Larbanet and Ligier, 2010). Also, this way of distribution forces luxury brands to reveal their prices, providing consumers with the possibility of making easier comparisons with competitors. Dall'Olmo Riley and Lacroix (2003) state that there might also be a risk related to the fears expressed by luxury brands' managers who could be threatened by the loss of spontaneity of buying on the Internet because of conscious decision-making.
- The visual appearance of the websites of luxury brands is another factor that can affect the purchase online. At the beginning of the Internet and e-commerce, a high heterogeneity of websites was observed. At that time, most websites were aesthetic, but not very operational. They did not offer online sales or areas reserved for privileged members, and most of their clientele had only limited contact with the brand.
- Lack of experience appears to be a fundamental limitation of the use of e-commerce for luxury brands. E-commerce does not convey the emotions or provide the sensory input that is essential in luxury. Consumers, therefore, have a preference for in-store luxury experience, wherein they feel considered and immersed and well-served in a luxurious universe.
- The risk of insecurity of online payment perceived by some consumers reinforces the mistrust of luxury brands in the adoption of e-commerce. These various risks are relative to the categories of products. The luxury hotel business sector would sell very well on their websites and the Internet. The same would be true for fashion accessories, wines, or spirits. On the other hand, e-commerce would not be suitable for fine jewelry, for example.

Twenty years later, luxury brands have developed their own websites with forceful e-commerce strategies to capture an ultra-connected clientele. In fact, luxury brands are now accelerating their online development in a highly competitive marketplace. According to a study by Altagamma-McKinsey Digital Luxury Experience Observatory, the share of e-commerce in total sales of luxury brands is expected to reach 12% by

2020 (vs. 6% in 2015) and online sales of luxury goods could triple by 2025 (Catena et al., 2015). Although a significant increase, this figure remains well below other markets, such as clothing. In June 2017, after 18 months of development, the LVMH Group launched 24Sevres.com, its international online platform and mobile application dedicated to its luxury brands. This website, designed as the digital showcase for its famous Parisian Le Bon Marché store, brings together over 170 banners and offers the possibility to order from 70 countries. The objective is to attract online customers with new offerings. This e-shop brings a strong added value to the LVMH Group, which is different from most competing luxury brands and other pure players. Another example is from September 2017 when Givenchy opened its e-commerce website with the aim of making e-commerce one of the brand's top five boutiques in the world.

Nowadays, six out of 10 sales in the luxury sector are influenced by the Web in the form of direct or in-store purchases after online searches, according to the latest study conducted in 10 countries in 2016 by the Boston Consulting Group: "Digital or Die: The Choice for Luxury Brands" (Abtan et al., 2016), It is, indeed, a profound transformation for these luxury brands that will require maintaining an optimal level of service and high-quality customer experience that will reinforce their image and reputation, while dealing with the competition of digital players and their multi-brand luxury e-shops. But, the wait-and-see attitude of luxury houses has enabled high-end multi-brand websites, such as Net-a-Porter, Matchesfashion.com, and Farfetch, to become key players in luxury e-commerce.

Thus, 2017 promised to be a record year for the sector: sales worldwide (textiles, leather goods, accessories, watches, jewelry, etc.) represented 262 billion euros, according to a report published by Bain & Co. in October 2017 and which highlights the inevitable rise in online luxury sales. For example, the Kering Group announced a 60% increase in online sales of its luxury goods in the first quarter of 2017 after a growth of 12% in 2016, representing a growth rate that is larger than its physical stores. The e-commerce website of Gucci, the Italian luxury brand, even achieved a growth of 86%. Because of its pioneering work in e-commerce in the 2000s, Burberry is regarded as one of the first brands to have sold luxury ready-to-wear goods on the Internet. Today, this pioneer of the Web has a very aggressive digital commercial strategy. When the user arrives on Burberry's website, he/she lands directly on its own e-shop, while on other luxury brand websites, the user must first navigate advertising campaigns, videos of fashion shows, or content centered around the news of the brand. Twenty years later, we can say that the idea of incompatibility between e-commerce and luxury is now completely gone. Indeed, a luxury brand that does not sell online will no longer exist because of the change in the behavior of today's luxury consumers.

However, although the Internet and e-commerce is a source of huge opportunities and sales growth, this technology also generates strategic risks for luxury brands. In fact, for the past decade, luxury brands have been trying to strengthen their grasp on online distribution channels, which coincided with the growth of a global online market, fueling widespread fear of e-commerce threats to two fundamental pillars of luxury:

pricing and distribution. Yet, arriving late in this market has allowed luxury players to master the already established technologies and learn from the mistakes of the pioneers. Today, this industry is facing a new reality where the physical and virtual worlds are merging, representing a major new source of profit for luxury brands. However, exploiting these digital opportunities is not without risk. In fact, e-commerce increases the risk of conflict between the channels (physical and digital) and amplifies the problems of control over distribution. The worst-case scenario for a luxury brand is a wholesaler who sells its products over the Internet at lower prices than in the luxury brand's own stores. Previously, luxury brands might not notice, or would prefer to ignore, that wholesalers sold their products; now they clearly feel the difference when less high-end websites sell their products from anywhere in the world.

TREND 2.1

RAY-BAN AND THE DARK SIDE OF ONLINE LUXURY

Although the Internet provides several opportunities for luxury brands to increase sales and connect with their customers, it might also increase the risk of conflict between the channels: physical (in-store) and digital (company's website, social media, multi-brand e-commerce, etc.), thus intensifying the problems of control over distribution, fake products, and promotional offers. This is what happened to a premium brand of Italian sunglasses and eyeglasses. Ray-Ban, as wholesalers, used to sell its products on the Internet at lower prices than in its own stores. Consequently, the company was eventually forced to reduce its presence in the United States and implement a minimum posted price policy, banning wholesalers from advertising Ray-Ban products at discounted prices in order to protect the reputation of the brand. Furthermore, e-commerce can also bypass the geographic price architecture that has been introduced in this sector over time. Thus, a brand that sells its products at a higher price in its stores in, say, China and that offers consumers the opportunity to buy the same product on its website for a lower price due to lower European or American tariffs will probably end up having negative consequences in terms of brand reputation and consumer trust.

SOCIAL DIGITAL LUXURY (2007–2012)

This era refers to the interactive Web 2.0, which moves away from the top-down model characterized by one-way, hierarchical mass communication. The emergence of social digital luxury and the development of social media platforms and forums have facilitated the delivery of content by users as well as co-creation and sharing between users. Unlike functional digital luxury, social digital luxury integrates the user into the heart of its strategy as an active participant and co-creator of content. Social digital luxury includes the following features:

- It is multichannel and based on a multiuser approach in which each user has the power to share information and communicate it in a positive or negative way.
- In social digital luxury, the success factors of digital luxury (e.g., speed of download or the appearance of the website) are no longer part of customer satisfaction. In fact, the new elements of user satisfaction are now human factors that luxury brands cannot control.
- Human factors can positively or negatively influence the image of the luxury brand, its marketing strategy, and its communication.

In the 2000s, the evolution of digital luxury marketing has undergone several developments. Although functional digital luxury used to adopt a rather practical vision according to which the company knows how to produce what is good for the consumer because it has the expertise and the consumer is considered naive, social digital luxury has a more customer-centric logic, the objectives of which are the following: co-creation, communication, and value delivery. These objectives are integrated into a strongly consumer-driven approach resulting from dialogues and interactions between the consumer and the company that increases the luxury brand's creativity. For Prahalad and Ramaswamy (2004a), changing the roles of consumers from isolated to connected, from ignorant to informed, and from passive to active, would go hand-in-hand with the change of their relationships with companies. Thus, the traditional system (value creation by the firm for passive consumers) would become obsolete (Prahalad and Ramaswamy, 2004b), for luxury companies would no longer be a "market to consumers," but rather a "market with consumers" (Cova and White, 2010) by integrating the consumer into the heart of the luxury brand's actions, and by promoting the co-creation of value (e.g., Ramaswamy, 2008), in particular with the help of social media to create and develop its own virtual brand communities (e.g., Kaplan and Haenlein, 2010). The definition of brand community, as acknowledged by many scholars (e.g., Andersen, 2005; Bagozzi and Dholakia, 2006; McAlexander et al., 2002, 2003) and established by Muniz and O'Guinn (2001), is a specialized community that is not geographically delineated but based on a series of structured relationships surrounding brand admirers/enthusiasts. The features of social digital luxury marketing are summarized in Figure 2.3.

Although the creation of such a community is possible for all brands, it is important to note that brand communities are most often formed around a strong brand that involves the consumer emotionally, such as Louis Vuitton. In the social digital luxury era, the Internet allows new possibilities for luxury houses to create their virtual brand communities. Rheingold (1993) defines virtual communities as a social group emerging from the

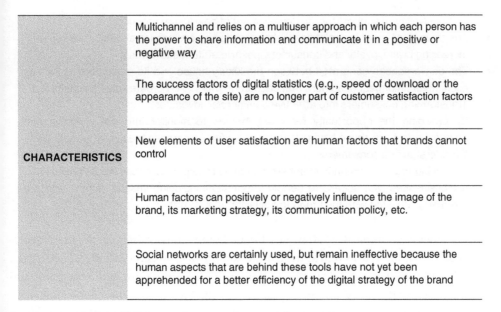

CHARACTERISTICS	Multichannel and relies on a multiuser approach in which each person has the power to share information and communicate it in a positive or negative way
	The success factors of digital statistics (e.g., speed of download or the appearance of the site) are no longer part of customer satisfaction factors
	New elements of user satisfaction are human factors that brands cannot control
	Human factors can positively or negatively influence the image of the brand, its marketing strategy, its communication policy, etc.
	Social networks are certainly used, but remain ineffective because the human aspects that are behind these tools have not yet been apprehended for a better efficiency of the digital strategy of the brand

Figure 2.3   Characteristics of social digital luxury marketing

Internet when a reasonable number of individuals support public discussions long enough, with enough human feelings, to form a network of personal relationships in cyberspace through various social media platforms (Facebook, Instagram, Snapchat, YouTube, etc.). For Park and Feinberg (2010), these virtual communities have the potential to reshape the way consumers learn, understand, form an opinion, and process information about luxury products and services for their decision-making. Spreading viral information or a positive e-WOM (online word-of-mouth) rather than passively consuming products is one of the advantages of virtual brand communities.

The effects of e-WOM are more significant for virtual brand communities (e.g., De Valck et al., 2009) than for traditional communities, particularly in the effect, speed, and duration of information (Park and Feinberg, 2010). The e-WOM is not only limited to the knowledge of the source, but now extends to users of websites around the world, thus crossing important physical barriers. Therefore, e-WOM helps consumers report their experiences of products and services in a very easy way and the community to convey a message in an extended way. The comments provided on the Web are therefore quickly disseminated inside and outside communities (Brodie et al., 2011) and the duration of the e-WOM officially stops only when the texts are erased (Park and Feinberg, 2010). According to Shang et al. (2006), virtual communities can be divided into two types: commercial and non-commercial communities. There are several reasons why luxury brand managers may create a virtual community around their brands. Amongst the benefits of online brand communities, the following are considered:

- The possibility of support for the development of new luxury products;
- The strengthening of the relationship between luxury businesses and their customers;
- Increasing brand loyalty and consumers' positive attitudes towards it;
- The conversations generated between the luxury house and its customers as well as exchanges amongst consumers that encourage them to co-create value for the brand;
- Transforming consumers into effective commercial advocates;
- By providing the opportunity for luxury brands to monitor information exchanged amongst members, these types of communities would increase the luxury brand's ability to understand its consumers;
- By making brand community members' identities transparent, social media provide luxury businesses with access to certain information, including images of fans who are voluntarily affiliated with the brand (e.g., Naylor et al., 2012).

Through their communication strategies, luxury brands convey their values, their ideologies, a particular lifestyle as well as the culture and the history of the brand (e.g., Danziger, 2005; Joachimsthaler and Aaker, 1997) in order to attract the most elite consumers and advocate exclusivity, rarity, and inaccessibility. In the Web 2.0 era, two main challenges are part of the digital strategies of luxury houses, namely, the preservation of a strong reputation as well as the strengthening of their exclusive personality amongst their elite customers. With social media and through virtual communities, luxury brands should be capable of charming the masses and creating desire while preserving exclusivity.

For Hoffman and Novak (1996) and Kozinets (1999), these online communities evoke one of the most exciting advancements of the social Web in which the human dimension, co-creation, and interactivity are crucial for luxury brands that are trying to enhance their relationships with their customers. Therefore, involving consumers in the co-creation process of luxury items and experiences is not an end in itself. Nowadays, a luxury company may engage in the co-creation process if the participation of the consumer is considered as a value. The involvement of the consumer requires favorable conditions allowing the transformation of ideas into innovation and products as they respond to existing needs. Today, more and more actions should be taken by luxury companies to engage the consumer and benefit from his/her knowledge and creativity by involving him/her in the company's offer and its improvement. For luxury businesses, it is, therefore, important to understand at what stage they should involve the consumer and by what means. The idea of co-creation has been a rather new concept in the luxury domain that adds a relevant understanding regarding the difficulties of the experience and exchange value expected by customers. This perspective provides a clear vision of the participation of customers who can also be considered as co-creators, or even employees who are remunerated, and thus play an important role in the production and the delivery of offers. In recent years, consumers have become more integrated into the process of designing products and services; innovations are, therefore, a more consumer-oriented logic.

Prahalad and Ramaswamy (2004b) describe the value of co-creation as a joint initiative through which providers (companies) and recipients (consumers) create value together. In the co-creation process, value is created reciprocally for each of the market actors (consumers, organizations, and networks) who engage in the process by interacting and exchanging their resources. The interactions take place on an engagement platform where each market actor shares its own resources, integrates the resources proposed by other actors, and potentially develops new resources through a learning process.

This definition emphasizes the importance of the Internet and online platforms in the construction of the relationship between companies and customers. Thanks to the development and democratization of technology, today, luxury companies no longer have the monopoly on information, or even an exclusive benefit from access to information. Consumers and luxury businesses have the same information, which reduces the power that firms hold over consumers.

In fact, the Web 2.0 has allowed consumers to express themselves and engage actively with luxury businesses, thus becoming a new source of competence. Furthermore, Prahalad and Ramaswamy (2004b) emphasized the idea that today's consumers are more connected, informed, empowered, and active, and they have new tools that help them to make choices, resist, collaborate, or even negotiate with companies. Therefore, maintaining a dialogue between the company and its customers in the co-creation process is very important for guaranteeing a positive and satisfying customer experience.

In the Web 2.0 era, consumer participation in the creation of the offer was first considered as an approach to increase efficiency by using the client as a free workforce, and thus attaining a lower price (e.g., Fitzsimmons, 1985; Mills and Morris, 1986). In the consumer culture paradigm, most research suggests enlarging consumer participation and expanding it in the experiential sphere, since it benefits to lead the consumer towards a consumption experience and provide him/her with satisfaction, values, and reward. In this perspective, co-creation is connected with a dynamic participation that suggests that consumer engagement helps in determining the luxury brand's offerings, which is perceived by the customer as a value-in-exchange since he/she plays an active role in the creation process, and thus is considered legitimate and competent. Beyond products and services, luxury companies should offer their consumers a real experience of co-creation. Value is no longer unilaterally created by the company, but co-created with the consumer. This model is consistent with the theorization of Da Silveira et al. (2001) because, regardless of the level of mass customization, and therefore the degree of consumer involvement in the process, in order to co-create value with the consumer, the company will always need to engage in a dialogue with the consumer by making certain tools available to generate interest and share information.

Finally, social media have been shown to produce feelings of we-ness, that is, feelings of fellowship and togetherness in a group, and to allow the development of strong social relationships, providing consumers with pleasurable experiences of social integration. When consumers become core members of a community, they gain status in the group and receive approval and praise from their peers in the community, generating pleasurable experiences of social enhancement. Because communications on social media are digitally mediated, consumers can bond with like-minded individuals with whom they could not have otherwise connected because of geographical and time constraints. Altogether, digital technologies, therefore, facilitate the emergence of relational value in consumption.

EXPERIENTIAL DIGITAL LUXURY (2013–PRESENT)

Experiential digital luxury is about taking into account the customer experience with its functional, emotional, and relational dimensions in the digital strategies of luxury companies that seek to differentiate themselves from the competitors by creating unique, effective, and enjoyable digital luxury experiences. These digital experiences, whether online or connected via the Internet of Things (IoT), contribute to improving the quality of the physical luxury experience (in stores, hotels, restaurants, etc.). With the evolution of digital technologies and social networks, luxury businesses are faced with a key issue in creating the ultimate online luxury experience. The goal for luxury brands is to engage users and make them experience memorable digital experiences and emotions through immersion and co-creation in virtual worlds using the latest digital innovations.

Experiential digital luxury is then very important for luxury brands because it helps to improve the quality of both online and offline experiences. With the evolution of digital technologies and social networks, luxury brands are confronted with a major problem related to the creation of a coherent and effective online luxury experience with the added value of the physical experience lived in-store. In the era of Web 3.0 and 4.0, online social interactions can be facilitated by immersive technologies, such as 3D and 4D, avatars, augmented reality, connected objects, 3D printing, etc. However, while the role of immersive technologies as a tool for creating the digital luxury experience on websites is confirmed every day, there are still many questions as to the elements that can bring to life online luxury experiences for individuals. Implementing luxury experience that has been studied in a physical environment and adapting it to a virtual context raises two questions:

- How can luxury brands integrate the components of the physical luxury experience into commercial and non-commercial websites in order to create a pleasant and memorable virtual luxury experience?
- How can we translate sensory, emotional, cultural dimensions, etc. (characteristics of the luxury experience in a real context) in a digital context?

The starting point of any successful digital experience strategy is not the creation or the use of an innovative technological tool, but rather the creation of the digital experience from the consumer standpoint in order to understand when luxury brands should incorporate digital devices, and what kind of needs they are aiming to satisfy (e.g., social, functional, or emotional). It is, therefore, essential to know the new consumer, the way he/she uses digital technologies in his/her consumption, and his/her expectations when it comes to using technology in the luxury consumption and purchase process. Figure 2.4 shows how luxury businesses can create innovative and effective digital luxury experiences by taking into account the consumer's point-of-view.

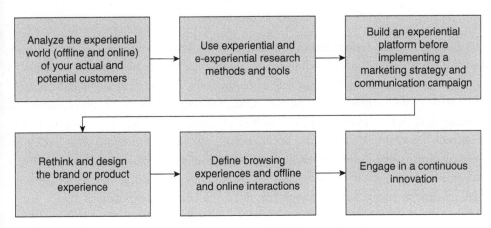

Figure 2.4   Steps for creating an innovative digital luxury experience

By changing their practices, luxury brands will, therefore, have more opportunities to understand the online needs of users before implementing a digital luxury marketing device to ensure the development of the luxury brand. Furthermore, to be efficient, the experiential digital luxury concept should incorporate three key characteristics: immersion, co-creation, and efficiency (Table 2.1).

Table 2.1   Three key characteristics of experiential digital luxury

Characteristic	Definition
Immersion	Immersion in the digital world should be designed to allow users to live virtual experiences by incorporating immersive and interactive technology tools linking the physical environment of the luxury brand and the virtual context. These two elements bring a realistic dimension to the online luxury experience. Thus, customers can live virtual experiences similar to experiences in the real context (in-store, hotel, etc.) because they can interact with online brand virtual agents and physical agents (staff, salespeople, etc.)

(Continued)

Table 2.1   (Continued)

Characteristic	Definition
Co-creation	Users should be involved in the process of co-creating the luxury products or services, as well as in the marketing strategy and communication of the luxury brand. They can give their opinions on products and services and customize the products according to their needs
Efficiency	The marketing of experiential digital luxury should provide a cognitive response (e.g., convenience, time savings, comparison, customization) and an emotional response (e.g., pleasure, hedonism, online socialization)

Emerging research has started to characterize how digital experiences are qualitatively different from their physical counterparts. Digital experiences have been characterized as virtual and imbued with transience, instability (e.g., Watkins, 2016), fragmentation, and a sense of augmented reality. Social media experiences have also been characterized as networked and polyvocal (e.g., Kozinets et al., 2010), wavering between private and public conversations. Therefore, for luxury brands, the digital context creates a practical convenience for consumption practices, which should not be in contradiction with the experiential dimension of consumption. Two main issues for luxury brands that are interested in implementing a digital strategy focus on the customer experience:

- The quality of customer service within a human dimension is crucial, but quasi-inapplicable to the digital universe, which represents a rather pragmatic, effective, and fast-paced side of the experience.
- The emergence of a new generation of "digital natives" (see Chapter 3), whose behaviors drive luxury brands to rethink their communication strategies, and thus adapt their digital schemes by combining both online and offline experiences in order to attract and retain this generation of consumers.

TREND 2.2

ASTON MARTIN DIGITAL AND EXPERIENTIAL APPROACHES

For the luxury car brand Aston Martin, owning a luxury car like an Aston Martin should be more than just providing mobility. The owners are not just buying a car, they are also joining a family and, as such, the car company ensures the experience lives up to the promise of the brand. For example, Aston Martin believes that there is not much value to its customers in providing a concierge service, as they typically have this already in their lives. However, its customers do want to have interesting and engaging experiences with the company that are unique to the ownership of an Aston Martin. That could be a private visit to the factory or access behind the scenes at a Formula 1 race. The customer experience is, then, based on personal contact between the company and its customers alongside a digital relationship. In fact, in 2016, the car company undertook a total overhaul of its website and configurator technology. Today, Aston Martin has a website that has richer content, a more sophisticated and luxurious user experience, and is enabled for viewing on multiple devices. The parallel investments in configurator technology were equally important, as this is where its customers will come and start to create their personal Aston Martin. To enhance the continuum and the fluidity in the customer journey, the luxury car brand has also extended this technology into its retail network, and is now working on next-generation technologies, incorporating virtual reality to offer more immersive online and offline experiences.

Although the introduction of the digital customer experience is important, most luxury companies' digital strategies rely on digital content marketing, which is not enough today to convey the specificity and exceptionalism of the luxury brand. For this reason, luxury businesses have to guarantee a multichannel continuum of customer experience by taking into account the specificities of digital tools and their diversity. In fact, the digital luxury experience reflects all the interactions between a luxury brand and its consumers that take place through digital channels (email, social networks, online advertising, etc.). Digital channels can create value in various ways, such as improving customer knowledge, facilitating the customer journey, or enhancing the consumer connection to a brand. Thus, luxury brands should draw on the digital data obtained from the exploitation of social media data to enrich their knowledge of customers in B2C or B2B experiential settings. They can also involve consumers by asking them to share their experiences with their digital connections, whether they are fashion products, like Burberry, or travel experiences, like luxury hotels. Luxury companies can also decide to launch their own online communities and use the Internet of Things to add social value to their products similar to mass brands, such as Nike does with its jogging community, or American Express with its entrepreneur community. Finally, by creating online contests, luxury brands can create social dynamics and increase their experiential reputation, which goes beyond the brand reputation, amongst their consumers.

The success of a digital luxury experience principally relies on two complementary pillars. On the one hand, there is the careful assessment of customers' digital data in order to understand their journey and create luxury experiences that meet their expectations at each moment of their journey; on the other hand, luxury brands should understand and use the social dynamics that enhance the community aspect of purchasing behavior and, thereby, amplify the impact of the proposed customer experience. For example, not only does the L'Oréal Group systematically use digital data to imagine and set up model customer journeys, but it also relies on influencers, such as YouTubers (see Chapter 3), to amplify the messages of its brands at different points of the customers' journeys.

TRANSFORMING LUXURY BRAND EXPERIENCES

Digitalization is not only about the use of the Internet and marketing techniques applied to websites. It can also be associated with several activities, techniques, and tools used according to two key elements: the objectives of the company and its global digital strategy. These two elements, defined upstream in the luxury company's digital strategy, influence the type of tools and platforms used to deliver an effective and optimal implementation of the digital strategy. The fields of action of digital transformation are multiple, and are related to its content, which can become operational through the use of several digital channels: social media, emails, mobile phones, tablets, etc. In order to facilitate the implementation of an effective digital experiential strategy, it is important for luxury companies to understand the specificities of digital marketing and its digital resources for selecting the right digital channel. Thus, understanding the specifics of digital marketing leads luxury brand managers to make a more informed decision about which digital tool will be best suited to meet brand goals at different levels: strategy, marketing, communication, sales, etc. Indeed, each digital tool has a characteristic that directly or indirectly influences the way it is used.

The use of tools, therefore, has an impact on the goal of the luxury company's digital strategy. The implementation of digital marketing strategies that are focused on the customer experience allows the luxury brand to locate the customer at the center of its strategy. This placement helps marketing and communication managers reduce the discrepancies that may exist between different experiences (e.g., the experience expected by the consumer must not be too far from the experience desired by the company). Therefore, the accomplishment of a successful experiential digital marketing approach requires the development of two organizational skills: (1) the ability of the company to intervene on the elements that constitute the consumer experience in order to adjust the digital offer to the symbolic and emotional needs expressed by consumers, and (2) the aptitude to guide and assist customers in their own luxury experiences lived in physical places or/and in digital spaces. In order to design an optimal experience, Pine and Gilmore (1998) propose five main factors of experiential marketing (Figure 2.5), which luxury companies can take into account when designing the experiential offer both online and offline.

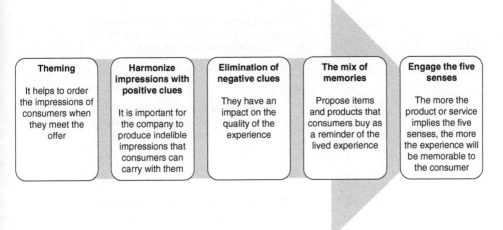

Figure 2.5 Five factors of experiential marketing

The digital luxury experience logic is, therefore, the only effective strategy that offers companies a differentiation of their offerings from competitors, the creation of a sustainable competitive advantage, and the loyalty of their customers. Thus, creating a luxury experience in the digital world is a winning strategy that allows luxury brands to respond to the transformations of the economic and digital environment. At a time when the competition is ever more intense, the digital experience has become a key factor for luxury brands when attempting to attract and retain customers. To meet the demands of the new consumer's increasingly digital and emotional needs and expectations, luxury companies should incorporate the digital customer experience by offering a package comprising five main features:

1. Deliver offline and online experiences that are useful, exciting, emotional, and interactive;
2. Allow consumers to choose their experiences and the way in which they would like to interact with the luxury brand;
3. Luxury brands should reserve a space for improvisation and customization of its offers;
4. Establish a continuum between in-store and online experiences;
5. Collect immersive and deep data to better understand the online behavior of the target.

Today, more than ever, luxury brands recognize that a positive online customer experience is essential to the success of the global digital strategy of the company. Several factors can explain the importance for decision-makers to use digital tools to deliver a satisfying and profitable digital customer experience. Figure 2.6 summarizes the advantages of the use of different digital tools in creating successful digital experiences in luxury.

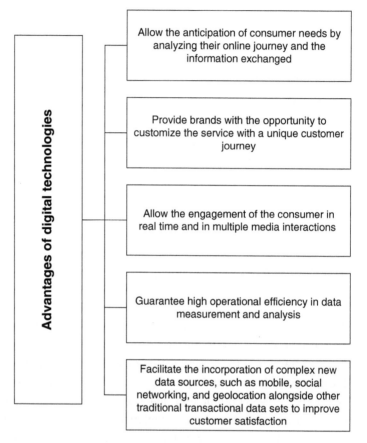

Figure 2.6   Digital tools used in the customer experience

HOW CAN LUXURY HOUSES IMPLEMENT A DIGITAL STRATEGY FOCUSED ON CUSTOMER EXPERIENCE?

The luxury experience lived in the physical environment is affected by various elements, such as the quality of the offers (products and services), emotions, relationships, well-being, learning, training, and marketing tools, that help to support the customer in his/her experiential journey through the incorporation of digital technologies, and tools that help improve the quality of the customer experience. In fact, consumers enjoy physical experiences, such as attending concerts or buying in concept stores, as well as digital experiences, such as playing video games.

MAIN COMPONENTS OF THE DIGITAL LUXURY EXPERIENCE

In order to guarantee a consistent customer experience continuum that extends the real-life experience through the integration of digital technologies, luxury brands need to identify the key components of the physical customer experience in order to incorporate them into the implementation of their digital strategies. Luxury companies can, therefore, select digital solutions adapted to the digital luxury experience they have defined. The components of the digital customer experience that luxury companies should focus on when designing their experiential offerings both online and offline include the following:

- Individual (customer/consumer);
- Environmental (physical and digital);
- Marketplace (competition, policies, industry, etc.);
- Temporality (anticipated, lived, required, and memorized), which defines the needs of the customers according to the stage of the digital experience.

In order to extend the customer experience to the digital context, luxury brands should think of the digital luxury experience according to three levels of reflection: What are the drivers of the digital luxury experience? What are the values associated with the digital experience? And, what is the goal of the digital experience? The success of the experiential digital strategy involves aligning and balancing the three components of the digital luxury experience (Figure 2.7). These components are directly or indirectly related to the customer experience, and might have a positive or negative impact on the global luxury experience as well as on the image of the luxury brand, depending on the consumer values.

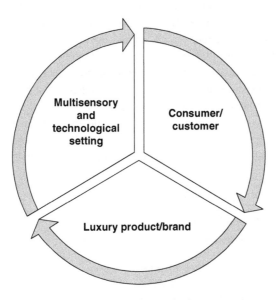

Figure 2.7   The three components of the digital luxury experience

- **Customer/consumer**. The question that the luxury company should ask before the development of its digital strategy is the type of value sought by its customers that the company can incorporate into its digital strategy in order to offer an unforgettable digital luxury experience. In fact, the value perceived by the customer is a key element that can help luxury brands, especially from a consumer perspective, improve the overall digital experience. Amongst consumer values (e.g. Holbrook, 1994, 1999), the following should be considered by luxury companies:

    o   Utility value (efficiency and excellence). Refers to a functional value based on the attributes of the product. It is about the quality and unique know-how of the luxury brand;
    o   Ideology value (ethics and spirituality). The purchase of a luxury good (product/service) is based on consumer consciousness and his/her value system;
    o   Experiential value (playfulness, affection, and aesthetics). Looking for fun and surprises through escaping everyday life. It is also characterized by the beauty and emotions related to the consumption of luxury;
    o   Social value (status and esteem). Refers to the social bond sought by the consumer. It is a consumption of certain luxury products to reinforce the consumer's self-esteem and self-confidence.

- **Luxury product/brand**. Digital brand content is a key strategy in creating digital luxury experiences. The brand content allows the online luxury brand to create a strong connection with its customers. It is an inbound marketing (content marketing) strategy that consists of producing online content in order to communicate, not only about the product, but also about the brand universe, its values, and its identity. Digital brand content enhances the luxury brand's culture, know-how, DNA, authenticity, history, and values. In the digital customer experience, brand content is key to differentiating itself from the competition and creating online proximity to the customer. The objective of digital brand content depends on the function that brand managers will assign to it (Table 2.2).
- **Multisensory and technological setting**. To create a memorable and rewarding digital customer experience, luxury brands should take into account a multisensory and technological environment that provides an intense and continuous immersion of the consumer into the digital experience. An immersive and multisensory digital experience translates into the five senses: olfactory, auditory, tactile, visual, and taste. Of these five senses, only the visual and sound elements are used as part of the digital experience. The olfactory element is still in the process of experimentation. The taste and tactile elements are very difficult to reproduce in the context of the luxury brand's online website, however they can still be achieved through other approaches and technological tools.

Table 2.2 Functions of digital brand content

Function	Characteristic
Identification function	Guide customers in their choice of brand to meet their needs for quality, use, price, etc. The digital brand content also plays a role of memory marker to recall the previous experience related to the brand
Decision function	Digital brand content provides customers with credibility and trust-based information to guide choice and decision-making

Function	Characteristic
Value function	Digital brand content is directly linked to the values of the brand
Justification function	The digital brand content also has as a main function the justification of the price of the products and services offered by the company
Positioning function	The digital brand content makes it possible to position the brand and to differentiate it from its competitors – its symbolic distinction that marks the spirit of its customers

TREND 2.3

"LE PETIT CHEF": AN IMMERSIVE LUXURY DINING EXPERIENCE VIA MINI-MAPPING TECHNOLOGY

Traditionally, visual mappings are considered an important means of expression that apply to buildings on the occasion of major events. Yet, the Belgian Skullmapping studio, directed by Antoon Verbeeck and Filip Sterckx, with its interest in scenography and experience design, has used high-resolution Panasonic projectors and mini-mapping to create new customer experiences by introducing the concept of "Le Petit Chef," or "The Little Chef." According to its founder, the concept comes from a request from a client who wanted a table mapping for an event. Table mapping is not a new idea, but so far, it was mostly graphic.

The studio created a human animation, with a little animated character that moves around the restaurant table and cooks the client's food. Initially, the mapping only concerned the preparation of the main course, but the video, posted on YouTube, went viral (4.3 million views in the first 10 months), and Skullmapping added an entrée, a fish dish, etc. Now, the mapping describes the design of a complete meal, including appetizers, the main course, and dessert, in addition to a culinary journey of the dishes to make the wait times at the restaurant more enjoyable. After the huge success of "Le Petit Chef" on the Internet, the Skullmapping agency has been approached by several luxury hotels and restaurants around the world, from Russia to Dubai, wishing to acquire rights to use the animation or make new animation projections to create luxurious, entertaining, and immersive dining experiences.

Furthermore, customer experience in a physical environment is determined by a large number of personal, interpersonal (including salespeople and other customers), and extra-personal factors (e.g., the overall atmosphere of the environment, its geographical location, its olfactory dimension, its temperature, its lighting, its ambient noise, its music). These factors are often beyond the direct control of the company and may be a barrier to making a purchase, or may negatively influence the consumer experience, and thus increase customer dissatisfaction. However, unlike the consumer experience in a physical environment in which customers can tolerate a few minutes' waiting, online users are much less patient and tolerate no technical failure when downloading a product sheet or the validation of a shopping cart. The hypersensitivity of consumers online is explained by the promise and the technical specificities of the Internet: speed, practicality, and simplicity (e.g., clicking on a mouse to buy a product is much easier than going to a store in the city center). Moreover, as Borowski (2015) states, a wait of more than 10 seconds for a page to load can mean that 50% of the users will abandon the site, thus making the website lose its attraction. The technical problems associated with the use of digital technologies are not the only reason that explains the poverty of the digital customer experience and the dissatisfaction of online consumers. Indeed, the adaptation of sensory, emotional, relational, and cultural components of a luxury experience lived in a physical environment (e.g., in-store, hotel, restaurant) within a digital setting is a major challenge that luxury companies should take into account in the implementation of their digital strategies. Although the customer experience is an important element for guaranteeing significant results with more customers, more sales, and more loyalty, many luxury companies still struggle to identify an action plan to implement the ultimate luxury experience in the digital world, and thus guarantee the success of their digital strategies.

THE CHALLENGES FACING DIGITAL LUXURY EXPERIENCE OFFERINGS

There are many challenges related to the digital transformation of luxury companies wishing to implement a digital strategy focused on the customer experience. One of the main changes that luxury companies make at the time of digital transformation is the transition from a digital marketing logic with a technical orientation to that of a digital customer experience that requires new skills as well as adequate human and economic resources for its implementation. In this section, I identify seven main challenges related to a company's implementation of a successful digital strategy to offer the ultimate luxury experience offline and online (Figure 2.8).

TECHNOLOGICAL AND TECHNICAL CHALLENGES

The digitalization of the customer experience requires technological tools and specific technical skills that luxury companies should acquire and master. Beyond the importance of using social media, such as Facebook and Twitter, to establish an instant and lasting relationship with their customers, the technological challenges for luxury companies in creating and delivering digital customer experiences are related to two main

Figure 2.8   Seven challenges of digital luxury experience design

aspects: multichannel and the omni-usage of mobile phones. These technological challenges bring a multiplicity of solutions and relational channels in order to offer the best digital customer experience before, during, and after the purchase.

- The intensification of multichannel usage is one of the most important issues in replicating the physical luxury experience within the digital world. With the proliferation of digital channels used by customers to interact with luxury brands (SMS, emails, mobile applications, chat, forums, communities, social networks, e-commerce, etc.), luxury companies have an obligation to apply a multichannel strategy that guarantees a consistent and seamless customer experience between the different digital channels. In fact, the behavior of the consumer who is constantly switching from one channel to another encourages luxury companies to develop a multichannel customer journey by offering a satisfying customer experience that should be both functional and emotional, regardless of the channel used. The multichannel logic should be to link the different digital channels to each other as well as to the physical stores. For example, customers should be able to search for information on their computer, register the product on their tablet, confirm their order on their connected watch, and receive an SMS indicating that they can pick up their parcel in the closest store.

- The omni-use of the mobile phone. The digital equipment of today's consumers is growing at a steady pace, giving priority to the mobile phone, which becomes the reference equipment. The rise in mobile phone equipment reflects consumers' enthusiasm for smartphones and their various usages that now go beyond the simple call or sending messages (e.g., browsing the Internet, downloading applications, geolocation, or mobile video viewing). Therefore, the smartphone has revolutionized the uses of consumers and, even more so, their experiences of consuming and purchasing luxury items. The new usages linked to the mobility and interface of smartphones represent a major challenge for luxury companies that would like to offer functionalities and content adapted to smartphones. This presence is not only about a responsive website or mobile applications, luxury brands need to build an effective and sustainable strategy with a high-value user experience that includes associated services. Thus, luxury companies looking to deliver a quality digital luxury experience need to integrate the mobile channel into their experiential journey thinking by improving the mobile customer experience beyond responsive design or SMS communication, as is often the case.

TREND 2.4

WECHAT, A MULTIFUNCTIONAL CHINESE APP FOR DOING EVERYTHING VIA A SMARTPHONE

WeChat may be the Chinese app that will replace all the other apps available on smartphones for users all around the world. In the space of six years or so, this app, which was created in 2011 for the simple purpose of instant messaging, has become the app to do anything for 900 million Chinese users. Amongst the features of WeChat, we can mention the following:

- Exchange photos and audio content;
- Send short voice messages;
- Integrated camera usage for videos;
- Geolocation services;
- Reading QR codes;
- Advanced chat services with call and video conferencing;
- Microblog service allowing users to post images in a message and brief texts;
- Emoticons library management service;
- Pay for purchases on the Internet or in stores;
- Order a taxi;
- Pay water and electricity bills;
- Buy tickets for trains, planes, and more;
- Book movie tickets, etc.

WeChat is unsurprisingly the most popular application in China and far ahead of its US competitors. Chinese and international brands are increasingly interested in this app, which they can use as a communication tool, as a database, as a tool for collecting customer information, and as a sales channel. For the Chinese, WeChat has become an unavoidable platform for daily use, and now attracts luxury brands, such as the French house Dior, which became the first luxury brand to sell high-end bags on WeChat. After opening its e-shop on WeChat on August 1st, 2016, Dior put online a limited edition handbag, the Lady Dior Small China Valentine, on its account. The objective was to celebrate the Chinese Valentine's Day on Tuesday, August 9th, and to trigger sales. The Dior site was stormed and stocks of the handbag model depleted in a day, despite a price of 28,000 yuan ($4,370). Dior's communication campaign was also successful: a huge number of articles about Dior were read on WeChat the day of the campaign launch.

The technological and technical challenges of the customer experience in the digital era of multichannel and mobile ubiquity lead luxury brands to rethink the digital experience by using a multi-device approach in which present and future exchanges are closely linked to past, present, and future luxury experiences, thus avoiding the break-up of the relationship, and creating a relational coherence between the customer and its brand through the different digital channels.

ANALYTICAL CHALLENGES

Big data and customer analytics issues are not only limited to data collection, but also include data analysis and understanding, data exploitation, and multidisciplinary analytical skills that use alternative methods to create or improve the customer experience. The data allow luxury companies to understand the experiential journeys identified on several platforms according to modes of navigation specific to each individual. The collection of data is very important, but it has no purpose if the analysts are not able to interpret and, especially, contextualize the data. According to the experts, in 2020, 30 times more data will be produced than in 2010. This evolution is due, in part, to the multiplication of digital channels as well as to the intensification of the use of connected objects in everyday life. Although big data are important for luxury brands, it is essential to be able to analyze them in a relevant way in order to reuse them to create effective and profitable digital and physical experiential strategies.

Luxury brands should, therefore, acquire the means to analyze, organize, contextualize, exploit, and make visible the data by implementing satisfactory and efficient, economic, strategic, and creative customer experience offerings. If big data contribute to customer knowledge and adapt pre-sales and post-sales marketing, it is the same during the buying experience. Intelligent multichannel data management around the customer allows luxury companies to identify the elements of dissatisfaction before the customer expresses them to the company, or on its social media. Today, the big challenge for luxury companies is to move from a logic focused on algorithms that generate and collect data (big data) to a more efficient approach in which "immersive smart data" (this idea is developed in Chapter 10) are at the heart of the customer experience offering. The interest for luxury companies is, therefore, to understand how big data can contribute to creating a quality and profitable customer experience, and thus guarantee customer retention.

HUMAN CHALLENGES

The place of the human in an experiential and digital setting is essential in the creation of a satisfying customer experience. In terms of relationships, the community logic that exists in exchanges on social media does not allow for the translation of the full dimensions of customer experience in the digital age. Customers appreciate luxury brands that interact with them and listen to them. For an effective human presence on social media, the luxury brand should offer a customer-oriented digital experience by allowing instant exchanges via community managers and interaction channels that are both adapted to and responsive throughout the experiential customer journey offline and online. Today, the challenge for luxury companies is to master the human aspects that constitute an integral part of the customer experience, and that are likely to differentiate the luxury company's offer from its competitors, and guarantee it a sustainable competitive advantage. Indeed, human dimensions play an important role in the sharing of values between luxury brands and their consumers as well as in the immersion of customers in a context of virtual consumption, or during their online purchases. In fact, consumers want to live immersive experiences in themed digital environments involving the five senses; luxury brands should, therefore, turn to disruptive and experiential designs when planning their digital platforms (mobile applications, website, in-store digital devices, etc.). Tools such as augmented reality, virtual reality, gamification, 3D, and 4D could be integrated into the creation of an immersive and emotionally charged digital luxury experience.

ORGANIZATIONAL AND MANAGERIAL CHALLENGES

The implementation of an experiential strategy in the digital age requires the participation of all the functions of the company as well as new managerial skills. The shift to a customer-centric logic and digital experience requires the involvement of different departments and profiles in creating and improving the digital customer experience. This represents a great challenge for managers, who should rethink their managerial methods as well as the synergies between the different functions of the organization. Indeed, the involvement of the various departments and functions of the luxury company (R&D, marketing, sales and commerce, finance, etc.) allows all the actors of the organization, regardless of their department and function (engineers, salespeople, computer scientists, etc.), to better understand the functional and experiential needs of customers, and thus optimize the creative, digital, and commercial resources by merging their knowledge in a collaborative and multidisciplinary work. This initiative can be achieved within the framework of the creation of a new "digital customer experience" department dedicated to the design and improvement of the customer experience in both real and digital contexts.

Luxury employees in all departments of the company should also be trained according to the specificity of this business to better capture consumers' values and respond to customers in order to provide them with a quality luxury experience where the challenge is to serve the customer in a human way that also includes a digital channel (Twitter, Facebook, etc.)

CORPORATE CULTURE CHALLENGES

The integration of a culture within a luxury company that places the digital customer experience at the center is an important stake for the success of the digital transformation of the organization. It is difficult to define an organizational culture in which the digital customer experience is uniformly shared across departments. Yet, this is a critical element in creating a satisfying digital luxury experience that should be both functional and emotional. The cultural issue is as important as the global digital strategy initiated by the luxury company. However, the commitment of the company's staff to the digital customer experience culture is not obvious. Although this topic is integrated into the company's project and communicated to all employees throughout several departments, the customer experience expressed through the luxury company's digital strategy seems rather abstract, with no concrete purpose or intelligibility. Today, the challenge for luxury companies is to explain to their employees the content and objectives of their digital strategies focused on customer experience in order to break down the barrier between the different personnel that are supposed to work together (e.g., between data scientists and marketers by connecting big data to strategic decisions, marketing, communication, and so forth).

For luxury brands in the digital age, a cultural transformation is required in order to deliver an online customer experience. The integration of digitalization has been favored by the development of an organizational culture following the arrival of new professional personnel (e.g., engineers, computer scientists, community managers) in luxury houses.

Faced with the noticeable reality of the digital world and the importance of taking into account online shopping behaviors, luxury brands have initiated several projects focused on providing a customer experience, or rather, user experience, to their customers online. For luxury houses, the challenge of digital transformation is not only linked to the creation of an e-shop or to the development of a mobile application, or even to be present on social media, such as Facebook and Instagram; it is also about offering continued experiences connecting physical stores to online shopping. However, while there are concrete examples of this digital transformation in luxury, it is not easy for luxury houses to implement all the dimensions related to lived physical experiences in-store. Additionally, the actions offered online are often limited to improving the user experience and navigation, customization, and other convenient services. Here are some examples of luxury brands that make efforts to connect with the consumer by offering practical online services:

- Saint Laurent launched its application "color shade Yves St Laurent";
- Guerlain has set up a makeup color chart on its website to provide users with a digital experience focused on finding the right product match online;
- Louis Vuitton offers its customers the possibility to customize their bags on its website;
- In the luxury retail sector, The Printemps Paris offers its customers a personal shopping service through online booking, which gives the customer personalized support in-store and a tailored welcome in its private and exclusive lounge.

Therefore, adopting and developing a corporate culture focused on the digital customer experience philosophy enables luxury houses to take full advantage of the digital channels and the resulting data to improve the offline and online customer experience. A customer-oriented digital culture is achieved, firstly, through bringing data analysts into the business and involving them in strategic decisions and, secondly, through the training of managers and marketers in the analysis and interpretation of big data and algorithmic language. Building a corporate culture that places the customer and his/her digital experience at the center of the luxury company's strategy is a long-term mission that involves the planning of actions as well as the training of employees in terms of the strategic and business challenges of an experiential and digital transformation in order to make them adhere to this new philosophy. The reality in the luxury business today is very different. Although it is important for all departments of the luxury company, marketing or interdepartmental teams often drive the customer experience, and the degree of maturity of the culture of the digital customer experience is not the same depending on sectors and different structures in the same sector of activity. During its transformation, every company goes through different stages, from the awareness of the primacy of customer experience in its digital transformation strategy to the implementation of concrete actions in terms of marketing and communication plans as well as operational actions and digital strategies. Figure 2.9 summarizes the steps of the digital transformation of luxury companies.

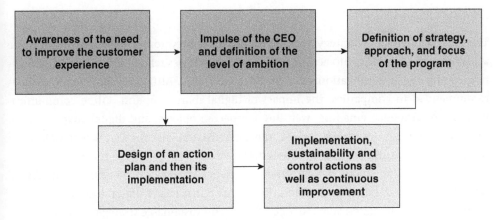

Figure 2.9   Five steps of the luxury digital transformation

In order to achieve a successful digital transformation while improving the customer experience, the luxury company should gradually rethink its organization by creating functionalities, departments, and processes allowing each function in the organization and each profile to contribute to the digital customer experience project at the heart of the scheme and the culture of the company.

ALLOCATED RESOURCES CHALLENGES

For luxury companies, embracing a corporate culture centered on the digital customer experience requires investments and allocated resources. Although investments often focus on innovation and new products and services development, the success of the digital customer experience requires investment in tools and skills to engage the customer throughout the experiential journey online and offline. Investing in digital customer experience offerings is, therefore, important for what it represents in terms of ROI, as well as in terms of the sustainable competitive advantage it creates. However, there are still gaps between the intention to integrate a philosophy centered on the digital customer experience and the execution of the action plan. While most luxury businesses believe that customer experience is essential for their growth and competitiveness, only a few of them have developed an effective and profitable customer experience program. This discrepancy can be explained, on the one hand, by the complex and abstract dimension of the customer experience and its ROI, and, on the other hand, by the lack of resources and skills allocated to the implementation of a global strategy involving all the departments of the luxury company.

ENVIRONMENTAL AND SOCIAL CHALLENGES

The development of a strategy focused on the digital customer experience cannot be achieved without taking into account environmental issues related to the impact of technology and the intensification of digital device usages. Although dematerialization is recommended in companies, the impact of digital marketing and online communication via social media, emailing, websites, connected objects, and digital advertising on the environment is not minor. Indeed, the conventional wisdom that dematerialization has no impact on the environment is simply wrong. The challenge for luxury companies wishing to implement the customer experience strategy at the center of its digital transformation is to better understand the impact of the use of digital tools on the environment in order to design adapted, operational, and sustainable strategies and programs. The implementation of an experiential and digital strategy can, therefore, contribute to the intensification of the use of digital multichannel tools. In order to ensure an efficient and ecologically responsible digital customer experience, luxury houses should take into account three main elements:

- Understanding the impact of Information and Communication Technologies (ICT) and their lifecycle;
- Developing eco-responsible digital communication practices, at least internally (e.g., avoid sending emails to communicate with colleagues in the same office as much as possible);
- Developing eco-friendly websites and blogs, for instance by improving content accessibility, providing responsive content, and resizing visuals.

TREND 2.5

WATTVALUE, A GREEN ENERGY WEB SERVICE THAT CERTIFIES GREEN WEBSITES

Founded in 2006, WattValue is a French company specializing in the European certification of renewable electric energy. WattValue represents electricity producers in the main renewable sectors: hydroelectricity, wind, and biomass. The company encourages electricity consumption that promotes the development of environmentally responsible production methods within the context of demand management and the limitation of energy wastage.

Inspired by the Naturemade quality label, WattValue is one of the first digital players to implement the green electricity label on the French market, an initiative led by the Renewable

Energies Liaison Committee and WWF-France. Amongst the brands that have chosen to certify their websites, we can mention the following: http://assurance.bnpparibas.com, www.assurance-credit.cardif.fr, www.assurance-sante.cardif.fr, www.bouygues-immobilier-mayenne-capucins.fr, www.concorde-hotels.fr, www.garnier.com.ru. Thanks to the WattValue certification, consulting the pages of these brands' websites has a reduced impact on the environment.

THE DIGITAL LUXURY TRIANGLE (DLT) TOOL

The Digital Luxury Triangle (DLT) tool is fundamental for luxury companies that wish to create and improve their digital luxury experiences. In order to make the most of this innovative tool, luxury brand managers should follow the steps summarized in Figure 2.10 to develop a global digital strategy aimed at improving the customer experience at the functional, relational, and emotional levels. The figure presents the DLT tool, its content, and the related strategies that help luxury houses optimize their digital customer experience offering.

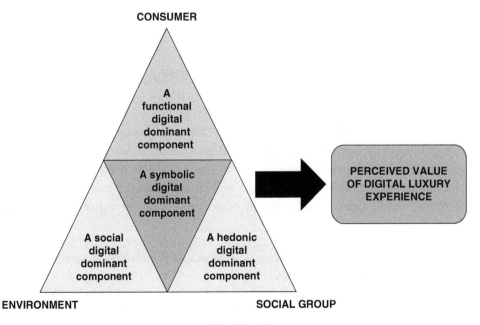

Figure 2.10 The Digital Luxury Triangle (DLT) tool

Therefore, DLT is a strategic tool that luxury companies can implement to design a digital experiential offering based on the four dominant components tailored to their customers and which allow them to win new customers. This tool provides luxury brand managers with three main strategies: (1) a predominantly utilitarian strategy, (2) a predominantly social strategy, and (3) a predominantly hedonistic strategy. The first strategy is intended to meet the functional and practical needs of customers. It reflects the offer made by the luxury company to its customers (e.g., e-commerce website). The two other strategies (social and hedonistic) aim to improve the digital customer experience as well as to answer, beyond the utilitarian dimension of the digital experience, the consumer's relational and symbolic needs (e.g., social media) and fun (e.g., online gaming websites). Figure 2.11 presents a classification of digital tools according to their dominant dimension (utilitarian, social, and hedonistic) that luxury professionals can use to design a comprehensive and overall digital luxury experience online and offline.

Functional digital strategy	Social and symbolic digital strategy	Hedonistic digital strategy
• LinkedIn and Twitter • Brand website • Search engine • Browser • Wikis • ...	• Facebook • Instagram • Snapchat • Periscope • ...	• YouTube • Online games • Advergame • ...

Figure 2.11   Digital tools for designing luxury experiences

In addition to its strategic dimension, the DLT tool incorporates three main elements: the individual (customer/consumer), the social group (friends, Internet users, peers, and family), and the environment (professional, cultural, institutional, etc.) within the design of the digital luxury experience. There are mutual interactions between the individual and his/her social group as well as with the other actors of the environment and the marketplace according to four main areas:

• The micro-environmental space refers to digital usages in the private sphere of the individual in his/her family environment.
• The meso-environmental space is the local setting shared with other individuals (semi-public spaces, neighborhood, workplace, shops, etc.), and reflects digital usages within the framework of interpersonal exchanges.

- The macro-environmental space reflects digital usages in public collective environments (e.g., cities, rural areas), and refers to collective digital usages (e.g., the characteristics of digital usage of city dwellers versus those in rural areas).
- The global environment area refers to the context in its entirety where sociocultural, historical, religious, and political variables, amongst others, shape users' profiles and digital practices.

These distinctions help luxury companies to understand and analyze the triptych relationship between individuals, groups, and the environment in terms of the usage of tools and online channels in designing suitable and satisfying digital luxury experiences. Indeed, the design of a digital customer experience should include different dimensions according to the spatiotemporal scale in which the customer is located and, therefore, define the typologies of the digital experience in line with its cultural environment and digital equipment, a consumer's digital usages, and his/her socio-digital needs in terms of efficiency and effectiveness, autonomy, economy, self-fulfillment, socialization, entertainment, immersion, well-being, and performance.

THE BLUE SUNFLOWER MARKETING APPROACH TO DESIGNING SUCCESSFUL DIGITAL LUXURY EXPERIENCES

BLUE SUNFLOWER MARKETING: WHAT IS IT?

Blue Sunflower Marketing is a disruptive strategy combining customer experience, digital marketing, and breakthrough innovation. It is a hybrid and evolutionary process based on an analytical logic guided by critical and experiential design thinking. The metaphor of "Blue Sunflower" reflects the complexity and the multidimensional aspect of the digital customer experience. Furthermore, the characteristics of Blue Sunflower Marketing revolve around three major elements: consumer perspective, uniqueness, and subjective emotion.

Digital marketing that focuses on customer experience should include the consumer perspective and follow the customer in his/her experiential journey online and offline by adapting its tools to the needs of customers that can vary throughout the journey. The idea of Blue Sunflower Marketing follows the same logic of a sunflower, whose movements and orientation vary throughout the day. The petals of the sunflower follow the sun all day long. In the early morning, the sunflowers are facing east, during the day, they follow the sun, and in the late afternoon, they look to the west. The Blue Sunflower Marketing approach, when applied to the digital luxury experience, is, therefore, not static; luxury brand managers should rethink the tools and their digital strategies to make them evolve in the direction of the customer in order to offer him/her a suitable and adaptable evolving digital experience.

The metaphor of the blue color reflects the unique and descriptive aspects of the digital luxury experience. In fact, in order to offer value to consumers, the luxury experience should be both unique and distinctive compared to dominant digital offerings. Indeed, no one would notice a yellow sunflower, especially in a field where all were alike, all of the same yellow color. In contrast, a blue sunflower in a field of yellow sunflowers will be instantly noticed by its blue color, and perceived as fascinating, intriguing, seductive, or disturbing. Like the blue sunflower in a field, the new digital marketing based on the Blue Sunflower Marketing logic can make the digital customer experience a pleasant, seductive, or provocative experience. It is, in fact, a deconstruction of what exists in order to rebuild it again in a digital context with other sources in order to generate the WOW effect that is an integral part of a successful digital luxury experience. The third characteristic of the experiential offer in the digital era refers to the creation of positive emotions in the digital world. In order to succeed in its digital customer experience strategy, the luxury brand has to include components that generate positive emotions for the consumer. The luxury brand should then place the peace of mind of the consumer at the center of the digital experience. This dimension is very emblematic of the cultural significance of sunflowers in the language of flowers. The sunflower expresses a sincere message of support, a desire to bring some sun to a person in difficulty; this is the goal of the digital customer experience.

The Blue Sunflower Marketing paradigm challenges the traditional digital marketing logic that focuses on digital tools, by taking into account the disruptive, subjective, and emotional dimensions of digital tools and their impact on consumer behavior according to the context in which the product or service is purchased or consumed. Blue Sunflower Marketing explains how classic digital marketing should evolve from a logic that is centered on the use of digital technologies for the implementation of the offer to the creation of a unique luxury experience while guaranteeing a continuum offline and online in a phygital environment (see Chapter 11). The Blue Sunflower Marketing approach is the basis of a successful digital strategy positioned upstream of the creative process of the luxury brand offerings, and is based on the idea of creating an exceptional luxury product/service that is perceived as unique by the customer while offering him/her a memorable and satisfying customer experience. In order to implement this new marketing strategy, the luxury company should develop and enhance an organizational culture based on risk-taking – in other words, by proposing products that shock, challenge, intrigue, generate emotions, etc. Luxury brands should then offer products that do not leave customers indifferent. Beyond the culture of risk, the passion and the desire to surpass and challenge oneself as a member of the luxury staff are essential components of a disruptive and experiential digital strategy that allows the differentiation of the supply of the product, the construction of customer loyalty, and the creation of a sustainable competitive advantage.

BLUE SUNFLOWER MARKETING: A DIGITAL DISRUPTIVE STRATEGY

Blue Sunflower Marketing is founded on the idea of "experiential disruption" through the creation of digital experiences that generate an interruption of existing offers and innovations by integrating emotions. To understand the idea of experiential disruption, we first need to understand what is meant by disruption prior to explaining the experiential disruption as the foundation of the Blue Sunflower Marketing paradigm, and its contributions to the success of digital luxury experience offerings.

The idea of disruption is not new. It finds its first origins in the natural sciences where it is used when describing disasters. Its introduction into economics and management dates back to the early 1940s, and termed "creative destruction" in the writings of economist Joseph Schumpeter with the publication of his book *Capitalism, Socialism, and Democracy*, published in the United States in 1942. This idea was later taken up by Theodore Levitt in his book *Innovation and Marketing*, published in 1969. In the early 1990s, the term "disruptive technology," or "technological disruption," was introduced and defined by Clayton Christensen, inventor of the disruptive innovation concept and prominent professor at Harvard Business School, in research articles and then in a book entitled *The Innovator's Dilemma*, published in 1997. It was in the 1990s that marketing scholars and practitioners witnessed a proliferation of the use of the concepts disruption, disruptive innovation, and disruptive technology. This proliferation led the worldwide communication group TBWA to patent the concept of DISRUPTION® in 1992. The contributions related to the definition of the disruptive approach and the perspectives according to which disruption has been defined are summarized in Figure 2.12.

Destructive creation	Disruptive innovation	Creative disruption
• A process continually at work in economies • It is linked to the simultaneous disappearance of sectors of economic activity giving rise to new economic activities	• Breakthrough innovations (e.g., digital disruption) • Disruption is considered as a goal in terms of innovation	• Disruptive innovation is a breakthrough innovation • It is opposed to incremental innovation, which is content to optimize the existing product

Figure 2.12   Definitions of disruption

According to the Blue Sunflower Marketing logic, disruption is approached from an experiential perspective, "experiential disruption," as well as from a customer-centric perspective and with regard to its functional and emotional needs in order to create singular and unforgettable digital luxury experiences. This new marketing strategy can be used to design efficient, unique, and memorable digital luxury experiences by integrating three fundamental criteria: the project leader, the culture of the organization, and the environment.

- The project leader is the holder of the disruptive idea. This digital experience can be directly influenced by the knowledge, career path, beliefs, personality, lifestyle, consumption practices, values, habits, ideology, and life philosophy of the project leader. All these factors have a direct or indirect impact on the emergence of the disruptive offering and the design of the digital customer experience so as to offer a unique and appreciable experience linking real and digital spaces.
- The culture of the company is another important factor in the process of the creation and design of the experiential and disruptive luxury offering within the digital era. The culture of the company is defined by the entrepreneurial model, the diversity of internal competencies, the commitment of the organization's staff to the logic of experiential disruption. If the employees do not believe in the logic of disruption with the risk that this can generate, they will not be able to adhere to the values related to the creative step of the project manager, making its realization impossible. Furthermore, to enable the fulfillment of digital projects that are experiential and disruptive, the employees should have various skills (see Table 2.3). The sum of these skills is the fusion of ideas generating experiential disruption at the heart of the Blue Sunflower Marketing approach to create a unique digital experience.
- The environment includes several actors (customers, institutional, government, industry, etc.), and is influenced by numerous macro-environmental variables (digital, economic, sociocultural, ecological, etc.). Three important conditions should be considered by luxury companies for the success of a digital strategy integrating the Blue Sunflower Marketing logic:

  o   A digital environment that is ready to welcome the disruptive project;
  o   A company that has an ability to understand the disruptive project;
  o   Customers who are ready to adopt digital and experiential innovations in response to their tangible (functional) and intangible (emotional, symbolic, relational, relational, social, etc.) needs.

BLUE SUNFLOWER MARKETING: HOW DOES IT WORK?

In order to implement a digital luxury experience offering, Blue Sunflower Marketing needs to incorporate several types of skills that luxury brand managers should employ to design an effective digital customer experience: analytical, critical, and collaborative. Table 2.3 summarizes these three skills and their characteristics.

Table 2.3 Three types of experiential disruption skills

Type of competence	Characteristics
Analytical competence	A mastery of immersive and exploratory methodological techniques to grasp the experiential dimension. In contrast to quantitative and qualitative studies, immersive tools such as self-ethnography, ethnography or subjective introspection offer a thorough and exhaustive understanding of experience – a foundational element of experiential disruption
Critical competence	An intellectual ability to develop critical thinking by performing back-and-forth mental gymnastics that alternate between subjective and analytical phases
Collaborative competence	The ability to co-create in a logic of knowledge management. It is about the organizer's ability to make different skills work in the organization in a "cross-skills" way that favors collective intelligence

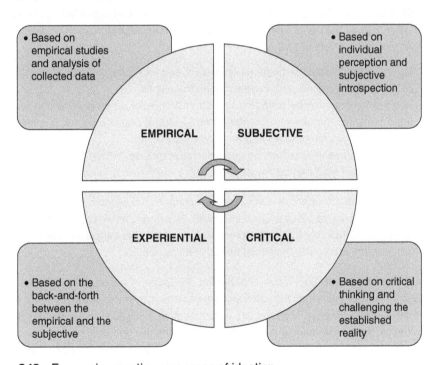

- Based on empirical studies and analysis of collected data

- Based on individual perception and subjective introspection

EMPIRICAL   **SUBJECTIVE**

EXPERIENTIAL   **CRITICAL**

- Based on the back-and-forth between the empirical and the subjective

- Based on critical thinking and challenging the established reality

Figure 2.13 Four major creative processes of ideation

Blue Sunflower Marketing used in the creation of the digital customer experience highlights the disruptive experience as an essential element to make a mark on the minds of the targets: to challenge them, to excite them, and thus to differentiate the luxury company from its competitors. This strategy, based on the concept of experiential disruption, is therefore the foundation for the emergence of new products and services and, especially, a new philosophy of life for luxury brands by implementing a creative process that relies on the launching of new and unexpected ideas. These ideas can find their origin in several sources whose use varies according to four major creative processes of ideation: subjective, empirical, critical, and experiential (Figure 2.13). Thus, luxury companies can follow one or more of these creative processes to carry out their marketing and communication strategies based on fashioning a profitable digital customer experience using a logic of experiential disruption and delivering unique value and shared meaning for their customers.

- **An empirical approach**. This process is a crucial step in setting up the Blue Sunflower Marketing approach to create a satisfying and effective digital luxury experience offering. It is a rational and analytical approach involving several validation and counter-validation steps. The process is based on a reasoning characterized by the five essential stages of experiential disruption (see Figure 2.14). The empirical creative process allows luxury brands to offer a digital customer experience based on the analysis of the sociocultural context as well as the benchmark of direct and indirect competitors in the marketplace by following three levels of analysis:

  o Macro-environmental: through the analysis of economic, cultural, social, ecological, political, environmental, and technological dimensions;

  o Meso-environmental: by analyzing the direct and indirect competition and the different targets: consumers (potential, direct, indirect, prescribers, etc.), companies (B2C) or (B2B), institutions and governments (B2G), etc.

  o Micro-environmental: by analyzing the internal actors related to the company or the brand (current staff and customers).

  Through this in-depth analysis, luxury brand managers will be able to define a digital customer experience strategy in coherence with the offering as well as with the tangible (functional) and intangible (relational, emotional, symbolic, ideological, etc.) attributes of the luxury brand, in line with the social trends of its customers.

- **A subjective approach**. Subjective experiential disruption is based on a personal and introspective approach that the individual will implement consciously or unconsciously to come up with creative, experiential, and disruptive ideas, concepts, and products. Experiential disruption reflects a creative idea that originates in the subjectivity as well as in the personal interpretation of the individual. It brings together three elements: several solutions are produced to answer a problem, the solutions produced can be dissociated from each other, and finally human creativity is at the center of the process; subjective and unfounded ideas are also considered.

- **An experiential disruption through learning**. The experiential learning disruption process at the center of the digital experience integrates the empirical and subjective approaches mentioned above. It is a cyclical process that evolves and adapts according to the evolution of customer experiences between real and digital spaces as well as in a phygital environment. This dynamic back-and-forth process aims to propose an idea of experiential disruption for

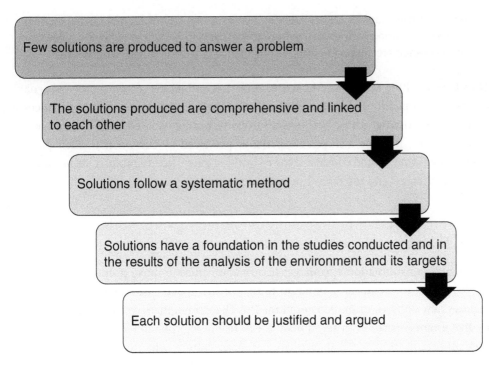

Figure 2.14   Stages of experiential disruption

both the company and customer, a concept, or a product/service. The experiential learning disruption approach refers to personal experience as a source of creative and disruptive skills development using two sources of creativity: an intellectual source and a basis of creativity through experiential learning (knowledge developed in lived experiences). An experiential disruption approach based on lived experiences highlights a dynamic process through two complementary processes: "top-down" and "bottom-up." These processes offer a continuum between the two processes previously developed in this section: empirical and subjective. This approach is the most complete and the most efficient for implementing a process applied to the design of digital luxury experiences because it allows luxury companies to integrate the cognitive aspect represented by the analytical dimension, but does not neglect the role of the emotional dimension that is at the heart of the Blue Sunflower Marketing paradigm.

- **A critical experiential disruption approach**. This process is based on the development of a critical thinking about reality, and the questioning of already established social realities. Critical thinking is the key element in implementing a Blue Sunflower Marketing approach based on a critical experiential disruption logic. This approach can be likened to an apprenticeship that brings together three main elements: a multitude of social, transgressive, cognitive, technical and digital skills; theoretical and practical content; and the critical capacities of the project leader. Critical thinking should, therefore, be encouraged at each stage within the creative teams, and also in all services. Even usual daily activities, such as taking notes at meetings, can be a source of critical thinking. During note-taking, individuals use their critical thinking to judge whether the notes they have selected are consistent with the emergence of a creative and disruptive idea.

Therefore, the Blue Sunflower Marketing approach and its four creative processes enable luxury companies to design and deliver breakthrough digital customer experiences in terms of experiential ideas, products/services, technologies used, and luxury concept creation. Thus, it is the disruptive experience perceived by customers in their phygital environment that should command the creation of a new luxury product, its positioning, its digital strategy, and the discourse associated with it.

SUMMARY

The digital transformation encourages luxury companies to move from a digital marketing logic with its technical orientation to that of the digital customer experience, which requires new skills for its implementation. This chapter emphasized the challenges related to digital transformation in seven main areas: technological and technical, data analysis, human, organization and management, corporate culture, allocated resources, and environment. In this chapter, I also introduced the Digital Luxury Triangle (DLT) tool, which reflects all the means and strategies that luxury companies should implement in order to design a global experiential digital offering that is effective and adapted to their customers. A new digital marketing strategy, "Blue Sunflower Marketing," and its four creative processes should also be considered by luxury business to deliver breakthrough and disruptive digital customer experiences.

3

CONNECTING WITH DIGITAL NATIVES AND SHARING LUXURY EXPERIENCES ON SOCIAL MEDIA

INTRODUCTION AND SCOPE

The relationship between digital natives and social networks is a subject that is both very current and particularly complex. Digital native generations were born in the 1990s when the Internet and social media really began to spread rapidly. These young people were, therefore, the first to be really at ease with technology devices and hyper-connectivity. However, young people's behaviors on social media are too complex for luxury businesses to grasp because of the diversity of tools, the wealth of opportunities, as well as the social, psychological, and economic influences that come into play. Therefore, it is important for luxury houses to understand how they can collaborate with this digital generation to create and share social experiences through the use of social media. The dissemination of online information by digital natives who exchange on blogs profoundly changes the communication conditions for luxury brands. A new ecosystem is needed in which bloggers, followers, as well as luxury brands interact. Bloggers, influencers, and a brand's fans are all parts of a digital generation that are considered to be full-fledged players in this ecosystem in which luxury brands need to reinvent their way of contributing and generating value as well as the way they connect with young people through shared, meaningful experiences. Beyond their belonging to a digital generation, these young people are also characterized by their age, from 15 to 25 years: they are, therefore, at a very special stage of their lives. If they do not see themselves as teenagers anymore, they may not consider themselves completely as adults, especially because they are often still financially dependent.

Gradually emerging from the family identity, they will seek to assert their personality freely. The formation of the youth identity involves exploring several possibilities and making choices in a more autonomous way.

The purpose of this chapter is to identify how digital natives are taking ownership of blogs and developing new relationships with luxury brands. To that end, I will, first of all, present the specificities of the digital native generation that will have an influence on its usages of social media: the construction of self-identity, the exploration of new horizons, the integration of communities, and the need for recognition. Next, I will discuss how young people who belong to this digital generation are using social media to develop their online "person-branding," how they connect with luxury brands, and how they share experiences with their followers. I will conclude by examining the modes of collaboration, and the new relationships that are created on blogs between digital natives and luxury brands.

WHO ARE DIGITAL NATIVES AND WHAT KIND OF LUXURY EXPERIENCES DO THEY WANT?

For luxury brands, each advent of a generation raises new questions about the transmission, continuity, and breakdown of social behaviors (work, consumption, daily life, etc.). In the early 1990s, there was a paradigm shift in society accompanied by the emergence of a new generation of "digital natives," which had its own values and beliefs acquired during its early years of socialization. In addition, the technological revolution has had a powerful impact that has created a wide gap in terms of the values and characteristics of consumption between the digital natives and other generations.

DIGITAL NATIVES: WHO ARE THEY?

We can find this concept under different terms, such as generation Z, the Net or Web generation, post-millennials, Nexters, Generation Next, the connected or digital generation. The rise of a digital native generation is a consequence of the democratization of the use of digital technologies and their integration into the daily life of a Web 2.0 generation whose members share a common digital culture. These young people are part of an Internet generation, and are inventing a new culture of consumption, whose codes are specific to them, and are breaking with the codes of previous generations: generations X and Y.

Digital natives are a particularly strategic target for the luxury industry and services. Indeed, not only does this generation represent a significant weight for the luxury market, but it is also a deeply globalized consumer segment, which is a major asset for international luxury brands. Raised in an environment of political, ecological, and socio-economic crises, the digital native generation, meanwhile, is lacking values. Swapping from one channel to another, or from one brand to another, this generation seeks advice from virtual communities and searches the Web for a way to consolidate its choices by instantly sharing its buying experiences or personal relationships with luxury brands. I can summarize the common features of this digital generation that group young consumers together by the following:

- Growing interest in brands, friends, hobbies, and digital culture;
- This generation is confident, relaxed, and engaged;
- The members of this generation have a very high level of education compared to previous generations;
- This generation shows a strong need for security;
- Young people in this generation are viewed as impatient, focused on their well-being while enjoying team spirit and collaboration;
- The members of this generation have been spared from wars, but are under great pressure from society to succeed in working life.

Additionally, one of the main features that distinguish digital natives from other generations is "multitasking" or the art of combining several tasks at once. These multitaskers often work as a team through online social networks and are influenced by friends, online communities, and peers. All these characteristics depend on the interactions between digital natives and the social and economic settings that exist during their first years of socialization, which are influenced by previous generations. These bring in community policies and practices, thus forming the traits of this generation. These influences, as noted by Fields et al. (2008), refer to the fact that digital natives as a group have a growing influence on our culture, with a powerful impact on the workplace and the marketplace. Digital native members are identified as representing a "cultural phenomenon." Any individual born before this generation is called a digital immigrant (Prensky, 2006). In fact, digital natives were brought up with technologies and the Internet; they are individuals who have an unconventional and accelerated pace of life compared to the average individual; they operate randomly rather than stepwise; they combine different parallel processes rather than a single linear process; for them, it is the graphic design first and not the text; they are connected and exposed to several screens (TV, computers, mobile phone, etc.); and they spend a lot of time indoors.

As this generation is sometimes connected simultaneously to upwards of five screens (TV, mobile, desktop, laptop, and MP3) and while the previous generation uses only two, this current youth generation is distinguished above all by its overconsumption of the Internet and social media as well as by its ability to switch from one medium, one distribution channel, or one brand to another. Without a doubt, omnichannel digital natives place image and aesthetics at the heart of their luxury buying process – an experience that only makes sense if it is dubbed so by their peers and their community as shared through stories or online games in which they are staged with the brand.

For this youth generation, the dream of luxury is transmitted by its virtual community while for other types of customers, the desire for luxury is fed by the endorsers who wear or use it. During the purchase process, youth generations are constantly connected to others. After the purchase, these young people are staged with the luxury product to intensify the pleasure within their community; while the traditional client sees the luxury product as a means of social esteem and compares his/her choices with the other customers or sellers in the store.

WHAT DO DIGITAL NATIVES WANT FROM LUXURY BRANDS?

Overall, digital native consumers have a compulsive buying behavior that is less reasoned and less faithful than the previous generations. They favor experiences with luxury brands and their desire or pleasure in the instant guides their buying preferences according to a customer journey that is increasingly complex to understand for luxury houses. What digital natives want from their experiences with luxury brands can be explained through expectations, such as swapping, immediacy and instantaneity, showing-off, authenticity, experiences, and gamification.

- **Digital natives are brand swappers**. These young consumers are referred to as omnichannel buyers. They explore, compare, and become experts on luxury products and brands through the numerous platforms that make information immediately available (laptop, computer, smartphone, and tablet). They make their purchase decision online and according to their desires at that moment, and then they choose their place of purchase. Digital natives also have no scruples about switching from one brand to another. Indeed, this generation is interested in embracing everything and every trend. In fashion or jewelry, as in haute cuisine, they could go from fast food to Michelin star restaurants, or from basic accessories to luxury jewelry. This generation switches from one luxury brand value to another. Thus, international renowned actors and actresses, such as Marion Cotillard for Dior or a rock-star from Metallica for Brioni, or even a transsexual makeup artist or a street graffiti artist, can endorse the values embodied by luxury brands, such as Burberry, Gucci, and Vivienne Westwood, who decided to merge all of their men's and women's collections from 2016 as a response to this generation that is socially liberated and in favor of "marriage for all."
- **Digital natives search for immediacy and instantaneity**. These young people select their point of sales according to what they consider the most convenient channel, which responds to their immediate need. Yet, the Internet remains the first luxury meeting space for youth generations, where companies might push luxury brands to offer cheaper products in their stores. For some categories of luxury products, such as cosmetics, makeup,

or fashion and accessories, the Web channel is preferred over physical shops by young people, and half of them prefer to buy their clothes online. Similarly, for the more masstige brands that are consumed by younger generations (e.g., Longchamp, Michael Kors), the weight of the Web, in terms of purchases, is more significant. Despite their overrepresentation on the Internet, these young consumers remain attached to luxury physical stores, but their motivations for visiting them have evolved, and luxury houses are now reconfiguring their offline/physical outlets to meet the expectations of this digital generation. Thus, the use of iBeacons to personalize the customer journey (e.g., Barney's in Chelsea, London), Google Glass for re-experiencing at home, the experience of trying on makeup in-store (e.g., Yves Saint Laurent), virtual reality headsets (e.g., Dior Eyes) for giving backstage access to fashion shows, etc., can help luxury houses to capture and retain digital natives. In fact, altogether, these innovative digital devices allow luxury houses to gradually reconnect to their youth targets within the traditional places of consumption (stores). The idea here is that there should be no break in the brand narrative throughout the different points of contact that these highly connected, young consumers use in their daily consumption experiences.

TREND 3.1

THE SWISS WATCHMAKER H. MOSER & CIE. ATTRACTS DIGITAL NATIVES BY DISRUPTING THE TRADITIONAL HAUTE HORLOGERIE INDUSTRY

H. Moser & Cie. is an independent, high-end, Swiss watchmaking brand based in Schaffhausen. It was founded in 1828 by Heinrich Moser, a descendant of a family of watchmakers in Schaffhausen. H. Moser & Cie. differs from other brands as it subtly combines tradition and modernism and has built a transparent online communication strategy targeting digital natives that is based on its values and desire to protect traditional watchmaking. H. Moser & Cie. came into the spotlight thanks to its advertising campaigns combining humor and provocation on important topics, such as Smart Watches – "upgrade to a mechanical watch" – or a Swiss-made watch – "Make Swiss-made Great Again." H. Moser & Cie.'s disruptive approach is unique in the industry for two reasons: (1) it is linked to important topics related to traditional Swiss watchmaking, and (2) it uses unconventional tools (social media) and communication techniques (humor and provocation). It is relevant because traditional watchmaking is not famous for its sense of humor and because there is a lack of transparency in this industry. As the Swiss watch industry grew very successful in the last few years, it became, in many cases, a pure marketing machine, which started to forget its origins and what had made the traditional Swiss watchmaking so successful. Furthermore, the most important thing for the watch brand is to keep the

(Continued)

(Continued)

connection with the young customers while remaining authentic, evoke emotions, and build a link to a traditional world where the brand can be interpreted as in opposition to a digital world, which is very abstract for most people.

Digital marketing is a tool that helps H. Moser & Cie. bring all those elements as close as possible to its young clients. If done well, it can be very real, emotional, and engaging. It also allows the company to better target its youth audience, which is a key element for brands with limited budgets. "I don't want to reach everyone, only the right people." Today, thanks to digital tools, the CEO of the brand can personally answer, within a few minutes or hours, any request or question from end customers around the world. This is the solution for getting connected to digital natives in order to build a human relationship with them. Beyond the product, this is the most important element.

So, luxury brands should use instantaneity as part of their luxury experience offering to capture and retain digital natives. For example, in 2016, Burberry announced that its collections would go on sale online and in-store within hours after its show. This logic evolves in parallel with the characteristics of social media, which are governed by the instantaneity and the culture of "I want everything and immediately." In fact, these online networks allow the luxury fashion industry to highlight perfect authenticity in real time. Hence, the instantaneous communication and constant interaction needed to build trust between luxury brands and digital natives can facilitate the customer experience. Thus, luxury fashion marketing professionals should prioritize spontaneous communication, as it allows instant and natural communication, ephemeral content applications, and services through Snapchat, Periscope, and Meerkat, which are popular amongst digital natives. Table 3.1 shows an example of communication modes using ephemeral social applications.

Table 3.1 Communication via ephemeral applications in the fashion industry

Social media	Functionality
Snapchat	Snapchat relies on the image to tell the story, behind the scenes of creating fashion items and fashion shows. In 10 seconds on Snapchat, a fashion brand can tell its everyday life in real time and authentically
Periscope	Periscope is often used for the creation of promotional videos, allowing a theming and a staging of the collections

By communicating instantly, luxury brands demonstrate their willingness to interact with digital natives and their friends – giving that immediate, imperfect, behind-the-scenes moment that evidently pleases young people. This is why social media networks are massively used by Burberry to communicate about future collections, new trends, celebrity news, photo shoots, etc. This strategy will boost the image of the luxury brand in social media to ensure maximum visibility in a universe occupied by young and connected, ultra-fashion conscious clients. Thus, in the age of digital transformation, marketing is based on the economy of attention (the propensity to produce added value) and the economy of the occupation (the capacity to put in place offers and messages contextualized). Therefore, luxury fashion professionals should learn from digital native customers' daily lives to develop content (fashion shows, model photos, behind-the-scenes creations, tutorials, etc.) on media, such as Instagram, Snapchat, YouTube, Pinterest, etc., especially since these social media directly affect the behaviors and purchase decisions of this young generation.

Clearly, conveying a good perception of the luxury brand also means persuading this digital generation via the luxury brand's ambassadors, which can be incarnated by popular influencers. Accordingly, the luxury industry has every interest in recruiting the most interactive stars on social media as well as connecting them with digital natives. To do this, luxury houses should seize the instantaneity of digital social networks to promote the participation of followers in the events they may organize and stimulate interaction with influencers, such as fashionable celebrities, bloggers, and fashion YouTubers.

TREND 3.2

DOLCE & GABBANA TARGETS DIGITAL NATIVES BY INVITING INFLUENTIAL FASHION BLOGGERS

Dolce & Gabbana has always been at the forefront of adopting digital innovations, and today, it has a mission: to seduce the next generation of young consumers and digital natives. And, as always with this Italian brand, marketing efforts towards young people are not to be underestimated. During the Milan Fashion Week in the fall of 2017, the brand recruited an "army" of more than 49 influencers and celebrities to appear on the catwalk in place of the "traditional" models. Celebrities like the YouTuber Jim Chapman as well as young entrepreneurs such as Luka Sabbat, Cameron Dallas, and Jimmy Waterhouse took part in the show, generating thousands of clicks and likes from their own followers and drawing attention to the Italian brand. Later on, Dolce & Gabbana proposed an even more spectacular runway show for its women's ready-to-wear collection: Pyper America Smith, Kenya Kinski Jones, Kristina Bazan, Aimee Song, Harley Viera Newton, Pixie Lott, Oliver Cheshire, Rafferty Law, Isabel Getty, and Princess Maria Olympia of Greece were amongst the personalities who took part on the podium to model a collection inspired by animal prints and a very Sicilian decor.

(Continued)

(Continued)

The American blogger Aimee Song shared backstage snippets in a YouTube "vlog" that was viewed nearly 93,000 times. Other bloggers, such as Kristina Bazan, Shea Marie, and Negin Mirsalehi, have created visual stories on their Instagram accounts, and shown fittings with Stefano Gabbana and Domenico Dolce. Each image has collected more than 20,000 likes. For Dolce & Gabbana and its influencers, the relationship goes far beyond a merely sponsored content. Just like any event, the parade surprised many and generated buzz on social networks. Although some fashion addicts and experts were skeptical about the integrity of the brand, claiming instead that relying on Instagram celebrities to make its brand talk rather than the collections themselves was problematic, for the brand, the parade and the operations around it are the representation of a new phase that the company called #DGRinascimento (or rebirth), which will ensure its future.

By complementing the show with influencers and bloggers, Dolce & Gabbana demonstrates that it is ready to engage the digital natives and go beyond the classic brand–influencers partnerships that are limited to sharing sponsored content on Instagram, by involving personalities other than professional models. Moreover, the brand has launched a new line of products to satisfy its young customers, from handbags with cartoon illustrations and logos, like "All I Need is Love and Wifi," to a new collection of sneakers. Customers can customize their own pair of sneakers by adding patches and embroidered slogans, like "I am the Queen." To promote the launch of these products, animated videos revealing the production process were posted on Instagram and events in stores were organized. More recently, the brand invited its customers to discover its new collection of sneakers at an event in Milan on Via Della Spiga, which was attended by its favorite influencers, such as Pelayo Diaz and German blogger Caroline Daur. Thus, by combining online and offline strategies with more targeted products for digital natives, Dolce & Gabbana has significantly increased its visibility on social networks, achieved a significant conversion rate, and built a special relationship with its young audience.

- **Digital natives use luxury for showing-off**. In their mode of communication, digital natives are usually more attentive to images than texts. Therefore, any visual staging that sends them a strong and instant emotional message is relayed spontaneously by this generation as digital natives decide to capture it and share it with peers and followers. Aesthetics, emotion, and experience with the luxury brand only make sense when young people can share them with their communities by placing themselves in the spotlight. As a result, luxury houses are revising their communication policies and feeding social media not only with more traditional content (events, advertising campaigns, new collections, news related to their muses), but also with interactive information for their young fans (commercial offers, contests, questions and answers, advice, tutorials, etc.).
- **Digital natives value exclusivity**. Far from the unrealistic aesthetics offered on Instagram media, the Snapchat application is very popular amongst these young people who use

it to exchange real and instantaneous moments. The ephemeral dimension associated with the "raw" and voluntarily untouched nature of the shared photos does not seem to be in line with the codes of the traditional luxury logic. Burberry or Valentino have come to understand the interest of this place of exchange, which privileges the spontaneity of the "beautiful moments," the exclusivity, and the instantaneousness of the contents posted for users, over the traditional retouched glossy aesthetic. Burberry's spring-summer collection 2016 was first revealed to Snapchat users around the world, who had access to runway images, backstage events, and visual collections before the actual show. Users then relayed the information across social networks, creating a much bigger buzz than any other media. The Snapchat effect, whose shared images mix staging, chance, and strong emotional power, has also motivated other platforms, such as Instagram, to change its format to benefit more natural, authentic visuals, even those punctuated by flaws.

- **Digital natives are in search of emotional and memorable luxury experiences**. These young people also expect a pleasurable purchase and need to be immersed within an enjoyable as well as experiential setting, ranging from physical stores to e-commerce websites and other multi-brand websites, through promotional websites and sites for second-hand items in which the luxury codes are perfectly embraced. For this digital generation, the luxury experience is not lived in an individual manner; it is collective and only makes sense when it goes beyond its place of consumption. Social shopping is the favored buying method of this generation; digital natives use Tweet Mirrors and other interactive displays available in the shops to instantly export the look on social media, and seek the opinion of friends before buying the product. Purchases are increasingly connected, and despite the strong reputation attached to luxury brands, the products and services in this universe are related to feedback from their young customers. To respond to this, certain luxury brand websites have also created social media consultation buttons next to the products on their e-commerce website.

- **Digital natives use games in their luxury experiences**. This generation uses games to connect with luxury brands. An effective re-enchantment of everyday life through the incorporation of imaginary elements into the real world needs strong emotional experiences, focusing on visuals. Youths also need games to feed their relationships and connect with their chosen luxury brands. Therefore, inspired by the joint success of video games, the explosion of social media, and the collective activities within this youth generation, some luxury houses have come to understand the need for new approaches, such as that of gamification (this concept will be developed in Chapter 6) to engage with this target, and guide it towards their products and services: smartphone applications (quizzes, virtual fitting, etc.) or quizzes followed and shared through social media have become very popular amongst luxury houses. This is also about bringing luxury brands and young people together around a sporting, playful, or simply entertaining event inspired by the success of augmented reality games that allows young consumers to virtually immerse themselves in the universe created by the luxury brand. Thanks to immersive gaming experience, the luxury brand can have a more active audience, one that is immersed in its narratives and codes, thus allowing the brand to engage its younger audience for a longer duration.

HOW ARE INFLUENCERS RESHAPING LUXURY BRAND EXPERIENCES?

Since the emergence of social media, influencers have taken a new liking to social platforms such as Facebook, Snapchat, Twitter, or Instagram, which have facilitated and "viralized" interactions amongst users. This phenomenon affects all ages, whether they are bloggers or addicts to social media; their opinion counts and they have a real influence on the visibility and the popularity of luxury brands. Influencers are, then, considered as major persuaders, since they can modify the behaviors of the audience in a certain way (adoption or rejection of the luxury brand).

WHO ARE INFLUENCERS?

Whether via a direct or indirect impact, the influencer's online publications engage, draw attention to, and convey a message that unites his/her community. The influencer often has a large audience, spread over various social networks, which allows him/her to capture and attract readers wherever they are (e.g., a blog post, which will be relayed on Snapchat, then on Instagram, and next on Twitter). The strength of these influencers exists in having an audience that listens to them because of their expertise in a field, and an audience that can be convinced through the influencer's publications; in this way influencers stage luxury brands as well as their personalities. In fact, the staging of products and luxury fashion accessories through the use of everyday individuals or celebrities is a recurrent practice. Indeed, achieving an awareness of the influence that these people could have on the clothing of digital natives is imperative. As a result, luxury brands have joined with influencers to better establish their marketing strategies. This is because these influencers provide, beyond their notoriety, principles of seduction connecting them to a process of consumption that the advertisers solicit from them. Influencers become, therefore, the "boss-model" who can be a global archetype. In doing so, influencers (stars or non-celebrities) have the power to seduce their audiences and make them want to identify with them. For instance, the thigh gap, a social media phenomenon consisting of forming a space between one's thighs of up to five centimeters in order to create a geometric shape between the legs, is indicative of this imitation and identification process as well as the influencers' power of persuasion. Obsessed by their physical appearance and convinced that the thigh gap is an ideal canon of beauty, some teenage girls, especially Americans, rushed to adopt this practice by engaging in a fierce competition on social media. Thus, for this digital native generation, influencers are individuals who embody the ideal representations, or what is known in sociology as the vertical diffusion of tastes, which is developed by the popularity of online influencers. Table 3.2 shows the main influencers and the related emerging trends.

Table 3.2 Influencers and emerging trends

Type of influencers	Influencers are mainly singers, actors, bloggers, sportspeople, and models
Emerging trends	The figure of the influencer has evolved. Now it is measured by the number of subscribers one has and is accompanied by new players, like bloggers and YouTubers. These actors only exist according to their activities, which are evaluated quantitatively (number of subscribers, "likes," friends, tweets, posts)
Main features	The influencer works as a medium with an impact (depending on his/her popularity), a credibility, and especially, an influence on his/her group
Social networks used	Influencers are particularly fond of social networks (Facebook, Twitter, LinkedIn) and platforms for broadcasting images, videos, and other content (Pinterest, Instagram, Snapchat)
Example of influencers who have become brand ambassadors	With more than 100 million subscribers on Instagram, Selena Gomez, muse for Louis Vuitton, broke Taylor Swift's subscriber record (91.4 million), making her as powerful as the brand itself

Since they influence their group, influencers are regularly asked by the luxury and fashion industries to promote their brands on various social media and broadcast channels. If Burberry has used Brooklyn Beckham (17 years old) to promote its perfume, it was certainly because his parents (Victoria and David Beckham) are global stars; but it is also because he has 6.4 million subscribers on his Instagram account. Thus, in order to capture the attention of digital natives, the luxury and fashion industries should rely on powerful influencers: Selena Gomez, Taylor Swift, Justin Bieber, or Christiano Ronaldo, to name but a few. For luxury brands, it is clearly effective to rely on these new figures, especially as they control the codes that govern social media, and more particularly the culture of LOL (laughing out loud), which refers to a particular humor born within the Internet and shaped by the digital native culture. Furthermore, influencers also know which profile to choose for a more attractive selfie, or what kind of messages to highlight and stimulate a better interaction with their peers, as they are part of the same consumption culture.

THE ROLE OF SELFIES IN PROMOTING LUXURY EXPERIENCES

As an ego booster, the selfie, often taken with a smile or a grimace, allows digital natives to show themselves in their best profile. It has also become the best way to feel known, even recognized for one's clothing style, in a way that allows these tech-savvy young people to create different styles, to stand out from the crowd, and, therefore, to assert themselves as individuals. Having the purpose to be published on social media (e.g., Instagram, Facebook, Twitter, Snapchat) in order to be massively liked and shared, the selfie is undoubtedly profitable to luxury fashion companies, especially as it highlights items associated with various outfits, and is embedded within a pleasant experience that show how the influencer is having fun.

The particularly attractive photos allow digital natives to display their aspirations in order to experience new sensations after the purchase. In doing so, the self-portrait becomes an extension of the experience of luxury and fashion items. By publishing selfies on social media and highlighting the looks they, themselves, have composed, these digital natives have become not only showcases, but also models of inspiration for the luxury fashion industry. Luxury brands no longer even need to advertise their products by using global communication budgets as customers are promoting the brands through social media on their own. The influence of the selfie in the luxury fashion industry is all the more remarkable as digital natives lend themselves more and more to the game. There are many influencers (public persons or anonymous) known for their selfies, in which they showcase their physique, lifestyle, and fashion choices. Furthermore, some young consumers can also be inspired by an influencer's selfies to get the same product (e.g., bags, dress, shirt). On a more extreme level, they can use their own selfies modified by filters to ask plastic surgeons to get the same physical look.

Influencers, therefore, often allow luxury houses to achieve a communication not centered on the company alone. As a result, luxury and fashion brands should identify words that positively represent their products in social networks, relaying them into privileged online spheres in which the generation of the digital natives is hyperactive and committed. Fashion YouTubers, whose tendency is to broadcast videos in which they unwrap their purchases of accessories and fashion items in front of a camera, are real stars and are communication sources as effective as the women's press and magazines. For example, the Californian Bethany Mota, who is barely 20 years old, has more than 10 million followers on YouTube. The influence of the icons of the Web is, then, very significant, and should be considered by luxury brands to promote true and real experiences. In a study of the influence of stars on young American women (13 to 18 years old), *Variety* magazine (Ault, 2014) revealed that five YouTubers precede celebrities, such as the actress Jennifer Lawrence, in popularity and subscribers. In fact, the proximity (these girls are accessible and look like the young generation of digital natives) that these YouTubers weave with their fans is the foundation of their success.

Leveraging these YouTubers, otherwise known as "vloggers," that is, bloggers who use video, allows luxury brands to get closer to, and engage their audience with original and creative content. However, in order to create a successful association, the fashion and luxury items popular with YouTubers in their videos should blend naturally with the decor so that there is no break in tone. In this exercise, luxury fashion bloggers have become ideal partners. Their popularity, acquired from their "media capital" manifested through a number of interactions and expressions of identity, contains deliberate strategies of self-exposure giving them a hegemonic influence in the marketing of luxury fashion.

By partnering with fashion bloggers, luxury brands can gain additional media coverage online. The most followed columnists of the fashion blogosphere have several ways to promote fashion items, amongst which we can mention: collaborations, advertisements on blogs, sponsored articles, or affiliate links. All in all, young people who are digital natives are inspired by celebrities who go on a fashion journey. It is in this context that influencers, whether they come from the cinema, modeling, sports, or social networks, often venture into this stylish trade with more or less success. Rather than giving customers the feeling of buying a piece of clothing simply because a star wears it, they are now selling products that (they say) have been created by the customers' idols. This is how many influencers have created their own collections, which are most often in partnership with brands and/or major fashion designers.

THE POWER OF PERSUASION AND INFLUENCERS' STRATEGIES

While the luxury brand encompasses three main components: functional (e.g., product, design), relational (e.g., relationship with customers, personal), and symbolic (e.g., values, DNA, logo, personality) that are powerful elements of brand differentiation, positioning, and competitive advantage creation, the power of persuasion requires the ability to change not just action, but attitude towards the luxury brand. For example, a luxury brand that creates a range of new products with accessible prices (e.g., masstige and co-branding H&M and Karl Lagerfeld) may gain new customers, but it has not necessarily changed how it is perceived. Luxury brands can also use influencer marketing as a powerful tool of persuasion. While marketers have long recognized the importance of using celebrities and celebrity products as a source of value influence, in the digital context consumers can also become influencers and brand endorsers who may have billions of followers. Thus, there is a multitude of factors (e.g., psychological, sociological, economic) explaining the "why" of the power of persuasion of online ordinary individuals. These individuals may become icons in their own right, they may be endorsed by popular brands in implicit or explicit ways, and, even more, they may create their own brand and recommend it to their followers. Pitkin (2011) suggests three principal ways in which online influencers can make other consumers like, share, buy, or even hate brands: influencer connectivity, influencer product adoption, and influencer authority.

- **Influencer connectivity**. This refers to the separation of social media influencers from standard social media users. Influencers can be divided into two main groups according to their social networks: connectors and specialists.
- **Influencer product adoption**. Influencers are often early product adopters. They are well positioned to disseminate product information through networks. Innovative influencers can even test out new products before other early adopters and the mainstream adopt them. They then become advocates for new consumers.

- **Influencer authority**. Influencers foster trust between each other because they are viewed as credible and competent.

BLOGGING: AN OPPORTUNITY FOR DELIVERING LUXURY EXPERIENCES

When talking about social media, the vocabulary is quite broad and nonspecific given the multiplicity of available media (Twitter, Facebook, personal blogs, Instagram, Pinterest, WeChat, LinkedIn, Tumblr, etc.). It is therefore essential for luxury companies to specify the purpose of their social media and blogging strategies, and it is better to concentrate in depth on one tool rather than act too quickly on developing several tools. In this section, I refer to blogs and blogging as a contraction of "web-log," which is a personal page containing notices, links, or columns periodically created by its author(s) in the form of posts. A Rich Site Summary (RSS) feed or email alert service usually allows users interested in a blog to be notified of new posts. Blogs allows their authors to share personal, free, and critical opinions and preferences on topics of interest. Thus, a blog is particularly interesting because, firstly, it allows digital natives to generate content and to be in contact with people who will consult the blog regularly (their "followers") and, secondly, it is a space controlled by its author and the information therein can be directly related to the blogger's intentions. Digital natives posting textual and visual content on their accounts generate attention to develop cultural, social, and ultimately, economic capital. In this context, blogs can be used as tools to allow digital natives to search for their own identity. Thus, blogs provide a platform to explore and express the different facets of the blogger's personality, removing barriers, such as outward appearance, physical abilities, or social status.

The blogging activity enables digital natives to participate in different online communities, follow other bloggers, react to information, and share their experiences and preferences about luxury brands and other things. They are in a state of tension and transition during which they will extend and confirm their identity. Furthermore, digital natives are divided between opposing forces: discovery and commitment, confusion and synthesis, and gradually, they will evolve towards a more stable identity (e.g., Schwartz, 2005). The blog is a tool at the service of this personal expansion. The theory of self-expansion, developed by Aron and Aron (1986), argues that each individual has an intrinsic motivation for reinforcing his/her personal effectiveness through the acquisition of new resources, perspectives, and identities that will enable him/her to facilitate the achievement of his/her objectives. One way to meet this motivation is to develop new and enriching relationships with others who promote personal development. This motivation explains why digital natives want to create new relationships in order to access different activities and perspectives.

This theory has also been applied in the context of a relationship between consumers and a brand. Luxury brands can enrich new experiences and discoveries that expand one's knowledge and capacity. The relationship with an innovative luxury brand with a rich history and strong values can meet the growth motivation of these young digital natives. Therefore, the creation of blogs allows digital natives to expand their horizons by developing new interactions with luxury brands and "followers," acquiring new skills, fostering the creative activity necessary for the blog, and finally, affirming their identity by expressing their opinion to their audience and beyond. Blogs allow digital natives to share their passions and develop knowledge. The work they provide on their blogs enriches their knowledge, since they are both a place of content creation as well as a space of exchange with the community that reads, comments, and responds to their posts. Digital native individuals are then discovering new passions and would love to share them with others. This motivation is particularly true in the luxury fashion industry where bloggers like to share their passion around tracking trends, styles, and brands. Thus, this digital generation uses blogs and blogging for different purposes:

- **Blogging is used by digital natives to affirm one's personal identity**. These young people are still independent of a social role, and they are in a transitory phase where self-concept is developing. Through their blog, they can develop and communicate their identity as well as manage their personal image, just as a luxury brand would do. The information posted by the blogger creates a digital trace that communicates impressions and shapes a positioning. The members of this young digital generation are aware of their own image, and they want to control it and make it even more attractive by using the communication techniques of online visuals and discourses. These young people are tempted to manage their image as a brand, to become a "person-brand" with a structured approach to defining their brand positioning. The creation of an online profile and the management of content and its related visuals allow the blogger to communicate his/her positioning. In a similar way to product marketing, it is about creating one's image and communicating it actively. Moreover, the objective of this digital generation is to create an image close to the "ideal-self." To define its model, it is sometimes based on representations, such as archetypes (a set of symbolic representations related to the collective unconscious). Each archetype acts according to a pre-established and recognized pattern of behavior.
- **Digital natives use blogs to define a social role for themselves in relation to their audience**. The theory of social identity (Tajfel and Turner, 1979) underlines the idea that individuals define their concept of the self through their connections with groups or organizations. In their quest for identity, digital natives will assume a role in order to define themselves in relation to their group. The created social role refers to a set of expected behaviors that identifies and differentiates them at the same time. De Kerviler and Demangeot (2016) conducted research with online bloggers to better understand the role this digital generation wishes to play within the community. The results show that there are three main possible roles, or 3Cs: confidant, critic, coach (Figure 3.1).

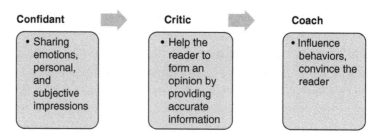

Figure 3.1   The 3Cs: bloggers' roles on social media

    ◦   The confidant. The blogger wants to tell his/her intimate story and develops topics that fascinate him/her. He/she presents a very personal description of his/her experiences and emotions. He/she is in a dynamic of building an intimate relationship with the reader based on emotions, as if the young blogger spoke with a familiar person.

    ◦   The critic. The blogger is positioned on topics that seem interesting to his/her community and will give and argue for his/her opinion in pursuit of the goal to convince his/her readers. The tone of the author is objective and impersonal with an intellectual approach.

    ◦   The coach. The blogger uses the style of a guide who wants to advise the reader. He/she takes a direct approach providing advice in a prescriptive tone. The coach appears as a mentor, who personalizes the information and develops empathy with his/her audience by offering tools to guide followers in their future experiences.

•   **Digital natives use blogs to develop their self-esteem**. These young people have a strong need to belong to groups, and are particularly sensitive to the social pressure of members of their communities. It is recognized that peers in their own community have a strong influence on young people's references, opinions, and behaviors. This digital generation chooses one or more reference group and will want to integrate themselves in it. To do so, these young people need to understand the standards and adopt them in order to be recognized as legitimate members. At the same time, they want to build their own identity, to differentiate themselves, and to highlight a territory of personal expression. This generation is looking for the optimal point of distinction between oneself and others. According to the theory of optimal distinction (Brewer, 1991), it is a question for this digital generation of being able to belong to a group and, at the same time, to remain unique and different at the personal level.

•   **Digital natives use blogs to guarantee recognition by peers**. As young people are in a stage of stabilizing their identity, they pay attention to the fact that their positioning on their blog should be similar and coherent with the image perceived by their followers. Since the blog is made to be consulted and intended to be shared, these young bloggers develop an expertise in terms of offering attractive content in order to be not only visible on the Internet, but also recognized as competent and credible. To develop this recognition by their peers, digital generation bloggers seek to create original editorial content introducing new ideas to differentiate themselves from other bloggers. Sharing knowledge with those who consult the blog by informing them, advising them, or stimulating their curiosity, also reinforces the feeling that digital native bloggers' expertise can be useful to others – and especially to luxury brands that can collaborate with them to promote their products and their image.

THE PROCESS OF BLOG CREATION AND THE ROLE OF LUXURY BRANDS

The development of the luxury brand online reputation performed by digital natives goes through several key stages, where luxury companies can collaborate with young bloggers in different ways. The primary concern for luxury brands to find the appropriate blogger to partner with is to find a blogger who has the desire and motivation to create his/her own blog, and find sources of inspiration from other Internet users as well as from luxury brands. For luxury brands, it is vital that the selected bloggers know how to showcase themselves with a focus on the story told and its staging. The next section will examine the motivations of bloggers and their sources of inspiration in order to understand how luxury brands can collaborate with them.

WHAT DRIVES THE CREATION OF A BLOG BY DIGITAL NATIVES?

Several triggers, more or less rational or emotional, lead digital natives to shift from a passive posture of observer to an active role of contributor. The first trigger is linked to a particular event in which the young person is a participant and is marked deeply by the experience to the extent that he/she wants to share it. Thus, the invitation to an exceptional event or the beginning of a new exciting activity can generate the creation of a blog. The young person will detail his/her experience to make it known and encourage others to try. From then on, the luxury brand can create vocations by inviting consumers to exceptional private events. The second trigger refers to the need to react, rectify, or bring to light a different view of a phenomenon compared to what is said on social networks. Thus, the blogger sees him/herself as a critic who offers a different perspective on things. For example, a young person who is a fan of a brand criticized on social media will want to create a blog to convey more positive information by communicating his/her own experience. Here, the luxury brand can encourage loyal consumers to share their opinions.

A third trigger comes from a feeling of empathy that makes digital natives want to give other people useful information. This is especially true if a young person has an expertise in a particular field, for example, playing the piano, and wishes to guide other young people who would like to learn about this skill. The luxury brand can then recognize the experts in the brand and give them tools to facilitate their discourses and the dissemination of online content. The blogger's activity can therefore be encouraged by intrinsic motivations (related to interest and pleasure that the individual finds in the blogging activity without expectation of external reward from the brand) or extrinsic motivations (linked to an external circumstance). In other situations, luxury brands can play an active role in promoting the emergence of blogs in which messages about their values or products can be relayed effectively amongst virtual and physical communities.

SOURCES OF INSPIRATION FOR BLOGGING

Digital natives are comfortable with social media and they prefer, first and foremost, to be observers of the blogs that interest them. They seek to identify effective strategies for obtaining what they like before embarking on their own. They regularly follow several bloggers that they take as a model, and sometimes expand their horizons by occasionally consulting other blogs. In the first stage, young people will try to analyze how other bloggers, especially those who have a lot of followers, develop their personal website. They will then identify their positioning, the topics discussed, and how to get on stage. By selecting models to follow, they will also be able to identify what best suits them, and the identity they want to develop and display on their own blog. A study of seven bloggers (De Kerviler and Audrezet, 2016) shows that digital natives have a professional approach and pursue a progressive strategy of engagement.

Furthermore, luxury brands are also sources of inspiration for future bloggers who visit their professional websites and social media platforms. By providing discussion platforms, being creative about communication, and generating rich content around their brand values, luxury companies can participate in this inspiring search. Thus, for example, more and more fashion brands include visuals called "street style" on their websites; that is to say, they display spontaneous photos of individuals on the street with their products rather than professional photographs with models in the studio. This trend refers to an expectation that customers will project themselves more easily in this staging – a setting that seems more related to their daily life. In initiatives like "Art of the Trench Burberry," consumers are encouraged to be creative while being guided by the brand. In fact, Burberry encourages consumers to upload their photos in which they wear the brand's famous raincoat. The luxury fashion brand can then make a creative montage on its website of all the photos taken by its customers wearing its products. Consequently, luxury brands can serve as role models in the presentation of street style images and encourage the dissemination of photos or videos on consumers' personal blogs by extending their creative work with the brand.

ARTISTIC AND NARRATIVE ASPECTS OF BLOGGING AMONGST DIGITAL NATIVES

The presentation of oneself on a blog can be compared to a theater performance, where every young blogger can define the decor, the costumes, and the lighting in order to present him/herself under a certain identity. The creative dimension is important for bloggers in terms of bringing their personal touch and thus creating an attractive blog for both actual and potential audiences. The artistic and graphic talents of the blogger can help enhance the aesthetic and visual aspects to which followers are sensitive. The elements of web pages, such as text, photos, and visual editing, help the blogger's creativity while trying to maintain a certain coherence to communicate a clear positioning of the blog. Once launched, the blogger will be able to share personal stories and feedback. Indeed, blogs are places where stories are written and they can be understood as a means to produce content. The narrative form is used to relate a series of specific events with a beginning, a middle, and an end (e.g., Bennett and Royle, 1999). By telling their stories on their blogs, in which followers can recognize themselves, at least partially, the digital native bloggers can create and enhance proximity with their community. Therefore, the blogger can create and tell stories by using several elements: a particular style of writing, a tone, a content, a way to share his/her own experiences, for example by systematically referring first to the place of consumption, the people present, or the product/service. Thus, all these elements of content and staging will create a unique positioning for each blog. Once it is well defined and structured, the blog can be improved based on the comments of readers. Thus, some bloggers, especially those who aim to give a professional dimension to their blogging activity, evaluate the reactions of their readers to the various texts and photos they post in order to identify what pleases their audience, and so the writers can evolve their blog as a result.

BLOGGING AND LUXURY BRAND COLLABORATION

Once one understands what digital natives are interested in blogs, as well as the strategy they pursue in terms of exploration, identity creation, and inclusion in a community, it is important to look at and define the modes of collaboration for luxury brands and bloggers. For luxury brands, blogs represent a communication channel that is complementary to traditional media. Thus, partnering with digital native bloggers allows luxury brands to increase their visibility, promote their image and products, develop interactions with young consumers, and quickly reach a broad target. Several modes of collaboration between bloggers and luxury brands are possible. Co-branding, for instance, is a strategic alliance in which two or more brands are presented simultaneously to consumers (e.g., Geylani et al., 2008). Seno and Lukas (2007) emphasize that celebrity brand support is a form of co-branding since both entities are associated in a single communication.

The reconciliation of a blogger and a luxury brand could, therefore, be understood as a form of symbolic alliance that enriches the image of the luxury brand by transferring the qualities associated with the blogger to the luxury brand he/she promotes on his/her own website.

THE AMBIVALENT RELATIONSHIP OF DIGITAL NATIVES WITH LUXURY BRANDS

Digital natives perceive luxury brands as a sign of belonging and affirmation of their identity. Choosing to buy and use a luxury brand is a way to affirm their identity by sharing values. These young people are fans of certain luxury brands that represent the image they make of themselves and reject others that do not match. In addition, the luxury brand is a sign of external recognition that ensures a sense of belonging to a group. Thus, digital natives purchase luxury brands in order to be accepted and recognized by their peers. Since this generation is particularly sensitive to group pressure and social acceptance, the social benefit will play an important role in its relationship to luxury brands. However, while digital natives recognize the identity and social dimension of luxury brands, they are cautious about advertising messages. The members of this generation of young people learn about products, and often feel that they have a good understanding of the offerings and their own needs. They consider that it is useless for luxury brands to make purchase recommendations to them, and they are sometimes suspicious of advertising communications. Therefore, collaborating with bloggers is the appropriate approach to communicate with digital natives. Though, from the blogger perspective, it is important to evaluate the risks and benefits of his/her potential association and collaboration with a luxury brand.

KEY SUCCESS FACTORS OF LUXURY BRAND-BLOGGER CO-CREATION

Consumers are increasingly asking for co-creation proposals from brands, as highlighted by different studies on customer participation. Co-creation gives customers the opportunity to express their opinion to improve products, and thus feel respected by brands. The consumer becomes a co-creator of value and breaks away from the vertical relationship of the provider–user logic to privilege a collaborative relationship with the company. This digital native generation enjoys co-creation opportunities with luxury brands that ask them for their opinion on product developments or advertising communications, that have them test the offers before launch, and that associate them with the production of photos or messages, especially when the blogger has skills in graphics. These activities allow bloggers to understand the luxury brand and feel involved in the relationship. They will then be able to communicate better and make known the luxury brand products. Thus, before posting information associated with a luxury brand on their blogs, bloggers first need to understand and examine the values of the luxury brand they are aiming to collaborate with. Furthermore, collaborating with a luxury brand pushes the blogger to double his/her efforts when writing an article or considering the layout of a photo so that he or she feels the same level of rigor that a professional would in the field.

As stated by Bonnemaizon and Batat (2011), brands can facilitate the process of co-creation by helping young people to develop their skills through offering them editorial content, advising them on layouts, and giving them tips for improving the title of an article, for example. Therefore, there is a need to achieve a balance in the exchange between a luxury brand and bloggers. An exchange between two parties should be equitable to ensure satisfaction on both sides. According to the theory of social justice (Miller, 1991), everyone should feel that he/she receives as much as he/she gives to ensure the continuity of the relationship. Luxury brands and digital native bloggers together should then define "win-win" collaboration modes, as shown in Figure 3.2.

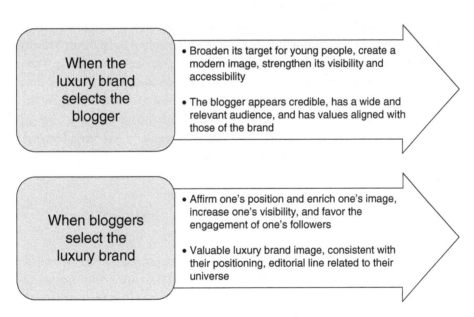

Figure 3.2   The luxury brand–blogger partnership selection process

When considering collaborating with bloggers luxury brands might choose them according to specific criteria, providing them with a return on their investment. These criteria may include the credibility of the blog, the richness of the content, the aesthetics of the formatting, the profile of the followers, and the cohesion of the image of the blogger with the values of the luxury brand. It is also important, before proposing a partnership with a blogger, to take into account his/her personality, his/her goals, and the quality of the dialogue with his/her community. The digital native generation also has its own criteria for choosing the luxury brands with which it wants to collaborate. The blogger can decide to associate with a brand that is strictly in line with his/her identity in order to reinforce his/her positioning, or the blogger may prefer to collaborate with luxury brands that are quite different from his/her positioning and personality to expand his/her audience, at the risk of making his/her image ambiguous. The strict application of criteria will be qualified and evaluated by luxury brands according to the notoriety of the blogger. Yet, when it starts, a young person may be tempted to accept any partnership that a brand could offer in order to develop his/her visibility.

Furthermore, it is important that bloggers also take into account the expectations of their followers in managing their blogs and working with brands. Regarding his/her audience, the blogger should communicate in a manner that is perceived as credible and transparent. People who follow a blog like to feel close to the blogger, to be able to identify with him/her, and to project themselves into his/her everyday life. Luxury brands that initiate partnerships with bloggers should, therefore, guarantee that the proposed collaborations will allow the blogger to maintain a close relationship with his/her audience while avoiding overly constraining the freedom of expression of the blogger. Moreover, a strong expectation of readers is being able to return to the site and find exactly what they need, including opportunities for new discoveries and personal growth. One of the difficulties encountered by bloggers is arousing constant interest. One solution might include offering greater variety and frequent updates to justify a frequent visit to a blog. In this quest, luxury brands can assist and guide the blogger by regularly providing him/her new offers or experiences that he/she can display on the blog.

HOW CAN BLOGGERS-BRAND COLLABORATION PROMOTE LUXURY EXPERIENCES?

Several modes of collaboration are possible between a blogger and a luxury brand, which can be categorized according to the degree of visibility of the partnership and the degree of personalization of the blogger's communication. In any case, it is important to understand the expertise of both the luxury brand and the blogger. Moreover, it is essential that the connection maintains an authentic dimension of the luxury experience so that followers will like it. In fact, digital native bloggers are aware of their skills as well as their strong influence on their followers. They know they have a great sensitivity and understanding of the trends in their communities as they live there every day. With their blogs, they consider that they are performing a genuine creative service by generating attractive textual and visual content that is useful for their readers. They also have a similarity and proximity to their community that gives them strong credibility when giving advice or recommending products. Furthermore, most expert bloggers have an in-depth knowledge of the topics of interest and forms of communication that are relevant to their community and followers.

However, one of the difficulties of luxury brand development on the Internet comes from the lack of experiencing the product in real life. Indeed, compared to a store, it is not possible to touch or try the product on a website. Presenting the product in a specific situation, that is to say, used by a blogger in which followers may also recognize themselves, can reassure them as to the adequacy of the product to their needs (e.g., social, self-esteem, functional). Therefore, luxury brands can benefit from working with a blogger to create greater experiential image accessibility in order to facilitate and simplify the purchase. As for luxury brands, they have expertise regarding their products, their values, and their history, and the information they provide to the blogger allows him/her to create and post editorial content that enriches the site with relevant elements about the luxury brand and its trends. The collaboration will be enriched from the moment when the expertise of the luxury brand and the blogger will respectively be recognized. Mutual respect is key to ensuring a balanced and successful partnership. The blogger will be very proud if a luxury brand indicates that it appreciates his/her work, and the luxury brand will appreciate that the blogger has a professional and creative approach when promoting its values and products.

As part of the collaboration, the luxury brand should first and foremost fit, in a natural and non-intrusive way, into the blogger's world and be consistent with its positioning. The relationship can be disinterested: the blogger freely shares his/her favorites with his/her followers and quotes the luxury brand, often in a discreet way, by a simple hashtag representing the name of the luxury brand used. Or, the relationship can be more commercial: the blogger signs a contract with a luxury brand and presents it in an almost advertisement-like manner on his/her site or blog. Between these two options, several possibilities exist, ranging from the most spontaneous to the most commercial. Amongst these approaches, I can cite the following:

- **Personal partnership**. If the profile of the blogger shows a professional status that is strongly influenced by the luxury brand, the strategy is then to send gifts/invitations to the blogger, who will write an article about the luxury brand or post a video with the products and the blogger. The content is largely influenced by the luxury brand, and is often accompanied by links that will redirect readers to its online store. Otherwise, if the blogger's profile refers to an amateur whose blog is highly personalized, the content (e.g., article, photo, video) is produced spontaneously without the intervention of the luxury brand, and is regularly accompanied by a hashtag that encourages readers to visit the website of the luxury brand.
- **Community partnership**. If the bloggers' profile highlights professional features, the luxury brand will implement advertising inserts (e.g., banner, pop-up). Paying for clicks or views, organizing game competitions sponsored by the brand, and relaying information on the blog featuring gifts for followers are but some of the ways luxury brands

will compensate or reward bloggers and their readers. If the profile is more amateur, the luxury brand should create a product placement strategy. It can invite the blogger to write an article or make a video in which its products are inserted, with a possible financial compensation.

The choice amongst these options depends on the maturity of the blogger, his/her number of followers, personal goals, and the sensitivity of his/her community. In any case, it is significant to clarify the rules of the collaboration to ensure transparency to the community in terms of the relationship between the brand and the blogger, whether of a contractual nature or not.

Before starting a collaboration, the blogger should be convinced of the relevance of the luxury brand and truly appreciate it. The blogger should make it clear that his/her choices are motivated more by his/her passions and the concern for his/her community than by purely commercial considerations. Thus, the blogger demonstrates that he/she gives primacy to the interest of his/her followers rather than to the profitability of the blog. It is also essential that the blogger maintains continuity in his/her positioning and that his/her approach to the community is not changed when the blogger engages with a luxury brand. The blogger can choose collaborations that express his/her values, such as defending a luxury brand that offers local products, or defending young artists and designers. Additionally, blogs are sought for their authenticity, sincerity, and speechless language. These are essential factors of differentiation in relation to the luxury brand site. A luxury brand that is perceived as authentic may encompass the following characteristics: maintenance of quality standards, respecting its ancestral heritage, preservation of the essence of its DNA, and the removal of an overly commercial approach (e.g., Spiggle et al., 2012). A celebrity will be perceived as authentic if his or her behavior is aligned with universal values (e.g., Moulard et al., 2015) and appears both as original/unique, and as stable over time. For a blogger, it is also about giving intimate information, offering an honest and personal opinion that is not influenced by luxury brands. The authenticity of a blog depends on its transparency, its continuity, and the concerns of its audience (e.g., Marwick, 2013). Therefore, luxury brands can have an effective strategy if they follow certain rules: (1) encourage the young person's immersion in the world of the luxury brand so that he or she understands its values; (2) privilege coherent collaborations in which the blogger or the influencer and the luxury brand share the same values; (3) allow the bloggers/influencers to be creative and stay consistent with their style in the presentation of the luxury brand; (4) help digital natives to professionalize and become known by allowing them to work with experts while using the power of communication of the luxury brand to be visible; (5) respect the influencer's/blogger's universe, his/her editorial content, and positioning; and finally (6) luxury brands should clearly define the rules of the game and terms of collaboration with digital natives, especially when the relationship is monetized.

SUMMARY

In a context where young digital natives are in a very special phase of their development and where they will use their blogs and social media to meet their needs for identity development, luxury brands should adapt their digital strategies and their experiential offerings targeting this youth generation in order to propose relevant modes of collaboration, connection, and the sharing of values online and offline. These young people continue, as they move from adolescence to adulthood, in the dual purpose of developing their own identity and belonging to online communities. Blogs and social media are, therefore, a tool for these purposes: they are an opportunity for self-expansion by providing a platform for personal expression and communication within a community. Nowadays, digital natives are able to take on a new role and acquire new skills in order to build their identity and develop their expertise in a luxury brand, or in the fashion sector, which will, ultimately, be recognized by their peers, thereby increasing their self-esteem.

In this chapter, I showed that the creative process of both digital natives and luxury brands in terms of blogging usually follows a progressive path from observation to personalization in gradually creating an original communication space. In their relationship with luxury brands, digital native youngsters are simultaneously attracted by the communication of luxury brands, which allows them to assert themselves despite suspicious marketing discourses, which sometimes seem manipulative to them. Therefore, to ensure effective luxury brand–digital native collaboration (co-creation), luxury businesses need to gain greater acceptance amongst these young people and demonstrate that they could generate added value for the digital generation. In fact, digital natives want to develop a balanced relationship with luxury brands that allows them to meet the expectations of their audience and to have fun. In the evolution of the relationship between the luxury brand and the digital native generation, it will be a question of moving towards an increasingly creative and personalized approach to communication rather than merely monetizing its influence.

PART II

REALMS OF THE DIGITAL LUXURY EXPERIENCE

4
IMMERSIVE DIGITAL LUXURY EXPERIENCES

INTRODUCTION AND SCOPE

Both researchers and practitioners advocate the immersion of a consumer in an experiential setting that is both physical (e.g., in-store) and digital (e.g., Internet and social media platforms). Their arguments are mainly based on three observations: immersion is a source of well-being for the consumer; immersion generates emotions that positively influence satisfaction; and immersion positively influences loyalty. The objective of creating immersive customer experiences by using technologies is to disconnect the consumer from his/her everyday life and to ensure that the consumer lives a unique and pleasant customer experience offline and online. Chapter 4 explores the notion of digital immersion and the way luxury companies can use different creative technologies as well as narrative techniques, such as digital storytelling and storydoing, to immerse their customers in pleasurable and emotional luxury experiences.

WHAT IS IMMERSIVE DIGITAL LUXURY EXPERIENCE?

An immersive digital experience is when a consumer interacts with a luxury brand's experiential atmosphere. We can define immersion as a mode of access to a pleasurable consumption experience. Thus, immersion suggests an activity wherein customers will get involved in an experiential setting (usually themed) to be transported by way of an experience sufficiently different from their daily habits to create an ultimate setting in which they will experience intense and unforgettable emotions. Bitner (1992) refers to immersive environments as a "servicescape" to underline the effect of the physical setting in which service is delivered. The servicescape can have a positive or negative impact on the quality of customer experience, as well as on consumers' behaviors and on the inter-personal employee relationships and interactions amongst consumers. The servicescape model includes facilitator, technological, functional, and sensory elements.

By changing these different elements, luxury companies can create whole "experience worlds," which become new tools for promoting brands and products differently. Carù and Cova describe immersion as "a feeling of well-being, development, and satisfaction" (2003). Thus, accessing a state of immersion is conditioned by consumers' ability to re-acquire the experience setting through which they change and customize the immediate setting to gen-erate a feeling of personal context. Carù and Cova state that the consumer can achieve the re-acquirement process through three major processes: nesting, exploration, and tagging:

- **Nesting**. Processes allowing individuals to personalize their environment and create a homey feeling;
- **Exploration**. Involves consumers exploring the service environment in order to identify the elements (services, activities, surroundings) that will allow them to develop their own personal experiences;
- **Tagging**. Refers more specifically to the personal meaning (inspired from one's own value system, history, and past experiences) given by consumers to various elements of the experience.

Immersion in digital consumption experiences is a relevant strategy for luxury brands, since it is viewed both as a process that allows consumers to access and live intense expe-riences, and as an outcome of a satisfying lived experience. This is particularly interesting for luxury professionals and brand managers, since consumer immersion is the key factor for improving and enhancing consumer satisfaction and loyalty. Consumers who expe-rience immersive consumption and purchase processes will be more eager to develop positive, pleasurable, and memorable feelings and thus re-experience the same feelings in future encounters. As stated by Cova and Carù (2003), what makes an experience pleasur-able is the consumer's whole immersion in one that is original.

While today's consumers are seeking varied and captivating experiences, authors such as Goulding (2000) and Ritzer (2004) argue that consumers will seek consumption expe-riences that allow them to escape their ordinary life by driving those experiences in a pre-conceptualized, pre-established, safe, and themed sphere. While certain authors argue that customers expect unusual consumption settings to produce strong, deep, and memo-rable experiences (e.g., Arnould and Price, 1993; Pine and Gilmore, 1999), others state that not all consumption experiences require an extraordinary dimension to attain immersion (e.g., Carù and Cova, 2003). Both "ordinary" and "extraordinary" consumption expe-riences can lead to the creation of intense immersion through special occasions (e.g., holidays are used by consumers who seek "farniente" [from the Italian "to do nothing"], to relax; they are not seeking leisure activities and extraordinary experiences, as they regard "farniente" as a non-extraordinary, calm, and relaxing experience that is highly immersive). Immersion in luxury consumption experiences, whether they occur within ordinary or extraordinary settings, creates emotions, and thus consumer satisfaction and loyalty. Ritzer (2004) argues that there is a need to examine the consumer experience from a "re-enchantment" perspective instead of only focusing on environmental and sensorial factors that may enhance consumer immersion, to generate positive feelings and unforgettable consumption and/or purchase experiences.

A successful offering of a satisfying cognitive and emotional experience can be achieved by luxury companies through the use of immersive digital tools and/or by focusing on immersive factors that can enable consumers to experience positive and memorable consumption settings that have several advantages for luxury brands:

- A positive influence of consumer behavior;
- Reinforcing the memorization of brand and product information;
- Helping consumers to be effectively involved within their experiences and social interactions with brands and salespeople;
- Generating pleasure and stimulating consumers' senses;
- Promoting exchanges and socialization within the marketplace.

CREATIVE TECHNOLOGIES FOR IMMERSIVE DIGITAL LUXURY EXPERIENCES

Immersive digital luxury experiences can include one or multiple creative technologies. Each of these technologies brings together specific digital tools tailored to the digital customer experience for the purpose of generating value for the company and its customers. For luxury houses, in order to create or reinvent the digital customer experience, the use of various creative technologies and immersive digital tools, including virtual and augmented reality, 3D and 4D, 360-degree video, and interactive digital screens, represents the challenge of connecting the real world to the virtual ecosphere, which includes guaranteeing a fluid, sensory, emotional, continuous, and satisfying digital luxury experience for their customers. Further, delivering a memorable and enjoyable immersive digital luxury experience requires the integration of technological devices such as smartphones, tablets, and connected objects. Luxury companies also have to meet three main conditions to design a successful, efficient, and profitable digital customer experience:

- Condition 1: create a contextualized, functional, emotional, and sensory digital customer experience.
- Condition 2: reinforce the link between the virtual and real experience across several media: laptops, tablets, apps, website, etc.

- Condition 3: offer engaging experiential content using storytelling techniques. The video and especially 360-degree video can be used to tell stories. This technique is very effective and does not require the effort of reading and is especially easy to share on social networks.

In fact, in art, the media, sports, and other sectors, 360-degree video technology refers to immersive and interactive videos that became very popular thanks to the advent of virtual reality headsets. The latter innovation goes hand-in-hand with 360-degree videos, which are becoming ever more popular. On a simple computer screen or smartphone, these videos allow the user to view scenes in 360-degree video by moving the cursor of his/her mouse or using a touchscreen – right, left, up, or down. Instead of merely viewing a video, the user lives an immersive and interactive experience. Furthermore, during the projection of the video, the user can have control over the direction in which he/she views the scene – up, down, or sideways. Usually, the only direction in which the viewer cannot look is in the direction of the camera that is recording the video. For luxury companies, the use of 360-degree videos will better immerse their customers within a sensory and memorable luxury experience.

TREND 4.1

THE EXPERIENCE OF PARIS REINVENTED BY YVES SAINT LAURENT, THANKS TO 360-DEGREE VIDEOS

For Yves Saint Laurent, beauty is part of a dynamic of innovations and commitments driven by a digital logic designed to connect with a generation of globetrotters and hyper-connected customers with the aim of reinventing the customer experience and the shopping experience indefinitely. In so doing, the luxury brand initiated a digital campaign that integrates a 360-degree video, "Mon Paris," to promote the launch of its perfume. The video shows 360-degree views of all the locations in Paris shown in the film. "Mon Paris" is the story of modern lovers around the world, inspired by the heart of the city of light – Paris, as one has never seen it before. The perfume targets the impetuous, passionate woman who lets herself be guided by her desire and lives with a vertiginous love that floods her senses and turns her world completely upside down.

So, how can luxury brands use creative technologies, such as augmented and virtual reality, to design valuable immersive luxury experiences? Augmented reality (AR) refers to augmenting a real-time direct or indirect vision of the physical sphere with virtual information (e.g., Carmigniani and Furht, 2011). It is an emerging technology that narrows the gap between the digital world and the real setting (e.g., Manuri and Sanna, 2016). According to Azuma (1997), the augmented reality system is defined by three characteristics: it combines real and virtual objects, allows users real-time interactions, and records information in three dimensions (3D). In other words, AR provides a real-time, direct or indirect view of a physical environment that has been augmented by the addition of virtual and computerized content. Thus, AR increases and enriches the user's perception and interaction with the real world. In addition, Azuma et al. (2001) note that AR is not limited to the sense of vision alone, it can also be extended to other sensory systems, such as scent, touch, or hearing. According to Tăbuşcă (2014), augmented reality is not entirely new as virtual and immersive technologies have been around for over 60 years. The chronology of its evolution, established by Beauchemin (2016), shows the stages that AR went through before becoming a tool used to create immersive experiences.

- In the beginning, augmented reality was part of virtual reality (VR), another technology that wholly immersed the user in a virtual world generated by computers. The first VR system was a head-mounted display consisting of one or two television screens and a motion capture system (e.g., Carmigniani and Furht 2011; Manuri and Sanna, 2016). Its primary function was essentially to change users' perception of their real setting so that they focus all their attention on the virtual world. The use of VR was limited to functional usages, such as simulators used by pilots or military usages.
- In 1962, Morton Heilig, considered the founding father of virtual reality, created the "Sensorama" (Beauchemin, 2016). Prior to real-time numerical computation, this multisensory device was intended to immerse the user in a virtual movie scene (McLellan, 1996) by adding sensations of breezes and vibrations, which was then followed by the use of 3D images that allowed users to see images while moving in their real setting.
- By the end of the 20th century, VR had gained notoriety amongst the public thanks to headphones developed by the video game and entertainment industries, such as Sony, Nintendo, Sega, and others.
- Today, new, more accessible and less expensive prototypes (Hale and Stanney, 2014) have appeared (e.g., Google Glass). The recent emergence of augmented reality has also been facilitated by a new generation of mobile phones. At the same time, other technological innovations (such as speed of information processing) have improved the functioning of traditional augmented reality systems.

Although there are still discussions within the research community aimed at obtaining a clearer distinction between VR and AR, most scholars argue that the concept of augmented reality is an extension of virtual reality (e.g., Beauchemin, 2016; Uluyol and Şahin, 2016), and the difference between these two technologies is related to the continuum from the digital to the real, and vice versa. On the one hand, virtual reality drives the user into an immersive experience by replacing the surrounding physical world with a virtual environment (Haller, 2006). The individual can thus discover a computer-digitized world by using a suitable device (headphones, laptops, immersive rooms, etc.). On the other hand, augmented reality promises a more interactive experience by superimposing computer-generated virtual objects into the real world (Azuma, 1997; Carmigniani and Furht, 2011). However, augmented reality seems more advantageous than virtual reality, as it requires fewer pixels and, therefore, has greater processing power (e.g., Caudell and Mizell, 1992). Furthermore, for both technologies, AR and VR, display techniques require the use of a suitable device. Zhou et al. (2008) identified three main technologies: movable devices, optical headsets, and projection displays (or holograms).

- **Movable screens**. Several types of portable devices are available on the marketplace. The most common are: smartphones, digital tablets, etc. These technologies have the distinction of being less intrusive, socially acceptable, and ready to use.
- **Head-mounted display**. Augmented reality overlays virtual objects onto the real world through optical technology or video to allow the user to see the real world through a screen on which is projected a holographic image containing digital information.
- **Projection displays.** This technology relies on the process of displaying graphic information on objects or surfaces of everyday life.

TREND 4.2

KENZO USES A DIGITALLY CONNECTED POP-UP STORE AGAINST OVERFISHING

Creating an ephemeral pop-up connected store allows luxury brands to create a buzz around a product or concept launch. An example of this is Kenzo's surprising and innovative digital pop-up store created as a result of the Japanese designer's commitment to the problem of overfishing and his close collaboration with the Blue Marine Foundation. As a logical continuation of his fashion show, and taking up the foundation's slogan, "No Fish No Nothing," Kenzo Tagada wanted to reiterate his support for the foundation through an ephemeral 2.0 interactive store. At the heart of this highly interactive and experiential pop-up store, customers can find a giant virtual aquarium and order online all the unique pieces of the Kenzo capsule collection. All of this boosted the brand's notoriety and also its image thanks to the retweets on the social networks of #NoFishNoNothing.

For luxury companies, it is then critical to incorporate these immersive technologies in the design of their digital experiential offerings and settings. Olsson et al. (2013) state that service customization is an important part of augmented reality applications and their personal and immersive dimensions. In addition, these creative technologies are clearly more persuasive and engaging by their innovative nature. Moreover, for these authors, mobile augmented reality applications are vectors of experience and positive emotions. Thus, they can offer relevant and contextualized information in relation to the exact location of the consumer. Therefore, the digital customer experience can be created by luxury professionals by using virtual reality or augmented reality technologies to extend the consumer's actual experience in the virtual world or the reverse of the virtual world to a virtual reality experience projection thanks to technologies such as 3D or 4D in the real world.

The objective is to bring the virtual world into one's daily life using connected objects, such as Google Glass, which are glasses that allow the projection of the digital realm in the real world. These two technologies, and in particular that of virtual reality, allow luxury companies to immerse a person in a digitally created, artificial world. It can be a reproduction of the real world or a totally imaginary universe. Thus, the digital luxury experience is visual, auditory, and sensory. When the person is equipped with the appropriate interfaces, such as gloves or connected clothing, he/she can even experience some sensations related to touch or other feelings.

DESIGNING IMMERSIVE LUXURY EXPERIENCES VIA DIGITAL STORYTELLING

Storytelling is a very important strategic narrative communication tool for luxury brands, and can be used to create a digital experience, promote brand awareness, and enhance its value by creating an emotionally charged digital universe that includes the brand's identity and story. These stories are made and told to reach targets and create a strong relationship with them. To create strong and emotional storytelling, luxury brands can also collaborate with artists and filmmakers to give the brand more human, emotional, and historical depth. The making of a story varies according to the perspective adopted and the digital tools used for its manufacture as well as the objectives of the luxury brand. The benefit of digital storytelling can be an asset to luxury businesses because it allows them to capture and share the experiential value of their customers. Indeed, storytelling is used to create experiential value in a digital context known for its functional and utilitarian dimensions.

Digital storytelling captures the value perceived by the customer, an important dimension that the luxury brand should integrate upstream of its digital strategy, well before developing the story and even before choosing the right digital tool. Identifying the dimensions of perceived consumer value, whether it is utility, economic, social, or experiential, helps luxury companies improve the quality of the overall digital experience from a consumer perspective. In other words, what the customer wants (perceived value) and not what the luxury brand would like to offer (desired value). Marketing studies have highlighted the importance of the perceived value sought by the customer in his/her consumption experiences. Perceived value is, then, a result of the customer's interaction with the luxury brand, its products/services, its website, its staff, and other customers in a phygital context. The value derived from these offline and online social interactions is considered a kind of gratification that the consumer derives from his/her digital customer experience. This gratification can take many forms, which can have a positive or negative impact on the customer's digital and physical (in-store) brand experiences.

WHAT ARE THE MAIN COMPONENTS OF DIGITAL STORYTELLING?

Digital storytelling draws its inspiration from the story it tells. Good digital storytelling with value to the customer should highlight stories that include the following elements:

- Strong and unique emotional digital content that enables the luxury brand to be identified and differentiated from its competitors;
- Theatrical and artistic staging of the luxury brand in the digital world;
- Visual and textual contents that are memorable;
- Brand content adapted to different consumption cultures without losing the identity of the brand in the logic's continuum between two contexts: digital (e.g., website) and real (e.g., shops).

In addition to these elements, the implementation of strong and impactful digital storytelling can use other sources of inspiration to feed the story told by the luxury brand in order to move the consumer or create a shared value with him/her. There are five key ingredients of digital storytelling that luxury brands and digital leaders should take into consideration when designing a digital experiential offering. Figure 4.1 introduces these five components, which are also explained below.

Figure 4.1   The five ingredients of digital storytelling

- **Unique know-how**. This is an essential element in the production of digital storytelling. Digital storytelling that is based on ancestral and intergenerational know-how highlights specific manufacturing techniques that are emphasized in digital communications. The know-how is also linked to a cultural specificity (e.g., Made in France, Made in Italy).
- **The story of the brand creator**. The history of the luxury brand is often linked to its founder, who, by his/her personality, personal history, life course, creativity and, above all, daring, helps forge the myth of the luxury brand and its originality. In digital storytelling, telling the story of the luxury brand is to tell the inspiring and moving story of its creator. Digital storytelling based on the story of the founder meets various objectives:

  o   Promoting the unique know-how of the luxury brand and related professions;
  o   Humanizing the luxury brand through the life course of its creator;
  o   Communicating the values of the luxury brand;
  o   Promoting causes supported by the luxury brand;
  o   Disseminating the ideology of the luxury brand;
  o   Highlighting the authenticity and historical anchoring of the luxury brand;
  o   Strengthening the legitimacy of the luxury brand and differentiating it from its competitors.

TREND 4.3

CHANEL'S DIGITAL STORYTELLING: "INSIDE CHANEL" OR THE MYTH OF COCO CHANEL

"Inside Chanel" is the emotional storytelling video that explores the myth of the founder of the Chanel brand. For almost two years, the luxury house Chanel has been telling and reinventing its story through a dozen web-series presented both on its YouTube channel and through a dedicated microsite, Inside Chanel. The idea of the creators of the web-series is to tell the story of the brand and its origins online in order to make it accessible to as many viewers as possible. It is also another way to make a difference and reaffirm brand values in today's world. The narrative of the storytelling that reinforces the myth is punctuated by "once upon a time" and traces a touching human story of a young orphan who became Coco Chanel: "There was once a little girl who all her life masked her peasant origins and preferred to invent her legend. Once upon a time, there was Gabrielle Chanel, born under the sign of the lion to a pedantic and huckster merchant father and to a mother who ironed and ironed and died at age 32 exhausted by life. Once upon a time ..."

- **Creative mindset**. The creative and disruptive spirit in digital storytelling aims to generate the WOW effect and to challenge the consumer. Luxury brands need to honor their creative mindset in their digital strategies to retain current customers and attract new ones. The luxury brand's creative mindset, communicated through digital storytelling, highlights the brand's potential and capacity for renewal, which is more likely to surprise its customers and provide them with new and unique digital experiences every time they visit the website of the luxury brand, or on social media and in its stores.

- **The strength of visual aesthetics**. The use of visuals and images in the development of digital storytelling makes it easy for luxury brands to express the values and the messages that they wish to communicate to their targets. Luxury companies need, then, to focus on the use of beautiful and elegant visuals in digital storytelling to offer their customers immersive and authentic digital experiences. The visual element is accompanied by a simple and concise spoken text to avoid flooding the consumer with functional information about the product. In order for digital storytelling to appeal to consumers, the visual aspect should be refined and original enough to entice visitors to the site and to start interacting with and integrating the product into their own story and identity.

- **The sound elements**. These are important for creating and amplifying emotions. They allow the luxury brand to create its own musical and sound identity. The sound elements also influence the emotions of the audience and allow them to share a similar sensation, thus coinciding with the target's own "brand" or tastes. Yet, the music chosen and the digital media are more important than the choice of the particular style of music (e.g., jazz, underground, classic).

DIGITAL STORYTELLING IMPLEMENTATION PROCESS

The building of a story can be accomplished in two ways: (1) by transforming the positioning of the luxury brand into a story and (2) by setting up a digital storytelling that uses "the hero's journey" as a tool. Regarding the first approach and how it relates to transforming the positioning of the luxury brand into a story, the brand manager should start with the DNA of the luxury brand and build narrative elements around it and that are associated with digital tools, which will highlight the values and positioning of the luxury brand. The hero's journey is a concept established by Joseph Campbell in 1949 and a classic of narratology studies that is still used today in narrative communication to build stories with myths (Campbell, 2008).

The hero's journey is about building a story by describing the initiatory journey of a hero who goes through several phases during which he/she is likely to meet moments of happiness as well as difficulties that will have to be overcome during this journey. By moving from a known world to an unknown universe, the hero is realized and creates a myth that fascinates, inspires, and touches the audience. In order to create a digital storytelling, luxury brand managers should follow four main steps: identity, relational, story, and incarnation. Figure 4.2 summarizes the questions related to each stage. For luxury brands, these four steps are necessary to build an authentic story that can generate positive emotions for customers.

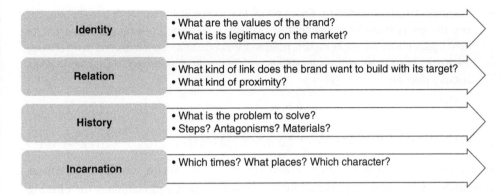

Figure 4.2 The four steps for creating digital storytelling

Furthermore, luxury companies can set up different strategies to create content that will enrich their digital storytelling. Amongst the major strategies for creating content for digital storytelling are the following: informational, emotional, immersive, experiential, and ideological.

- **Informational digital storytelling**. The strategies that use informational content are focused on the product/service and the brand news, which can feed its website and social media exchanges with practical and functional information content (e.g., information on product dimensions and their characteristics; the quality of their after-sales service and listening to customers; the dedicated teams; the simplicity and speed of booking or buying online; other products, offers and services available; other addresses where consumers can find the brand).
- **Emotional digital storytelling**. Those strategies involving emotional content aim to create a variety of emotions for consumers when they are on the luxury brand's website, or on social media. Luxury houses can use the emotional dimension in their communication strategies for several reasons: connecting with their consumers, establishing a strong bond with them, involving them and sharing values with them, creating proximity and a warm image, etc.
- **Immersive digital storytelling**. Strategies including immersive content engage the consumer through content and digital tools that require real or virtual interactions. In order to interact with consumers, luxury brands can use several approaches to immerse the consumer through experiences on their websites, or when buying from a connected digital store.
- **Experiential digital storytelling**. The goal of experiential content strategies is to project the consumer into a real or virtual world of the luxury brand and its products and services in an ordinary or extraordinary setting. This strategy can then anchor the luxury brand in the consumer's life or mind.

- **Ideological digital storytelling**. Engaged and/or ideological content strategies emphasize the luxury brand's commitment to a cause or ideology. For example, as part of its fight against discrimination, racism, pollution, violence against women, and homophobia, the luxury brand can express its values and its positioning through digital storytelling, sponsorship, etc.

FROM DIGITAL STORYTELLING TO DIGITAL STORYDOING

In contrast to digital storytelling, which consists of producing narratives to appeal to consumers, digital storydoing combines story with action and facilitates the offering of unique luxury consumer experiences. Thus, a question arises: Why do luxury brands have to transform their digital storytelling into storydoing through concrete offline and online actions? According to Batat (2019b), for luxury brands, transforming storytelling into concrete actions by involving customers helps brands to improve their performance and build strong customer loyalty. Telling stories is not enough today to retain customers, luxury brands should also engage in storydoing projects where they can engage customers within their stories.

Digital storytelling is, therefore, the starting point for any successful storydoing, a strategy that should cover all the company's actions and engage its various functions (marketing, communication, R&D, etc.). Furthermore, a digital storydoing strategy should place the customer and his/her expectations at the center of the luxury brand's story. It is clear that brands that adopt storydoing will perform better than those that limit their actions to storytelling. For example, unlike luxury brands, consumer brands, such as Red Bull, Apple, Coca-Cola, etc., are very successful in telling and sharing stories with their clients (storydoing). Digital storydoing is then an effective complementary strategy that allows luxury brands to differentiate themselves from the competition, and to be more successful in the long term. To implement a digital storydoing strategy, luxury brand managers can follow eight main steps:

1. Build the luxury brand story;
2. Define the experiential goals of customers;
3. Design the experience that the luxury brand wants its customers to live;
4. Select adequate digital tools and define the objectives of the digital strategy;
5. Make the experience accessible to customers;
6. Share a story and common values with customers;
7. Transform the experience into concrete actions;
8. Involve customers in the luxury brand's actions.

SUMMARY

This chapter highlighted the fact that luxury brands now believe that the digital transformation thrives on two performance drivers: customer relations and financial turnover. Thanks to the creative use of technologies, luxury brands can offer personalized profound, enjoyable, efficient, and emotional digital luxury experiences to their customers who can easily immerse themselves in a highly exceptional digitalized luxury experience. In this chapter, I explained the way luxury businesses can use both immersive technologies as well as narrative techniques, such as digital storytelling and storydoing, to reach the ultimate objective: customer re-enchantment.

5

CONNECTED DIGITAL
LUXURY EXPERIENCES

INTRODUCTION AND SCOPE

According to a study by McKinsey (2011), the economic stake of objects related to the Internet of Things (IoT) will be more than $11 trillion a year by 2025. Connected objects will multiply and enter into the daily lives of every consumer (Gartner, 2015a). There were 8.4 billion connected objects in 2017 and there will be more than 25 billion connected objects by 2020 (Gartner, 2017a). Connected objects are an integral part of the customer experience and create channels of direct communication with customers that businesses should integrate into the development of their digital strategies, which is at the center of the customer experience. IoT is, thus, changing the world and the way we consume and experience luxury consumption. The impact of this technology has already revolutionized areas such as communications, education, manufacturing, science, and many other areas of life. Clearly, IoT is evolving very quickly from concept to reality, transforming the way businesses operate and create value. The main developments and innovations in the IT world have had a significant impact on improving the digital customer experience.

Furthermore, according to IBM's statements at "The Genius of Things Summit" in 2017, the number of connected devices will rise to 30 billion over the next three years. This increasingly connected digital culture presents companies with a great opportunity to leverage digital connections to improve their products and services and, ultimately, to foster deeper human connections to enhance customer experiences and relationships. IBM put its IoT know-how and innovations into practice as part of its partnership with Visa to leverage the cognitive capabilities of IBM's Watson IoT platform. This collaboration allowed Visa to launch a technology that will enable customers to make payments from an IoT connected device, whether from an app, a car, or a watch. The new technology will not only eliminate the need for sensitive financial information on payment cards, but will also introduce a new level of simplicity and convenience for the customer's experiential journey.

Beyond allowing companies to collect real-time data, connected objects are a lever for the continuous improvement of the object itself, through a better understanding of its use by consumers in their consumption experiences in a continuous way. Nowadays, connected objects offer businesses the possibility of quantifying feedback on the customer experience and the usage of the object. This information needs to be complemented by other types of more immersive data that are closer to the consumer in order to be able to produce an in-depth analysis of the real customer experience and its tangible and intangible dimensions.

When objects enter the conversation, this inevitably impacts the user experience. To take a concrete example, if one's car and one's fridge are connected to each other, then if the individual passes near a supermarket on the way back from work, the car may suggest that he/she stop there to buy the product that is missing from the fridge at home. Connected objects can, therefore, be considered new databases that need to be taken into account in order to improve the experience within a specific setting when designing connected luxury experiences. This chapter explores technologies that luxury houses can use to offer connected luxury experiences, and thus collect data to better customize their experiential offerings and make them fit with their customers' emotional and functional expectations.

INTERNET OF THINGS (IOT): ORIGINS AND EVOLUTION

To date, there seems to be no clear and precise definition of connected objects in the academic world, although various papers deal exclusively with certain connected objects (e.g., smartphone, iBeacon). This lack of clarification leads to confusion between the concepts of connected objects, the Internet of Things (IoT), and pervasive technologies (ubiquitous technologies). The origins of the conceptualization of the Internet of Things (IoT) can be traced back to 1988, thanks to the work of Mark Weiser of Xerox PARC (Palo Alto Research Center Incorporated) who first suggested that computers weave the fabric of daily life, thus initiating the future of the sector. In 2000, the founding article "The networked physical world" (Sarma et al., 2000) gave birth to the concept of IoT, generating debate amongst scholars at the Sloan School of Management at MIT.

The Internet of Things means the "connection" of objects to a larger network, whether directly through Wi-Fi, through the user's smartphone (often via a Bluetooth connection) or through the intercommunication of objects with each other. It is this type of 2.0 objects that we call connected objects. Before defining IoT, it is important to explain what we mean by connected objects, a term that refers to a device that is not designed with the primary purpose of serving as a computer system, or as a Web access interface. For example, an object such as a coffee machine or a lock has historically been manufactured without integrating into the product itself computer systems, or a connection to the Internet. The integration of an Internet connection to a connected object enriches it in terms of functionality and interaction with its environment. It becomes an enriched connected object. For example, integrating an Internet connection into the coffee machine would make it remotely accessible. A connected object can interact with the physical world independently without human intervention. It has several constraints, such as memory, bandwidth, or power consumption, etc. That is why the incorporation of connected objects should be adapted to their intended usage. By definition, connected objects also have a certain form of intelligence, an ability to receive, to transmit data with software thanks to embedded sensors.

A connected object has a value when it is connected to other objects and software (e.g., a connected watch is of interest within a health/well-being oriented ecosystem, which goes well beyond knowing the time). Certain researchers refer to connected objects as "hyper objects" (Mavrommati and Kameas, 2003) that are able to pool their resources to perform everyday tasks; they are connected by "invisible links" within the same ecosystem. Therefore, connected objects, which are not necessarily connected to the Internet, are revolutionizing the life of the consumer (activity trackers, smartwatch, home automation, connected car, etc.). They are part of the recent evolution of the behavior of ubiquitous consumers who are connected and have access to a multitude of information from several supports (e.g., Hoffman and Novak, 2015, 2018). These new technologies are undeniably a step towards new usages in many economic sectors. Services (e.g., banking, insurance, transport, home automation) could, in this sense, benefit from the ability of these objects to collect, communicate, process, and exchange a multitude of data instantly and autonomously. This will pave the way for new business opportunities and the emergence of a new form of "smart service."

These smart services are connected objects designed with the aim of providing new experiences to the consumer that bring about changes in consumer behavior (mobility, ubiquity, connectivity, etc.) within the Internet of Things (IoT), which refers to a set of technological objects that are connected and implanted in their environment that work together to detect, process, store, and communicate information in a ubiquitous manner that meets the goals and tasks of their users. Therefore, IoT can be defined as an extension of the current Internet to all objects that can communicate, directly or indirectly, with electronic equipment, that is, connected to the Internet. The Internet as we know it today connects a variety of machines, ranging from computers to increasingly small, "smart," and portable electronic devices (phones, personal assistants, readers, etc.). However, with the development of technologies such as Radio-Frequency Identification (RFID) and sensor networks a whole generation of objects present both in the professional world and in everyday life (products, consumer goods, clothing, credit cards, temperature sensors, pressure sensors, etc.) opens up the path to the Internet of the future. In addition to RFID and sensor networks, companies should also take into account emerging strategies, often referred to as "Machine-to-Machine" solutions, and start to focus on relatively different measures of consumer behaviors.

Kevin Ashton, the co-founder of MIT's Auto-ID Center, used the term "Internet Of Things" in 1999. The term IoT combines the world of objects, devices, and sensors that are interconnected over the Internet. There are two aspects of IoT, temporal and spatial, that allow people to connect from anywhere at any time through connected objects. Thus, IoT should be designed for easy use and secure manipulation to avoid potential threats and risks while masking the underlying technological complexity. According to Hoffman and Novak (2015), there are four categories of connected objects:

- Wearable, as in connected objects that the consumer carries with him or her, such as calorie or step counters;
- Connected health objects, such as connected sphygmomanometers;
- Connected home, such as a connected alarm or smoke detector;
- Mobility objects (e.g., connected cars, GPS7 iBeacons).

The rapid evolution of this IoT disrupts the boundaries between the computer and everyday products. This is due to two factors: the generalization of computing resources and the appropriation of Web services by users. The applications of IoT are now practically affecting everyday life and the reactions of consumers to these connected objects are paradoxical. These reactions can be grouped into four main categories:

- **Easiness**. For consumers, the main benefits of connected objects are the simplification of daily life and the saving of time. However, certain studies state that IoT is made up of useless gadgets that are complex and time-consuming.
- **Intelligence**. Connected objects allow the individual to perform better. For consumers, IoT can allow them to better organize their daily activities, such as working out. However, connected objects also create dependency and give the impression that they are diminishing the skills of the human being.
- **Social**. On the one hand, these objects create social bonds because they make it easier to communicate, but they are criticized for maintaining an illusion of proximity.
- **Affect**. IoT can be a source of different emotional experiences. However, this experience is not always positive. Consumers oscillate between anxiety and fascination with connected objects.

The universe of connected objects is vast and has applications in health, home automation, transportation, industry, automotive, and many other sectors. In the customer and shopping experience, IoT refers to the incorporation of shopping connected devices to improve sales and customer experiences. From the customer experience perspective, the focus is on connected objects that can (1) receive contextualized notifications as well as communicate with other connected objects, such as the smartphone and the connected shopping cart (equipped with a touch terminal), and (2) have the ability to receive this type of notification and to make contact with other connected objects. As for notifications, they can also be considered mobile advertising, and some of them are contextualized through location-based advertising, which is defined as any application, service, or campaign that uses geolocation to deliver or improve a marketing message or service. Regarding communication, there is the example of how a smartphone can be used to compare prices on a product in a supermarket by scanning the QR code. Another example would be the possibility of having a shopping path traced on the smartphone, such as a global positing system (GPS) that allows the consumer to go directly to the products he/she has selected.

It would appear that the dichotomy between traditional commerce and e-commerce is bound to disappear in the coming years. Indeed, technological progress and the implementation of cross-channel strategies are gradually breaking down this physical and virtual barrier. Connected consumers will be more and more demanding, and the disappearance of borders (online and offline) will require the development of new services, such as the possibility of obtaining a product at any time. If companies aim to design consumer experience through the use of connected objects, it is because these have an impact on the experience itself. Indeed, we know that connected objects have a positive impact on the buying experience, which has a direct influence on customer satisfaction, and an indirect one on customer loyalty. The direct correlation between connected objects and customer loyalty, however, remains to be established in the specific context of mass retailing.

RFID can also improve the consumer buying experience. An interactive mirror and fitting rooms equipped with RFID positively affect the shopping experience. It also helps to better understand the customer and his/her needs. Another example advanced by Ngai et al. (2008) is the implementation of the RFID system PSA (personal shopping assistant) in a point of sale, which has shown to have a positive impact on the consumer's buying experience as well as resulting in a gain in efficiency thanks to consumers' access to additional information about the products. Furthermore, the use of Near-Field Communication (NFC) technology combined with others contributes positively to the overall consumer shopping experience. According to Kim and Forsythe (2007), the use of virtual technological products is motivated more by hedonistic than utilitarian factors. In fact, the installation of technological tools at the point of sale improves the image of the store, and positively impacts the experience and the value of shopping. These different examples show a real impact of connected objects on the consumer's buying experience.

CONSUMERS' ATTITUDES TOWARDS CONNECTED OBJECTS

The attitudes of the consumers towards connected objects include various dimensions of ambivalence and contradictory reactions vis-à-vis the use of connected technologies in their consumption experience and daily habits. Several kinds of ambivalence can be identified depending on the connection between the consumers, the user's relationship with connected objects (i.e., whether the user is an adopter or resister), and the function he/she gives to connected objects (e.g., utility, experiential, or symbolic). Ambivalent attitudes refer to a situation in which the individual is subject to contrary motivations and seeks to reduce the discomfort that this conflict generates. The consequences of ambivalence then depend on the strategy set up by the consumer. The purchase and use of the connected object are not hampered by ambivalence if the consumer succeeds in denying or rationalizing the contrary attitudes towards the connected object. But the ambivalent consumer can also choose to completely reject the connected object to no longer feel the discomfort of oscillating between contrary motives. Ambivalence is, therefore, decisive for the purchase and the repeated use of connected objects. Thus, the nature of a consumer's ambivalent attitudes towards connected objects can be classified into three main aspects:

- **Functionality and utility of the connected object**. Connected objects can be evaluated on their tangible attributes and incorporated according to their real characteristics and functions. The consumer relies on objective criteria and refrains from giving a subjective meaning to the object (associations of ideas, previous experiences). This utility is not dedicated to certain categories of connected objects. For example, a connected smoke detector and food processor are both perceived by consumers as being merely utilitarian. Consumers thus value the ability of these connected objects to provide solutions to a problem. When the connected object has a utilitarian function, ambivalence focuses on the easiness and simplicity for both users and non-users. Non-users recognize that these connected objects facilitate daily life, but that they do not respond to a real need, such as information on the weather. Connected object users also think that these objects are useful on a daily basis (positive on the easy dimension) even if they are too complex to use (negative on the easy dimension). The complexity does not discourage them from using the connected object because this technology allows them to respond to their functional needs and save time.

TREND 5.1

MONTBLANC AUGMENTED PAPER REVOLUTIONIZES THE HANDWRITING EXPERIENCE

Montblanc Augmented Paper is the name of the connected luxury notepad and pen launched by the German house. The passion for writing takes a different turn with the use of this innovative high-end accessory. Luxury pen creator Montblanc has decided to revolutionize traditional writing by connecting it with new technologies. Montblanc Augmented Paper is an innovative device for connecting a StarWalker ballpoint pen to one's smartphone or tablet. The main interest of this innovation is to never lose the experience of writing. Montblanc Augmented Paper allows users to recover notes placed on paper via a connected object. Whenever the user writes or draws on the Augmented Paper pad, the digital system instantly transmits data to a smartphone or tablet via Bluetooth technology.

Therefore, the Montblanc Augmented Paper experience combines the pleasure of writing with the convenience of technology. This connected luxury device allows lovers of traditional writing to set their keyboard aside and pick up a pen again. Montblanc Augmented Paper is supplied in a box containing the notebook, StarWalker ballpoint pen, and an Italian leather case. The user may at any time decide to transfer his/her notes in digital format. A simple push of the button on the leather case will transmit the data to the smartphone instantly. Montblanc is not the first to offer a connected pen, but the German luxury house has just created the most expensive digital pen on the market, retailing at around $700.

- **Experiential function of the connected object**. Connected objects can be incorporated for their ability to provide a particular user experience. The experiential dimension is a result of the consumer's greater emotional involvement. When the relationship with the connected object is experiential, the ambivalence of the consumer is based on both the facility and the intelligence of the object. Non-users might consider that these connected objects increase performance, but that they are too complex to use. These individuals are disillusioned with connected objects. They are fascinated by their technological prowess but know that the use is too complex to really make life easier. Users of these objects think that they facilitate their daily lives, but that they also make them less intelligent. They feel that technology reduces the cognitive skills of individuals. Users of connected objects might also feel locked into a form of dependency on such objects, but this does not prevent them from continuing to use the connected object, such as the use of GPS when driving rather than developing skills by learning how to read a road map.
- **Symbolic dimension of the connected object**. The connected object can be regarded as an assertion of the self, of one's integration into society. Consumers can use connected objects that allow them to establish a social link with others (e.g., a connected watch as a health object used to share information). The distinction is made between a more individual and self-centered use of the connected object, as opposed to a social use, in the sense that it allows the consumer to establish, reinforce, socially bond, collaborate, and communicate with others. The ambivalence towards symbolically connected objects is,

therefore, essentially related to the social dimension of the object. In this case, ambivalence lies in the opposition between openness to others made possible by connected objects, and the uselessness of connected objects, such as a connected bracelet to talk to others. Yet, the functional aspect of the object dominates the evaluation, and even users that believe that the connected objects create a social bond may not use them regularly if the connected objects do not facilitate their daily life.

Given the ambivalence of consumers towards connected objects, luxury companies cannot simply boast of the assets of objects without dealing with the constraints they also generate. The two aspects (positive and negative) of each dimension regarding the ambivalence of the connected object should be considered by companies when designing connected luxury experiences. Consumers' ambivalence calls into question the traditional marketing approach according to which some characteristics of the connected object would be barriers to the adoption of the product while others would be motivators for the adoption of the product. For the ambivalent consumer, the same characteristic can be both a limiting factor and a motivating factor for adopting connected objects. There is also a need for luxury businesses to assist and guide their customers in the use of connected objects, as users remain motivated when they really use them to satisfy specific needs (experiential or functional).

TREND 5.2

VIVIENNE WESTWOOD USES CONNECTED TECHNOLOGIES TO PROTECT ITS PRODUCTS

The luxury fashion brand Vivienne Westwood chooses TexTrace and its woven RFID labels for the protection of its products. Luxury fashion designer Vivienne Westwood adopted RFID technology for the authentication of her brand's logo. Its partner, TexTrace, has developed an innovative product authentication solution based on woven RFID tags, a technology that offers a unique solution that discreetly integrates RFID technology into the brand's woven labels, providing secure protection of the authentic brand. The brand of a luxury company is its most valuable asset, and brand protection is a growing issue around the world. Thus, the brand's TexTrace RFID woven label allows items to be tracked throughout the supply chain with easy authentication using standard RFID technology.

HOW ARE CONNECTED OBJECTS RESHAPING LUXURY EXPERIENCES?

For luxury houses, the integration of connected objects should go beyond the idea of connectivity by offering new services that entail the implementation of tailored customer experiences. The incorporation of technologies in luxury goods will also allow companies to collect useful information about their customers, and thus gradually enhance their marketing and communication strategies. Connected objects offer luxury businesses multiple growth opportunities if they position themselves as precursors in a marketplace by attracting new customers. In fact, offering connected objects could enable luxury brands to attract younger consumers as well as customers from Asian countries, in particular – customers with the profiles of early adopters and followers of technological products. Luxury brands have great experience in developing and launching new products. This expertise could be applied to connected objects. Companies in the luxury sector have a strong and unique legitimacy with consumers, and they have the ability to offer products that combine aesthetics and quality in addition to digital.

Although IoT is booming and different luxury brands are creating their own connected objects, consumers are not yet ready to massively buy these products, which are still mainly acquired by early adopters. This situation can increase competition from major digital pure players, such as in the example of the Hermes Apple Watch Edition, and other important digital players that are initiating the use of connected objects in the design of their luxury experience. The latter represent an important competitor vis-à-vis luxury brands and can claim greater legitimacy at the technical level. Another issue related to connected objects in the luxury sector is the challenging compatibility between two opposing lifecycles: IoT is constantly evolving and is characterized by renewal, while, on the contrary, luxury goods seek sustainability. Also, the acceptance by traditional customers is another challenging aspect, as there is a risk that traditional luxury buyers will turn away from brands that offer connected objects. Thus, some aspects are critical for luxury houses if they are planning to mix luxury and digital connectivity:

- **Technical aspect of connected objects**. It is important for luxury companies to work on improving three key elements specific to connected objects: perceived security, complexity of use, and technical reliability. First, it is important that luxury businesses invest in cybersecurity. A report from the manufacturer Hewlett Packard (2016) identified many weaknesses detrimental to the security of some of the most popular connected objects due to a level of protection that was quite low or even nonexistent. Second, luxury companies should work on functional compatibility between both the connected objects, themselves, and between connected objects and other equipment. Currently, the majority of consumer-connected objects are equipped with protocols unable to interact with each other. For example, it is impossible to synchronize the data of a connected watch with other equipment of different brands. It is necessary to develop a universal system of digital connectivity between the different objects. This could be accomplished through a partnership between companies and an exchange of technical information. Finally, luxury companies can improve the facility of usage through an ergonomic design and simplified functions. The objective is to offer a device that is easy to use and intuitive, thus giving consumers the feeling that they are controlling the connected object rather than it controlling them.

- **Commercial aspect of connected objects**. Amongst the factors that are specific to connected objects, the perception of uselessness is the one most current aspect perceived by consumers. The goal for luxury companies is, therefore, to develop strategies for countering the consumer perception (just a gadget) often associated with connected objects. A track that seems promising involves reinforcing the value added to connected products by associating them with a dedicated service. The idea here is to go beyond merely selling an innovative product by offering a package with personalized follow-up services, suggestions, and reminders, a direct relationship with an adviser, offers with other partner companies, etc. Another track would be to think of connected objects as an ecosystem in which all objects communicate together. So, instead of multiplying new objects, luxury companies should add intelligence to existing objects. One last track is to make connected objects a relational lever: in having greater access to a consumer's information, luxury businesses will be able to gain greater proximity to the consumer by offering personalized experiences and products/services as well as a privileged relationship.

- **Ethical aspect for more transparency in data management generated by connected objects**. This is a sensitive aspect of data that generates a fear of connected objects because they are seen as an intrusion into one's private life. Indeed, with the proliferation of connected objects in the years to come, an immeasurable volume of data will be collected (both with the agreement of the consumer and without his/her knowledge). In the next few years, almost all digital data will be produced through the Internet of Things. Therefore, it is essential to reflect on issues related to data management and information collected on the consumer (access, truthfulness, readability, etc.). Institutions and governments should then consolidate transparency laws and, in the case of a transgression, impose more sanctions with greater severity on companies. Otherwise, manufacturers of connected objects can propose their own biased guidelines on the use of personal data. Luxury companies should, then, think about the protection of privacy from the perspective of the object's design as part of the "privacy by design" concept, as proposed by Cavoukian and Jonas (2012). For example, the company could incorporate a feature that allows the user to easily erase the data captured by the object.

- **Communication aspect and taking into account the needs of consumers upstream of the design process**. Consumer resistance and ambivalent attitudes towards connected objects mean luxury companies should approach connected devices strategically. Consumers can express a rational resistance that suggests the need for concrete solutions to improve certain connected objects. Companies can implement online channels in order to be attentive to consumers and allow them to exchange information about the products through dedicated portals, a sort of community space calling on members to share their experiences and their questions. Furthermore, proactively, policies of co-creation involving the consumer before the development of connected objects would be interesting for luxury companies to set up. Indeed, it is important to involve the consumer in the process of creating and understanding his/her expectations in order to design new features that bring the consumer real added value. On the other hand, luxury companies should not neglect the power of Internet nuisance generated by the amount of information exchanged online. They can implement preventive strategies by putting exchange platforms in place to communicate with the community resisters and create collaborative strategies by inviting them to express themselves and to propose new ideas.

Therefore, the key success factors that allow luxury companies to offer memorable and satisfying connected luxury experiences should integrate the following fundamentals:

- Luxury houses should offer a real value-added service. They should supersede the fad effect where connected objects are mainly used as gadgets. In so doing, it is necessary for luxury houses to develop products with high-quality associated services, which respond to real customer needs.
- Luxury houses should manage data and obtain the benefits of the collected data. All data collected through the connected object should be utilized effectively to provide the best possible service and experience to the customer.
- Luxury businesses should also develop co-creation and strong collaborations with technology professionals and digital players.
- There is also a need to increase the effectiveness of marketing using the data collected through the connection of objects in addition to the guarantee of the protection of data.
- It is about meeting the expectations of a luxury product while guaranteeing the latest technological advances to consumers. For this, luxury brands should offer a sustainable product that has the capacity to be renewed at the technological level.

In the luxury automotive sector, a connected vehicle is a car that interfaces with systems and databases external to its own system and, as such, has the capacity to realize extended functionality beyond its organic, physical boundaries. For a driver, it changes everything. Indeed, as the situation of manual driving requires all the attention of the human being who is driving, a car that is connected to a consumer's digital life, for example, can offer him/her a playlist of favorite online music, inform clients of his/her temporary unavailability, calculate the most efficient route according to the driver's agenda, or book the nearest parking place at the user's favorite restaurant. Without connectivity or an interface linking the automotive world to the digital world, this level of intimate interaction with the consumer would be impossible.

The advent of autonomous driving is THE real revolution because it is not only disrupting our relationship with the automobile and other road users, but also life on board. Although we cannot do anything else while driving, it is clear that the use of digital connected objects is so addictive that they are today one of the main causes of danger on the road. Yet, thanks to the connected, intelligent, and autonomous vehicle, drivers who become passengers will be able to work, sleep, play, and network safely as if they were on a train. The real disruption will, therefore, come from these new uses that the automobile of tomorrow will present. The connected car, as a new mobile social robot, will have at its disposal many technologies to connect to the world around it: environmental sensors capable of interpreting it (cameras, lidar lasers, fusion and processing of big data, algorithm learning, etc.); a cybersecure cloud; and many APIs (Application Programming Interfaces) to access its own data, those of its partners, and those of its customers (such as cozycloud); a personal assistant who will play the user interface role with artificial intelligence that is able to understand natural language (like Soundhound); and hubs that ensure the interoperability of communication protocols of connected objects whatever the distance (in the manner of Artikcloud). The main barriers to a world of connected objects will, therefore, not be technological. The challenge of these complex systems lies, rather, in the ability to create fluid and efficient experiences for users looking for simplicity.

Beyond the social aspect of connected objects, many luxury companies have been interested in the use of blockchains as a tool that connects people and other databases to control the counterfeit of luxury items. After discussing IoT, the cloud, and big data, it is time to look at the blockchain, a technology that affects the financial, transport, health, and research sectors as well as the luxury and fashion industry. To define it, the blockchain is a technology of storage and transmission of information that is transparent, secure, and functions without a central control body. By extension, a blockchain is a database that contains the history of all the exchanges made between its users since its creation. This database is secure and distributed: it is shared by its different users without intermediaries, which allows them to check the validity of the chain.

Any public blockchain, by definition, works with a currency or a programmable token (token). Bitcoin is an example of a programmable currency. Transactions between network users are grouped into blocks. Each block is validated by the nodes of the network, called the "minors," according to techniques that depend on the type of blockchain. In the Bitcoin blockchain, this technique is called "Proof-of-Work," and consists of solving algorithmic problems. Once the block is validated, it is timestamped and added to the blockchain. The transaction is then visible to the receiver as well as to the entire network.

SUMMARY

Connected objects or IoT (the Internet of Things) are a real asset for luxury companies that are considering using them to better serve their customers. In the next few years, consumers will have more and more connected devices. Connected objects can help luxury brands in terms of knowing their customers better, guaranteeing customer loyalty, and enabling new experiences by providing a better understanding of user feedback. For luxury businesses interested in using these devices in the design of their customers' experiences, it is vital to understand what IoT stands for and what it involves. This chapter shows that IoT dramatically improves the user/consumer experience. Through connected objects, customer services will have the ability to receive, collect, analyze, and respond to requests from their users. Luxury companies can use IoT to reduce the effort exerted by their customers, improve their experience, and develop a bond of trust and attachment with their consumers, which will help retain them. In fact, with connected objects, the customer does not need to make a call about a problem. Connected objects have the ability to notify a support team of a problem before the customer even notices it.

6
PLAYFUL DIGITAL LUXURY EXPERIENCES

INTRODUCTION AND SCOPE

Gamification appeared with the first airline loyalty programs, offering air miles to reward frequent fliers traveling the world. Gamification, in short, is the use of gaming techniques to create an engagement in non-playful or uninviting settings. Beyond games, this chapter will introduce readers to playful digital luxury experiences and the role of gamification and its related technologies in creating immersive, emotional, and enjoyable experiences.

HOW DO GAMES CREATE FLOW PLAYFUL EXPERIENCES?

For game lovers, fun is one of the elements that makes a game a success, but it is not the only factor that can stimulate engagement and motivation. Behind these elements – the search for user engagement – are dozens of different hidden mechanisms, such as fear, fun, impatience, curiosity, glory and pride, and the feeling of accomplishment, that may be more or less effective. In other words, the game cannot be lived as a simple "fun" moment. In order to create commitment, the game should encompass three main aspects:

- Have a goal (something that the player should accomplish) and rules (which are the tools and the framework by which this goal can be achieved);
- Produce feedback, which can take different forms, but which allows the player to measure his/her progress or regression;
- Create frustration and conflict, the obstacles to overcome, the tests to be carried out; sometimes, the inevitable backward steps are all vectors of motivation and cause a legitimate joy when they are encountered.

Let's look at a very popular example of an intergenerational game called "Tetris" to understand the levers of gamification cited above and the way companies can use them in different sectors, especially the luxury industry, to create playful digital luxury experiences. How does the game handle these elements and how has it become a worldwide success? Tetris is a game that was created in 1984 by a Russian engineer. It has enjoyed many years of success in different media, and has never completely disappeared from our universe. What is the reason for this popularity? Tetris (like its clones) has many features that naturally create an engaging experience: quantified goals, voluntary participation, clear rules, immediate feedback, quick rewards, and a growing level of difficulty that allows players to challenge themselves at their highest level. The goal of Tetris is simple: create a maximum number of complete rows from blocks that descend from the top of the screen. The blocks have four positions, and it is a question of choosing the right orientation and precisely guiding its descent so the pieces nest perfectly and align in rows, thus causing the completed rows to disappear and the game to continue. Players can accelerate the fall of a block, which increases the score.

Social networks such as LinkedIn understand and demonstrate the motivations of users to play by creating a progress bar, which prompts users to fully complete their profile, breaking up each step and awarding users an all-star status for fully completing their profile. Many software applications already adopt this technique: Waze, Facebook, Tinder, etc. All seek to integrate this feature of "scores," true indicators of progress towards a goal. Also, with Tetris, every time users manage to erase a line, they earn points. Whenever they misplace one of their blocks, they get closer to the top of the screen and they are threatened. And every time they reach the top of the screen, the game stops. This immediate consequence is a peculiarity of fast-paced problem-solving games, just like Candy Crush, which belongs to a separate family in the world of gaming. Each time (about every three seconds) players put a block in the right place, their brain secretes a very small amount of endorphins and dopamine, two molecules that generate a sense of satisfaction and pleasure. In fact, people do like positive feedback, and waiting for it, they generate adrenaline that boosts their motivation. Another important aspect that makes the success of games, and thus the gamification experience, is the non-voluntary aspect of gamification.

At first glance, we cannot find anyone complaining of being forced to play Tetris. This is the major challenge of gamification: transforming an extrinsic motivation (updating one's CV on LinkedIn out of necessity) in order to motivate the user to achieve this task intrinsically (wanting to complete one's CV because one wants to progress and reach a better level, or feels that a progression in LinkedIn would generate more feedback, more likes, etc.). Like any game, Tetris imposes tests, errors, and failures. It becomes faster, more difficult as players progress. They must make the same decisions, but in a shorter and shorter time, under increasing pressure. However, and this is the strength of Tetris and games from the same family, they can become terribly addictive because they put users in a flow, which can last for hours. Tetris perfectly handles frustrations and instant rewards. Missing the placement of a block can quickly be corrected if players pick up and redouble attention.

THE GAMIFICATION OF DIGITAL LUXURY EXPERIENCES

For several years, the proliferation of forms of digital games in different sectors of activity has been accompanied by the emergence of several concepts and theoretical frameworks that describe, analyze, or even develop this phenomenon. In marketing and game design studies, the concept of gamification and its basic principles, defined by Zichermann and Cunningham (2011) as a process of using the state of mind and mechanics of the game to solve problems and involve users, are being applied in different contexts. Gamification is relevant to thinking about contemporary luxury consumption practices because it involves many challenges and opportunities in terms of designing immersive and hedonistic experiential offerings, but it also raises many questions about, amongst other things, its different meanings, devices, and usages and the way luxury companies can incorporate them into their global digital strategy.

One of the first fields in which the expression gamification appeared is that of marketing when it was presented as a "miracle solution" for companies. In fact, at the heart of gamification lies the question of the motivation and commitment of consumers in various activities that rely on the use of reward structures, positive reinforcements, and subtle feedback as well as mechanisms such as points, medals, levels, challenges, and leaderboards (Zichermann and Cunningham, 2011). Yet, Zichermann and Cunningham offered a particular meaning to the notion of commitment in their definition of gamification. Commitment, in a business perspective, indicates the connection between a consumer and a product or service rather than the idea of pushing the consumer to buy more. Thus, commitment based on gamification is about engaging the user to generate revenue and represents the profitable business model of the future. In this case, commitment is related to the consumer who invests with a company through playful strategies.

Initially, it is essential to develop new marketing techniques through the concept of gamification in order to strengthen the loyalty of consumers/users/players. For example, several companies use fun marketing strategies that cyberspace users have become accustomed to in order to introduce their products to those users more or less directly (e.g., Century 21, Mastercard, and many others). They invite participants to collaborate, to help each other, to exchange items, and to compare their results in order to achieve the objectives set in the design of the platform, the website, the video game, the installation, etc. Conversely, online socialization platforms are full of games in which various products are promoted. For example, the game The Sims Social, which is affiliated with the social network Facebook, invites players to try virtual products of well-known brands, such as

Samsung, Dunkin Donuts, Toyota, or Dove. Furthermore, according to McGonigal (2011), video games can also be used by companies to improve the world's economy through the incorporation of gamification in new settings, such as displacement and oil consumption. McGonigal argues that players are good at solving problems by collaborating – an advantage that can be used to find solutions by generating collective intelligence. The ability to collaborate not only encourages the power of players in problem-solving, but also enhances the appeal of play structures. Interest in interactions between participants, "shared pleasure," and online socialization could thus explain the use of these strategies.

WHAT IS GAMIFICATION AND WHAT ARE ITS FEATURES?

While professionals from the field of game design and video games have proposed the first conceptual clarification of the concept of gamification, its adoption by marketing professionals seems confusing because of its limited conceptualization. In fact, although gamification is mainly associated with the world of economics, this notion is, in fact, much broader and covers many contexts and meanings. The concept of gamification is regularly questioned and criticized, especially for its behaviorist approach to game design. As such, Deterding (2012) notes that a game is not interesting simply because it is a game, but primarily because it is well designed. Thus, the addition of a system of points or rewards cannot be enough to make an ordinary situation a game, moreover an interesting game.

In the field of marketing, Coll (2013) argues that the example of loyalty cards and bonus points, including air miles points, is an excellent one, which demonstrates that this gamification strategy is not a game at all, but rather a mode of surveillance, social control, and biopower. Other authors defined gamification as the way of integrating the mechanics from game design (video) into non-game settings (e.g., Deterding et al., 2014). Therefore, games are at the heart of the definition of gamification. Caillois (1962) defines games as a free activity (the player is free to choose whether or not to play and he/she is absolutely not subject to any constraint) that is separate (the game has a spatiotemporal frame of its own), uncertain (its outcome cannot be known in advance), unproductive (it does not create wealth at the end of the game), and structured by its own rules and fictional narrative (it takes place in a second reality). Based on this definition of a game, it appears that playfulness is not a specific feature of the game. The game itself is not a fun endeavor. It is not playful, however it can be a fun object. The game, therefore, encompasses two notions: the playful action that is the game and the object that constitutes it. For Caillois (1962), there is a need to separate the game environment (game) from the game entertainment (play). Thus, gamification is based on a specific architecture generally called gameplay. This term refers to the way the game is played, its rules, and mechanisms that increase the pleasure and satisfaction of players. Although there is no consensus on the definition of gameplay in the literature, a number of common features emerge and allow its definition. Hence, a gameplay is characterized by:

- The existence of a challenge that promotes the self-motivation of the player. It can be an enigma to solve or elements to discover.
- The presence of rewards to recompense the player for his/her commitment and encourage him/her to continue. These can be real (gifts, lots, etc.) or virtual (access to higher status, badges, and medals).
- The existence of a captivating scenario through a story unfolding around a theme. Storytelling is, therefore, at the heart of the gameplay. The story can be based on characters and real facts (historical or not) or fictitious (imagined for the game or inspired by a film, a comic, a novel).
- A blurring of the borders between fiction (game) and reality (a physical place), a mix between the real world and virtual realm. This immersion into the world of play favors the emergence of the experience of "flow" specific to the game experience – defined by Csikszentmihalyi (1990) as a mental state in which individuals are totally immersed in the action they are engaging in.
- A strong interactivity of the player as an active participant. The player is, indeed, asked to produce a real work of personal reflection to solve the riddle.
- A collaboration between the players who form a community at the time of the resolution of the enigma. They combine individual competence and collective competence and collaborate either virtually or in the real world.

However, in gamification devices, the gaming experience is central and although learning can be a consequence of experience, it is not the original intention. The purpose of these devices is to get the individual to act; to move; to go through hardships; not to learn, but to enrich his/her knowledge. The purpose is more intrinsic than extrinsic. In fact, gamification is a facilitator increasingly used in marketing strategies to engage consumers, change their behavior, and stimulate innovation (e.g., Hamari and Lehdonvirta, 2015; Hamari and Tuunanen, 2013). In the luxury sector, games are generally less sophisticated than those produced by major production studios and do not attract millions of players. Therefore, the main principles mentioned above should be implemented by luxury brands in order to encourage customer online and offline engagement and improve their digital experiences.

TREND 6.1

CHANEL GAMIFICATION EXPERIENCE THROUGH THE COCO GAME CENTER

Chanel Beauty is remarkable with regard to the use of gamification to immerse its consumers in a playful luxury in-store experience. After the 2017 hit "Coco Café," Chanel Beauty came up with another fun beauty concept to kick off the summer months: the Coco Game Center, which

(Continued)

(Continued)

features fun game stations named after popular products from the Chanel range, such as Rouge Coco, Chance, and Hydra Beauty. At the Coco Game Center, guests will get to engage themselves in entertaining arcade games with flashing screens and music that altogether add to the fun of it. First launched in Japan, where arcades remain a huge part of the culture, the French luxury house Chanel finally brought the Coco Game Center to Hong Kong after popping up in Seoul, Tokyo, Shanghai, and Singapore where many celebrities attended the exclusive launch event.

The arcade features six Rouge Coco game stations where guests can play either sound games, modeled after Guitar Hero, or Smash, which is like Pong. If visitors win, a game center guide will offer them a beauty consultation prize. There is also The Bubble Game, in which participants try to aim and catch a plastic ball containing special beauty gifts. In addition, the game center has the Beauty Ride where participants can drive the Coco Car, but not before reapplying their lipstick, which the glove pocket is stocked with. Participants can also rest in The Chance Lounge. To simplify things, Chanel Beauty has launched a microsite to facilitate reservations and priority entries. To book a slot one can simply visit the brand's site in order to avoid the queues at the entrance to the store.

HOW DOES GAMIFICATION WORK?

The idea that gamification is directly related to social media platforms emphasizes how much this playful strategy can effect changes in consumer/user behaviors (including visiting certain places because one can accumulate points with one's friends). Gamification can, then, imbue social relationships with playful dimensions in line with the "soft" persuasion tendency identified by Lipovetsky (1983). In the absence of traditional political, moral, or disciplinary ideologies, this trend consists in focusing on gratification and playfulness instead of other types of explicit power relations. As a result, new relationships with power are introduced not only within games, but also in the shaping and representation of social bonds. This dynamic is certainly not new, but it has grown since the advent of Web technologies, mobile platforms, and applications, accompanied by the rise of many ethical questions that should be analyzed in depth, as the play seems to interfere in all spheres of an individual's life. All the gamification platforms, which are part of daily entertainment, offer a range of benefits that can be summarized by consumer/user/player motivation. Positive effects on the lifestyle of the users/players, whether by regular exercise, stimulating repetitive tasks, or by coming out of a depression, are commendable and representative of a collective well-being. However, one should also keep in mind that this gamification operates through a behaviorist approach to the human psyche, where these systems impose a norm defined by the game designers. This normalization can be both infantilizing (regressive) and distressing, for example, if the objectives of the game are not achieved as they should be. But, normalization can also impose an ideological model under the appearance of play.

Nowadays, gamification works mainly through digital technologies that produce an astronomical amount of traces of identification of consumers who invest in, amongst others, the advertising market, referral systems, and insurance. The game then becomes a pretext for companies to keep the individuals connected for as long as possible, by producing a maximum of information in order to refine their profiling. The links between gamification and surveillance are numerous (e.g., Whitson 2013; Whitson and Simon, 2014), and now, this playful surveillance crosses every aspect of social life as evidenced, for example, by the plethora of games on television. It should be noted that this production of traces is done in part voluntarily due to a variety of fun applications that encourage the dissemination of information in which users participate in a motivated and transparent manner. In fact, this acceptance of sharing one's own information is done in exchange for a fun experience that aims to make life more exciting. However, this way of relating to the world comes at a price as well-hidden and often opaque social control mechanisms are produced where the behaviors of individuals are trained through the use of the playful.

In the same way, under the cover of a playful environment, companies can also use gamification strategies to motivate their employees (sometimes simply with the accumulation of points or badges), but with the main objective of increasing their productivity by putting workers in competition with themselves, or with each other. Therefore, in order to create successful gamification to enhance customer experience and motivate employees, luxury companies should set up a global strategy based on a successful approach of game digitalization. Luxury companies should first focus on the following issues: What kind of game can be selected? And, what are the key success factors when implementing an efficient and profitable gamification strategy?

Regarding game digitalization and its forms, Caillois (1962) mentions the paradox of the game in that it is simultaneously a creation of a culture, and also one of its results. The game is then the representation of a culture, and each culture has its own games. The arrival of the video game and the acceleration of the Internet, in a logic of globalization, lead to the advent of a new form of transnational acculturation of the game (e.g., Genvo, 2009): a new interpretation of games that is standardized, shares a common structure, and has a particular way of reasoning or thinking in the design (game design). This framework has favored the appearance of new types of games. For instance, the field of education has seen the emergence of serious games (e.g., Kasbi, 2012), that is to say, video games designed with a specific learning objective that favor the creation of intellectual capital. Developers are creating new, pervasive games that bridge the worlds of reality and fiction (e.g., Walther, 2005) and which rely on technology to take place in a new interface: reality. This new form of play is thus detached from the separate and fictitious features of games.

The game is also renewed with the appearance of brands. Advergames, or advertising games, are defined as a rich brand environment in which a video game (usually online) merges with brand communication. Since the appearance of the term in the early 2000s, it has become widely accepted as a common practice for brands, which spend millions of dollars on advertising games (e.g., Pardun, 2013). This type of game allows the brand to reach consumers from a new angle, spreading a positive message vis-à-vis the brand that offers a fun service. The consumer is no longer passive. He/she comes into contact with the brand and plays with it in a way that increases the brand's sympathy capital. The game is, therefore, an environment in which the brands come closer, as they have noticed the positive impact that it could create between the brand and the consumer. Reeves and Read (2009) suggest 10 key ingredients for designing good games:

- Personal representation through avatars;
- 3D environment;
- Narrative context;
- Feedback;
- Rewards, ranking, and levels;
- Marketplaces;
- Explicit rules defining the competition;
- Teams;
- Parallel communication systems;
- Pressure generated by a time limit.

Each of these elements taken individually could in no way define the game; it is the amalgamation of some of these ingredients that makes the game and allows classifying it as such. For example, the avatar is necessary for role-play, whereas in a game of cards it does not contribute anything to the mechanics. While the design of a game should be positioned in relation to these elements, the design of a gamified application will simply rely on some of them, without building a complete game. Gamification uses the mechanisms of the game to divert consumers to a different goal: to act on their behaviors. As Dale states, "companies seek to reduce their administrative costs and therefore, need [by this means] to influence the behavior of their customers so they adopt a process that is potentially more beneficial to them, the companies, than to their customers" (2014: 83). Therefore, while the play component refers to an entertainment function, gamification refers to a customer engagement function.

UNDERSTANDING GAMIFICATION IN CUSTOMER EXPERIENCE

Looking overall at the studies focusing on gamification, it appears that its effects on consumer engagement are mostly positive. The study conducted by Hakulinen et al. (2013), in the field of education, shows that gamification improves engagement in learning tasks and the motivation to learn. The activity is at the same time considered pleasant and entertaining. However, the study also points out that some aspects of gamification can be evaluated as poor: the difficulty of the tasks, the competition between the players, and the design of the game. Gamification could, therefore, if the device is too complex or misunderstood, depreciate the customer's shopping experience and limit his/her commitment. Furthermore, gamification is not an end in itself, but other devices and strategies, whose purpose is to contribute to the improvement of the customer experience and, more generally, to customer satisfaction, have to be taken into account by luxury companies in order to improve the overall customer experience.

In fact, research on gamification highlights the moderating factors of gamification efficiency, and thus of its ability to engage the user. These are essentially the motivation of the user, the type of service in which the game is implemented (for example, the authors demonstrate that gamification is not appropriate for purely utilitarian services), and finally gratification (points, levels, grades, etc.). The study conducted by Hamari and Koivitso (2013) also highlights the role of the age and gender of the players on the perceived benefits of gamification. The authors state that women perceive more social benefits than men and that the older the players, the more difficulties they perceive in interacting with gamified devices. Other studies highlighted an effect of gamification on different dimensions of lived customer experience: cognitive (learning, willingness to learn), commitment, and pleasure. They also revealed the importance of the type of service/product being gamified as well as the elements of the execution of the game (grades, levels, difficulty etc.) in the effectiveness of the device.

TREND 6.2

FENDI OFFERS A SOCIAL GAMIFICATION ON INSTAGRAM

The Italian brand Fendi created a playful activation program to announce its pre-fall collection of handbags by using the Instagram Stories video service. In a series of sparkling little movies designed by the Sky Pie studio, the user is invited to find a particular type of shoulder strap, to line up flowers, or burst bubbles by pressing pause, with messages prompting the user to return the next day to discover new games. The animations correspond to the different accessorization options of the bags. For Fendi, the use of the new Instagram tool creates stories that are a playful and a social way to reach its target using the principle of social gamification that simultaneously maintains the day-to-day relationship with its consumers, and above all creates visibility and proximity.

The use of video is deemed to increase the reach compared to a still image, and the positioning of stories at the top of the application makes them permanently visible to the subscriber. For Fendi, creating a gaming experience is a good tactic for getting fans interested in the brand's video content and giving them the satisfaction of sometimes winning, which can build affinity with the brand, at least unconsciously. However, Fendi could go further, as in its social

(Continued)

(Continued)

gamification experience currently nobody wins in the game, nor are they supposed to carry out a specific action at the end. To give more content to the operation, the brand could ask fans to send a screenshot with the correct answer, or to translate the participation in the game into page views or conversions. Nevertheless, the gamification experience is a key element in the digital communication of luxury brands and a strong trend in today's contemporary societies.

LEVELS OF GAMIFICATION IN THE CUSTOMER EXPERIENCE

Luxury professionals can implement gamification at different levels that refer to various stages of customer experience and engagement. The lowest level would also be the most current, such as a series of actions and decisions taken by the consumer to obtain bonuses. Gamification is seen here as a benefit that will be added to a global strategy to engage consumers on a particular issue. It is an integral part of the website while being easily deleted. Indeed, if its usefulness is not proven, it can be integrated at a different level of the website or completely removed. The community may be attached to this service, but it is not the essence of the website. This level is, therefore, a plus, which has the potential to be integrated into many areas. In itself, the use of gamification can be accessible to all, but the desired outcome will be a commitment and enthusiasm on the part of consumers.

The second level of gamification that luxury professionals can apply aims to integrate the mechanics into existing platforms, services, and products. The website of the brand can, by its nature, be social, however, the game may not be that obvious to users. Thus, luxury brand managers can integrate the mechanics from the video game into the website, thereby pushing users to comment more on the different product series and associated articles. This mechanism leads to the integration of a system through the accumulation of points: the more users post comments the more points they get. To generate value for the content posted, the points also depend on the number of people who like these comments. This system is similar to what Facebook and also Foursquare offer since the most committed users receive an honorary title.

TREND 6.3

FOURSQUARE, A SOCIAL GEOLOCATING NETWORK THAT OFFERS LUXURY BRAND USERS THE STATUS OF MAYOR

Foursquare is a social network created in New York in 2009 by Dennis Crowley. Its function is simple: it allows the network to geolocate directly via mobile, to indicate one's position to friends, recommend places, and share all this on one's Facebook or Twitter accounts. Foursquare also offers the possibility of using badges, thus making its content more fun. It has more than 55 million monthly active users worldwide and has logged more than 8 billion "check-ins" (DMR, 2018). The check-in is the action of geolocating oneself or others in a given place to recommend, for example, a restaurant, an exhibition to see, or even just the company in which one works. At check-in, users can write a tip on the place they tested and any user can become a guide for others' travels. In addition, when users write up their advice, their friends in nearby places will see their recommendations: "Why not go for a drink in the bar next door?" or "The music is really nice."

The second main objective of the check-in is to become Mayor of the place. Even if access to this function is not possible in real life, Foursquare allows users to become one in their virtual life. Whenever users geotag a place that they go to (their company, their favorite store, the café next door, etc.), they "check" this place, and once they have sufficiently "checked" on the place they will become the Mayor of this place. However, the competition is tough in popular places, so one will have to be patient to become the Mayor of one's favorite place if there are lots of other hopefuls on the list. The third objective of this social network is the use of badges. A badge on Foursquare is a "trophy" that unlocks a vignette with the image of a place, a city, or an activity. To be able to unlock a badge, users will have to make a number of check-ins on a given place. The luxury brand Louis Vuitton is ranked as the most popular place to visit thanks to an important number of users' check-ins on Foursquare, which in turn allows the brand to develop its visibility and offer people on Foursquare discounts or other special offers. As far as luxury brands are concerned, using this platform is a fun, interactive, and experiential way for users to enjoy good deals, promotions, or virtual loyalty cards. This social network is also a communication and loyalty tool that is especially entertaining and non-intrusive for its users.

In geolocation gamification, as shown in Trend 6.3, the objective is to develop dialogue and engagement that can be achieved rapidly. This example shows that gamification that requires a low level of commitment is very quickly effective in changing user behavior. So, would a stronger gamification make change more difficult and imply more marked behaviors? It is here that we unlock the third level of gamification, one that is more engaging: the one that will link the actions of one's real life to those of the digital one. Luxury brands will then ask consumers to perform physical actions and, therefore, make the experience more appealing. For example, Volkswagen's www.thefuntheory.com project is a good example of how to change a person's behavior through a simple action that is fun. To encourage people to use stairs instead of escalators, a staircase was laid out to make it look like a huge piano. The results show 66% more use of stairs compared to normal. In the same way, several other operations of this type have linked fun and game mechanics to a change of behaviors for an environmental purpose.

However, even more interestingly, these different operations have moved the company away from the main objective. At first sight, there is no link with the brand, but the more the luxury brand advances the more the actions will come closer to promoting a new product. In the end, as shown in the Volkswagen brand example, most consumers were open to the experience; but more importantly, they spent time with the brand. Therefore, a good gamification strategy is a gamification that is not visible; it is when the pleasure of the experience within the digital space as well as the physical place is linked to the luxury brand in a positive, non-intrusive way.

TREND 6.4

HERMES H-PITCHHH APP OFFERS A PLEASURABLE GAMIFICATION EXPERIENCE BETWEEN REAL AND VIRTUAL SPACES

To celebrate its 2018 theme of the year, "It's your turn!", Hermes launched H-pitchhh – a horseshoe throwing game app. Horseshoe pitching is one of the oldest games and still very popular in the United States. Throughout the three days of the competition, the participants were invited to play in the galleries of the Grand Palais, on a real playground with stakes and horseshoes. The virtual player has five horseshoes. With the tip of his/her finger or a movement of the arm, the player directs and throws the iron towards the stake. In order to immerse participants in an interactive playful luxury gaming experience, the player is guided by the game to evolve through five different realms: an immersion in an aquatic and fun space, a climb up the stairs of 24 Faubourg Saint-Honoré, a walk in a garden, etc. Each world is illustrated by a musical theme, from hip-hop to calypso to electro or rock.

H-pitchhh is also a live game where users can challenge their connected friends. To promote this downloadable app from the App Store and Google Play, Hermes has designed a trailer to the Western-inspired promotional video, where players dressed in the new collection clash in a desert landscape. For the luxury brand, this event app is in perfect harmony with its equestrian activity and its values of tradition and respect. But the experience of gamification within both real and virtual spheres also emphasizes another vital aspect of the luxury house: its creativity. Furthermore, the Hermes H-pitchhh app shows the ability of the luxury brand to adapt to new mobile usages and gamification.

Yet, even if gamification allows luxury companies to change a consumer's behavior so that it pays off in the long term, it will take more than a game. The sport, in this case, is a real activity that requires motivation and commitment over time. This brings us to the question of the duration of gamification. In the video game industry, the strength of video games is that the end gives the player a sense of accomplishment. Gamification for luxury brands, especially if it is based on a long-term strategy, should then have an end and move the customer/user/player to a renewal even if it is a new gamification.

Gamification, therefore, has its limits, and some practices can be risky. The consumer will feel cheated if luxury brands do not create new material, but rather copy other existing games. Thus, luxury brands should appropriate the codes of the video game universe and not only the playful dimension of games. Moreover, if a game is poorly designed, consumers will show more resistance to gamification. This raises the question of what gamification brings to the consumer experience. The answer lies between the pleasure of gambling and compensation, which can simply be honorific through virtual or physical rewards rather than real. The reward, in this case, can compensate for a weak design, for example, if a user collects all the badges from the mobile application to win a car. In this case, the treasure hunt is certainly fun, but what really leads to the retention and engagement of mobile users lies in the importance of the proposed compensation.

TREND 6.5

SWAROVSKI "DISCOVER YOUR LIGHT" TREASURE HUNT CAMPAIGN REWARDS BLOGGERS

Swarovski, an upscale brand known for its crystal jewelry, watches, Christmas ornaments, etc. launched its pioneering location-based mobile gaming app for a treasure hunt in London in 2011. Swarovski proposed to its fans, opinion leaders, and bloggers a real treasure hunt game, "Discover Your Light," in which participants could use their smartphones as well as social media platforms, such as Twitter, to discover 50 places in London, collect 42 clues, and win significant jackpots. The first prize was a trip for two to Florence and the runners-up won Swarovski jewels totaling £20,000 ($25,800). The game was part of a larger marketing campaign. Indeed, Swarovski throughout the month of September had broadcast this spot "Discover Your Light" in London cinemas. They sought to illustrate how the diamond accompanies a woman during the different stages of her life and reflects the different facets of her personality. Through the discovery of London via the treasure hunt and storytelling the young female participants would discover themselves.

Therefore, gamification is ultimately a question of dosage. Thus, to be effective, it should rely on attractive game mechanics or a sufficient reward to engage the player for the desired duration. The key to a successful long-term strategy will be for luxury brands to know how to renew themselves in order to retain their consumers. Moreover, luxury brands must be sincere and subtle in their approach. Indeed, the best gamification strategy is the one that is not visible, the one that merges seamlessly with the experience. In the luxury industry, Dior, Marc Jacobs, Lanvin, Jean Paul Gaultier, amongst others, have been convinced of the use of gamification through the incorporation of elements from video games to create playful experiences on the Web, or by using immersive technologies. Each brand approaches these new mechanics in its own way: for example, Dior clearly displays its references to the game, Lanvin hides them, and Jean Paul Gaultier refers to them in a humorous way. Table 6.1 offers a summary of the typologies of gamification experiences used by luxury brands, their characteristics, and the technologies used to provide users with playful luxury experiences.

Table 6.1   The typologies of gamification experiences in luxury

Type	Brand	Approach	Device
Advergame experience	Chanel	Chanel's advergame of Chanel displays its famous designer Karl Lagerfield with his glasses, which are part of his mystique and inaccessibility. The goal of the game is to take off his glasses	Web
	Dior	Dior is a brand that has clearly embraced positioned video games, beginning in 2011, with the campaign "Mise en Dior," featuring a pinball machine; then, a website offering a series of mini-games with its products	Web
	Jean Paul Gaultier	Through the game "The Unwise Children of Jean Paul Gaultier." The game for Christmas 2012 on the website displays Jean Paul Gaultier opening his big coat to present a creative advent calendar. Through various games and naughty animations, one can win gifts from the brand. Each day the website offers the possibility to open up to three pockets in which there may be gifts, by performing a short game beforehand; users can open more if they share the page with their friends or followers. The games are rather offbeat and in the spirit of the brand that does not take itself seriously. The Santa Claus Jean Paul offers players the chance to win perfumes, teddy bears, and many other objects	Web
	Breitling	The advergame "Reno Race," proposed by the luxury watch brand Breitling, is very interactive and innovative. It can also be used on mobile phones. Reno Race is an airplane race in the Nevada sky. The game offers players the chance to pilot and race flying sports cars	Mobile
	Lanvin	Lanvin chooses a dance game. Its models dance and play with Just Dance on a video games console	Xbox360
Immersive gamification	Valentino	Valentino's virtual museum is a 3D immersive video game. The 3D serves a game mechanic (the Battlefield fighting game) and/or a story (the interactive film Heavy Rain)	3D virtual reality
	Jimmy Choo	Jimmy Choo offers a treasure hunt augmented reality game in London with the help of social networks like Twitter or Foursquare. Once certain points in the city are reached, the player gains access to the last secret place to win a nice reward	Augmented reality
Social gamification	Marc Jacobs	The Marc Jacobs game on Facebook was part of the promotional campaign related to the release of his new perfume, Bang. The game consisted of "deconstructing" his profile picture and that of his friends. The picture with the most "Bang" wins a gift	Social media

THE CHALLENGES AND THE FUTURE OF GAMIFICATION

If experts do not fully concur on the definition or practice of gamification, there is one point on which everyone agrees: the future of gamification is technology. This technology can take many forms. Augmented reality will surely allow luxury brands to go much further in the gaming mechanics thanks to creative technologies. With sensors, for example, in the field of health, applications will allow us to follow a particular diet or enjoy sports activities without it being felt a constraint. Furthermore, Social Local Mobile (Solomo) and point of sale marketing can be combined with iBeacon technology by offering a journey to customers in the store and enabling them to achieve a particular objective; or stores can use technologies such as leap motion (which proposes to overcome the physical contact between the human and the computer through a box recognizing the different movements of the hand) to interact with passersby from the window.

Immersive technologies will also contribute to enrich the game and thereby offer advanced gamification experiences; examples include the Oculus Rift (a virtual reality headset for playing in augmented reality in 3D) and a more affordable version that has been introduced by Google. Low-tech, accessible, popular, and low-priced technologies will democratize the market, and thus allow companies in different sectors, especially in the luxury one, to offer playful experiences that are enjoyable, engaging, and profitable. As for connected objects, they are the first true manifestation of the digital world in the real sphere; in this sense, the connected object will become the real transfer of digital mechanics and truly transform a physical space into a playground (a treasure hunt with iBeacon terminals, for example). Beyond its development via technology, gamification will become more pervasive for its own sake. As the experts claim, the game has entered everyday life where everybody plays, so there will, de facto, be advertising in games. Thus, luxury brands should take part as well, paying particular attention to mobile-based advergames. More opportunities will then emerge and prove an effective way to change consumer/user behaviors and create new knowledge.

WHAT ARE THE LIMITS OF GAMIFICATION?

The first limit in the use of gamification by luxury brands is to make a simple copy-and-paste of the mechanics that have already proved effective in video games. This practice is the subject of criticism by video game professionals, for its being too reductive an appropriation of the concept by brands. Thus, gaming is not a question of integrating a badge, an avatar, a system of accumulation of points, or even a progress bar. The real gamification is upstream: it should result from a strategic reflection on the luxury company's target, its needs, and the reasons for it. Gamification, in that it borrows the mechanics of the game, should be designed as a real game: based on powerful storytelling and an attractive user experience. Gamification is a concept that is still poorly understood and its adoption can be compared with the learning process luxury brands have been through regarding the use of social networks.

Indeed, even if luxury companies have made efforts more recently, it is still the case that they offer in their communication strategies a Facebook page or a blog as an end in itself; but it is not always relevant for a brand to be present on this or that social network, some will be more appropriate, others should be avoided completely. On the one hand, luxury brands have to know their targets to be able to follow them and reach them and, on the other hand, they have to provide content to their offering. Thus, a luxury brand targeting seniors through Instagram will not be profitable because there are more young people on Instagram. Therefore, a luxury brand that invested in a social network without having a rich and adapted editorial line would not necessarily be successful. Having a Facebook page simply because companies have to have one, or because the competitors have one, or merely because everyone uses Facebook, makes no sense. It sounds logical today, yet how many luxury brands have fallen into the trap of poor social networking because they did not master its concepts. Now luxury brands will fall into the same trap through gamification if they do not master it first: they want to play without questioning the need for making the game and the way in which to go about it.

TOWARDS A GAMIFICATION OF EVERYDAY EXPERIENCES

If, on the one hand, luxury brands question the way to gamify their website, their products, services, or their community, on the other hand, technological progress is constant and continuously introduces new tools for digitizing everyday life. This digitization of daily life experiences relies in part on the development of technologies related to smartphones, including Wi-Fi or Bluetooth. The case of iBeacon technology is a major innovation in the development of indoor geolocation and it will enable luxury companies to turn any place into a playground. The system is still in its initial stages, but it is certainly a fundamental tool for certain sectors, such as distribution or tourism. Thus, iBeacon would take gamification further; it would no longer be a case of simple online gamification, but rather a "real gamification" in that the person interacts via his/her smartphone. When the user with the application passes close to an iBeacon terminal, a signal is sent, and he/she receives feedback providing content or compensation.

This is the beginning of the conversation. Instead of advertising to a consumer who is not receptive to the message, gamification by iBeacon technology assumes that the consumer has accepted the exchange via the download of the application dedicated to it. From then on, he/she is no longer a mere visitor to a store, but becomes an active visitor, the holder of the means to access privileged and rewarding content that is also entertaining. But the most important thing is that the visitor will spend time with the brand, he/she will manipulate the product without realizing it and will be all the more receptive. Additionally, without noticing it, the customer has spent more time in the shop or even discovered departments and bought products that he/she would not have thought of without this intervention. In-store gamification also affects the world of connected objects. It is a very broad ecosystem that emerges with the Internet of Things in order to connect everyday objects to the Internet through sensors and microprocessors that plot and record a multitude of data.

KEY FACTORS FOR A SUCCESSFUL GAMIFICATION OF LUXURY EXPERIENCES

In order to be successful, a gamification strategy should reach a delicate balance between experience and compensation. The poorer the customer experience of the game, the higher the reward, which is where luxury brands can compensate by offering real rewards to their consumers. It is a kind of easy solution for those who cannot afford to go beyond the game itself. It is also one of the limits that luxury brands risk running into with gadget-connected objects. Before long, every brand will want to implement connected objects, just as everyone previously wanted to invest in social networks – indeed, just as everyone wanted to integrate gamification. However, everyone does not have the means to develop real, attractive hi-tech objects. Thus, we might be seeing a wave of "gadgetization" of connected objects based on gamification experiences that are too insubstantial: that is to say that the user experience will not be developed enough and the compensation will not be sufficient.

Too many brands will not survive the likely saturation of the market by technology: it will separate the few big winners, future giants of the battle of the Internet of Things and GAFA (Google, Amazon, Facebook, and Apple), from the infinite number of outsiders in the luxury sector. Gamification can help to see these winners emerge amongst luxury brands: they will be those who bet on the user/customer experience and allow users to immerse themselves completely in the game and the universe of the luxury brand. The games will take up more space in reality in the sense that they will gradually come out of the screen. Many films and series use immersion to involve and connect with their viewers. Simply put, the recipe for a good gamification luxury experience, therefore, requires a compensatory mix between the user experience and the reward. In the design of a good gamification, simplicity counts just as much as the balance between user experience and compensation. The greater the difficulty of understanding, the more likely it is that the user will give up along the way and not achieve the goal defined by the luxury brand. Neither luxury brands nor even marketers are professionals in video game design and that is why they make mistakes.

Gamification is based on the mechanics of video games, so it should be conceived and thought of as such without becoming so. What makes a video game a success is the relationship between the complexity of the game and ease of handling. Thus, the more complex a gamification, the stronger it will be because it will be made up of elements that enrich it, such as ergonomics, history, content, or even mechanics. However, complex does not mean difficult, and luxury brands will often come up with a poor mix by creating a gamification that is both empty of content and difficult to comprehend. In the same way, simplicity does not mean poverty. Indeed, the simplicity of gamification lies in the fact that for it to be effective, it should meet a single and unique objective. Gamification aims to act on an existing behavior. The level of customer experience and engagement in the game will, therefore, have to be aligned with the luxury brand's goals and universe, otherwise, the message will be clouded by noise and disappointing results.

SUMMARY

This chapter underlines the importance of gamification to create playful digital luxury experiences. Indeed, for luxury houses, gamification is a powerful tool to enhance marketing strategies and the future of creativity and innovation in designing engaging customer experiences. Luxury brands should then apply in their customer experience design strategies, the fundamentals of the game, namely, the triptych of challenge–fulfillment–satisfaction. Each accomplished challenge generates in customers a sense of pleasure that drives them to want to continue playing in the entertaining universe created by the luxury brand. What explains the trend around gamification is its impact in terms of consumer commitment. Thus, this chapter shows how gamification boosts engagement because it associates in the minds of users the ability of the product or brand to challenge and fulfill. And retailers have understood this very well because they integrate a set of rewards, promotions, or gifts into their marketing strategies in order to offer a better customer experience. In this sense, many sectors "gamify" in order to offer an innovative and creative customer experience by recapturing techniques and tools that were around before the advent of the video game. In this chapter, I explained how leading luxury and fashion houses have been "gamified" to offer their customers new experiences that are playful, engaging, and emotional.

7

HUMANIZED DIGITAL LUXURY EXPERIENCES

INTRODUCTION AND SCOPE

Virtual agents, chatbots, artificial intelligence (AI), and robots or cyborgs are all new features of the future of digital luxury experience design. When Apple launched Siri in 2010, users began to get acquainted with virtual assistants based on artificial intelligence. Then, there was Alexa and Cortana. In 2016, Facebook Messenger helped popularize these virtual agents empowered and humanized by the use of AI. These conversational robots allowed companies to automate and personalize their messages to consumers in order to enrich their customer experience offerings. The question is, therefore, how can the luxury industry benefit from this technology? And, how can it be used to create humanized digital luxury experiences? Focused on the excellence of materials and craftsmanship, the top leading luxury houses have long distanced themselves from new technologies. However, in the digital and instantaneous era, luxury is presented with a more pragmatic question that goes beyond creativity and traditional know-how: that of the customer's experience in-store and online, to which these technologies can provide answers and solutions based on scientific data and artificial intelligence (AI). This chapter presents a profound analysis of technologies related to AI, virtual assistants/agents, chatbots, and robotics in order to understand how luxury professionals in different sectors can use them in an efficient and suitable way to design increasingly humanized, consistent, and profitable digital customer experiences.

THE ROLE OF VIRTUAL AGENTS IN LUXURY EXPERIENCE

Studies related to virtual agents have grown significantly in recent years in the marketing field. Numerous terms have emerged: virtual agent, intelligent agent, convergent agent,

agent of recommendation, agent of interface, incarnated conversational agent, avatar, chatbot, etc. (e.g., Chang, 2010; McGoldrick et al., 2008). The term "agent" refers, conventionally, to a person (for example, a real salesperson) who is authorized to offer advice or perform tasks on behalf of another person. Similarly, on the Internet, "an agent" can be defined as "a program that is capable of independent actions in a given environment on behalf of a user" (e.g., Qiu and Benbasat, 2009). These agents differ from conventional computer programs in that they can act independently of their users. In other words, the user does not need to enter an order or click on a button every time he/she wants a task to be performed (Dehn and Van Mulken, 2000). In addition to autonomy, scholars, such as Hostler et al. (2005), identified two other characteristics of a virtual agent: social skills and coping. Social capabilities refer to an agent's ability to cooperate and collaborate with other agents as well as with users to solve problems. Coping refers to the ability of an agent to adapt to the environment, including other agents and human users. Another important characteristic of virtual agents is the nature of their embodiment. Thus, it is possible to distinguish two major families of virtual agents: embodied agents and non-embodied agents. Cassell et al. (2000) define an embodied virtual agent as an animated character who has a certain capacity to act, react, speak, and move. Its behavior may vary over time, depending on the pages of the website and according to questions asked by the user. It is an animated character that is capable of pursuing a goal and adapting its behavior within a virtual environment. In addition, two terms are often used to refer to embodied virtual agents: conversational agents (chatbots) and avatars.

An avatar is a graphic representation in 2D or 3D on an electronic platform of a real individual (real person) or a fictional one (character). The "avatar" is not always animated and does not necessarily have the capacity to converse with users (Holzwarth et al., 2006). In contrast, a "chatbot" essentially possesses conversational abilities, but is not necessarily embodied. It might present itself as the spokesperson of an artificial intelligence system that uses a set of dialogue management rules and techniques to deal with user input (Semeraro et al., 2008). On the other hand, a "social virtual agent" results from combining the characteristics of animated avatars and chatbots, which means that it is an agent represented by a 2D or 3D character that possesses conversational capabilities. Referring to the work of Cassell et al. (2000), a social virtual agent can be defined as a computer-based graphic character that possesses the ability to engage in a face-to-face dialog with a user, using not only language, but other nonverbal (communication) modalities, such as gesture, gaze, intonation, and physical posture.

Since the early work of Cassell et al. (2000), several studies have been conducted on the impact of social virtual agents in e-commerce and show that the use of an embodied agent on a commercial website as a strategy can improve trust, the intention to recommend the website, and the satisfaction of the user. Punj and Moore (2009) state that this satisfaction stems from the agent's ability to facilitate the search for information, and to identify the product that corresponds to the needs of the user. Social virtual agents can also have a positive impact on online customer experiences, as they enable the creation of a close social bond between the customer/user and the online business. Furthermore, Holzwarth et al. (2006) studied the connection between the presence effect of in-store salespeople and the presence of commercial agents on e-commerce websites. The conclusion of their work showed that the presence of virtual commercial agents on a website should lead to an increase in satisfaction, improve the consumer's/user's attitude towards the products, and increase the purchase intention. Thus, faced with the development of omnichannel consumer behavior, it is important for luxury companies to understand the evolution of the role of the seller in the context of coexistence with virtual and intelligent social agents. Figure 7.1 shows three modes of coexistence between real and virtual agents and their impact on customer experience.

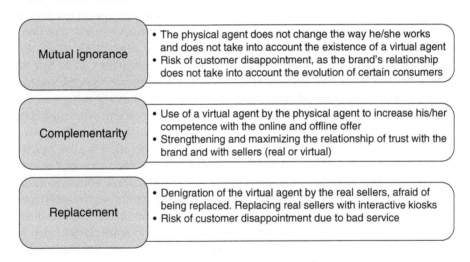

Figure 7.1   Coexistence between real agents and virtual agents

The adoption of social virtual agents by luxury companies is, therefore, important to consider when attempting to enhance the digital customer experience, and improve the portability of a brand's commercial website by converting each user into an online buyer who might also visit the physical store. Social virtual agents are characterized by different forms of digital representations of computer programs designed to interact with users – or even behave like a human. These virtual agents can thus be an asset for luxury companies because they help users and prospects sort out the right information in an efficient and friendly way. The Web self-service is of interest to any company that wants to ensure that the prospect or customer quickly finds an answer to his/her question directly on the website without having to make contact via telephone or email. Furthermore, social virtual agents have significant advantages because they can be endowed with a number of attributes that, until now, were reserved for human beings, such as vocal, writing, and intellectual abilities. Therefore, they can be entrusted with specific missions, such as navigation assistance, pre-sales assistance on information-rich sites, purchase assistance, and after-sales service. The evolution of emotional and artificial technologies allows social virtual agents to develop characteristics that make them, in some respects, similar to human beings while still retaining unique qualities of their own. Amongst the qualities of visual agents, luxury companies can consider the following in the design of their customer experience offerings that involve agents:

- **Virtual agents with increasingly sophisticated human qualities**. Technological advances have allowed the creation of virtual agents with human attributes. In fact, not only are they able to write and speak, but they also understand the customers and/or prospects who speak to them using natural language. One might reason that virtual agents merely pronounce or write sentences stored in a database in response to a query containing a certain number of keywords without, itself, being able to reason. This idea is now outdated. Nowadays, social agents have artificial intelligence. In the 1950s, Alan Turing predicted that by the year 2000 the intelligence of computers would rival that of humans. He had also proposed a test to distinguish the human from the machine, that is, to test whether or not an artificial intelligence is sentient, or self-aware. This elevated intelligence allows virtual agents to understand the meaning contained in questions formulated by customers thanks to a semantic analysis that allows the agent to answer them in a natural language. Overall, an intelligent virtual agent is a program that is capable of independent actions in a given environment on behalf of a user. It is a system that perceives its environment and is able to act on it. In addition, virtual agents gain intelligence with experience. A team of Taiwanese researchers has developed an agent named ISA (Intelligent Sales Agent) that is able to argue, make counter-arguments, and negotiate a price (Huang and Lin, 2007). Several experiments were conducted in the laboratory, and then on a website specializing in the sale of used cars. The online experience confirmed that the virtual agents had a positive impact on the perceived value of the product, willingness to pay, and satisfaction with the website.

- **Virtual agents that can overcome the deficiencies of the human being**. Virtual agents have certain advantages over humans; for instance, they are never tired or sick. As a result, they are available to customers and prospects 24 hours a day, seven days a week. In addition, social virtual agents do not lose patience and remain calm when confronted with an unpleasant or aggressive customer. They are also intelligent enough to be able to detect the emotional state of a customer and modify their interaction with that consumer accordingly. In fact, the virtual agent will use, in all circumstances, the appropriate tone and vocabulary. It will not resort to negations and will only use a vocabulary charged with positive meaning. It will also avoid technical terms. Another advantage of virtual agents is their ability to know when they can/cannot answer a question. Instead of making the customer believe that he or she is the one causing the problem – as hotline operators sometimes do – they will recognize that they do not have the answer and will switch the client to another channel, such as calling a physical agent in the store. Another quality of the intelligent virtual agent is that it can be multilingual and master several languages. Lastly, the virtual agent presents the advantage of not aging or becoming fatigued, unlike humans, and can improve its functionality, efficiency, and productivity according to the demands and expectations of customers/users.

- **Virtual agents with superhuman abilities**. Virtual agents do not only copy the qualities of human beings. In certain ways, they can also outperform them, such as in the case of being ubiquitous, which allows them to deal with multiple clients simultaneously. In contrast to a human being, a virtual agent can process a million simultaneous conversations per day, a feature that definitely sets them apart from humans. This quality enables companies to shorten the response time to the customer's queries. For example, eBay's virtual agent handles 50 million conversations per year in the United States. Moreover, a virtual agent offers great flexibility in physical appearance. Indeed, if this is desirable for the image or the identity of the luxury brand, for instance, a virtual agent can take on exactly the same physical appearance for all customers, from different countries and cultures (Asian, European, American, etc.) or any other country in which the brand is established. From a technical point-of-view, it is quite possible to customize the appearance of the virtual agent according to different criteria (contextual, choice of the user, the company, etc.), which can help the luxury brand create a sense of empathy, thus facilitating the identification with the agent. For example, an Asian consumer may prefer to converse with an Asian-type agent. The profile of the virtual agent can then be defined according to a set of specifications proposed by the luxury brand. The configuration of the virtual agent is not limited to its physical appearance; luxury brands can also define a very specific personality that is congruent with the desired personality for the brand.

TREND 7.1

GOOGLE DUPLEX, A POWERED VIRTUAL AGENT FOR HUMANIZING CUSTOMER EXPERIENCE

Imagine having a human conversation with a computer. Imagine that the computer does not need you to repeat what you just said; it does not require you to ask for what you just asked for. Imagine that the voice providing you with answers does not look like a robot. Google Duplex is an AI-powered virtual assistant that could be the most human computer built to date. In Google I/O, the annual conference of Google developers, Google CEO Sundar Pichai introduced this new technology by showing how Google Duplex and Google Assistant can handle calls like a human. The most fascinating thing is that it is not a reactive chatbot or an interactive voice system. This technology was not designed for a help desk, although it may do the task. It is actually a proactive assistant who can make calls, for example to book a table at a restaurant, or make an appointment at the hairdresser's. The assistant interacts with the person on the other end of

(Continued)

(Continued)

the phone as if it were human. It can even emit confirmation sounds like "mmm-hmm" and can identify human voice patterns, and adapt to the speed of the conversation. In his demonstration, Google's CEO presented the technology with a recording of two phone conversations. For the first call, the objective was to make an appointment at a hair salon, the receptionist in the presentation asked the client (Google Assistant) to wait. The Assistant responded with an "mmm-hmm," which caused applause and laughter in the room. There is no doubt that the hairdresser did not know he/she was dealing with a virtual agent. The recording of the second conversation showcased the Google virtual agent's ability to negotiate reservations at a restaurant. Despite the awkward responses from the restaurant employee, the Google virtual agent handled the phone call perfectly.

Luxury companies should think about the use of this powerful virtual agent or develop their own agents that have the same DNA as the luxury brand in order to design unified and consistent customer experiences. In fact, customers do not care necessarily which channel they communicate through, but they do need the same quality of response. There is, therefore, a requirement that identical identities and quality of service be presented at all points of contact, whether physical or digital. Luxury companies could then launch their intelligent virtual agent by collaborating with digital players, such as Google or Microsoft, to humanize the customer experience and help users discover the brand's identity traits, including humor.

Furthermore, in order to create a satisfying functional and emotional Web customer experience that integrates virtual agents, luxury companies need to go beyond the logic of e-commerce websites that do not bring any differentiation from the competition. They should, in fact, turn their e-commerce platforms into immersive Internet websites through the use of intelligent and emotional agents within an online setting in which the luxury brand incorporates the five senses: sight, sound, smell, taste, and touch. According to Batat (2019b), in order to implement such an e-commerce website, and thus offer an experiential and social setting for their users/customers, luxury brand managers can follow the following guidelines to enhance the online purchase experience:

- To enrich the visual website experience, luxury companies should design a homepage with strong visuals. It should have a strong impact upon the first visit to the site. There is also a need to put forward a concept and a design specific to the brand and its site. Luxury brands should use harmonized colors and HD images with a coherent graphic, be attentive to the style of the text font, and integrate interactive avatars.
- To design a tactile website experience, luxury brands should offer a global view with a selective zoom, integrate quality slideshows and full-screen videos, insert a 3D display of objects, a 360-degree field of vision, and augmented reality as well as integrate interactive and alternative views with demos.
- To create a gustatory website experience, luxury brands can propose a detailed description of the product, provide storytelling and strong content, organize tasting events on

the site so that the universe of the brand is associated with a taste, develop partnerships with chefs to create taste references in order to describe their products on their websites, and communicate about taste through quality images.

- To enhance the auditory website experience, luxury brands can employ a specific sound signature linked to the identity of the brand, diversify the music on the website and offer several options for the visitor to choose from, use sound control tools and a soothing soundtrack, integrate sound at a click, offer a choice of vocal narration and use a balanced tone, and offer the possibility of pulling text or narration in several languages.
- To create an olfactory website experience, luxury brands could use an olfactory signature, or they could also incorporate scent diffusers into connected objects in stores or on screens.

Therefore, in order to design an experiential e-commerce website that is both attractive and convenient for customers, luxury houses should use both embodied and non-embodied virtual agents for their social dimension. Furthermore, luxury companies can also use sensory digital settings involving the five senses to immerse their customers within a memorable and enjoyable Web experience. Indeed, the experience is what makes the customer return to the same website with pleasure and motivation rather than feeling inhibited or to merely fulfill a need. However, it would be an error to consider digital experience only through the prism of digital tools. Customer experience is primarily a business approach, an operational approach, which is then translated numerically. Luxury houses should therefore take into account the customer journey in a comprehensive way and then design an experience that follows the reality of this journey.

AVATARS AND HOW THEIR USE CAN IMPROVE THE LUXURY EXPERIENCE

Nowadays, virtual universes are offering original customer experiences that online users/shoppers can live and participate in thanks to their avatars. In fact, through their avatars, users can live an online playful consumer experience during which they discover aspects of themselves by interacting with other users. In such universes, the consumer chooses a character (an avatar) that serves as a virtual identity in which the anonymity and freedom of choice inherent in that identity are highly motivating for users.

Having long been criticized for its inhuman characteristics, the Internet now offers users the possibility to be represented on the screen and to be able to interact with other human representations. Each individual can thus today own one or more avatars in the form of a graphic representation of the user. As the virtual worlds become an increasingly entrepreneurial and commercial space, avatars become a key element in the browsing and online buying experience of users as they represent the individuals on the interface and reintroduce the users into the online space. Indeed, amongst the various rich media technologies and tools that can improve the online user experience, the avatar was very early identified as a key factor in the individual's engagement in the virtual world (e.g., Taylor, 2002). Authors such as Feldon and Kafai (2008) or Lim and Reeves (2010) showed the positive effect of the use of an avatar on the virtual experience as a whole. Their works show that the avatar allows the consumer/user to be fully immersed in the shopping experience. Thus, for luxury companies, consumer online involvement through avatars on their websites is a key factor in the success of immersion in a commercial online space.

Luxury companies can use avatars for different purposes, including playful, collaborative work, shopping, discussion, etc., depending on the profile of the chosen avatar as well as the place that the avatar is likely to occupy. Suh et al. (2011) emphasized the importance of the context and task in which the use of the avatar is embedded. According to Suh et al. (2011), any commercial context involving concrete consequences (purchase of a product that will be received at home or a financial transaction) usually motivates individuals to create an avatar that is as realistic as possible. Beyond this utilitarian aspect, some commercial websites, such as 3D commercial shopping malls, may have social and playful aspects. Even by walking through the shopping mall the online shoppers can meet other shoppers (avatars), talk with them, and participate in fun activities offered within the online mall. The personalization of the avatar will thus likely play the social role of self-presentation in the avatar's construction and transmission of its user's social identity, which is similar to the way in which the human body serves as a physical means of self-presentation and socialization. Therefore, the use of avatars can help luxury companies enhance the digital customer experience and optimize their e-commerce online experiences by providing effective connections with other avatars. In order to offer successful and profitable avatar experiences, luxury brands should follow five key rules:

1. **Capturing the traffic**. Most avatar users perceive the virtual world as a place of socialization. The luxury company should, therefore, ensure a sufficient level of traffic on its website to allow online socialization.
2. **Commission**. Living in a virtual world is not totally free and users need rewards or money to have fun. Luxury companies may reward the avatars (e.g., coupons, payment), which can serve to jumpstart the traffic.
3. **Innovation**. One of the main motivations of avatar users is to have fun online. Luxury companies should then find ways to provide users with innovative ways to distract themselves.
4. **Creating a learning environment**. For many users, avatars are an opportunity to learn and live new experiences. Thus luxury companies should offer online users experiences that allow them to develop knowledge and skills.
5. **Credibility**. Luxury businesses need to understand that this is more than merely a video game for most online users who are regularly within a virtual world; it is the extension of real life for them. Avatars should then be taken seriously on the merchant website of the luxury brand, or on other platforms.

TREND 7.2

NOONOOURI, DIOR'S VIRTUAL AVATAR

To promote its makeup on social media, Dior has chosen the influencer and fashion fan Noonoouri, an avatar created by a German branding agency. On her Instagram profile, Noonoouri describes herself as "cute, curious, and couture." For its cosmetic products, Dior posted on Instagram three videos in which one can see Noonoouri demonstrate eyeliners, mascara, and lipstick, generating all kinds of comments. Some of the users/consumers were doubtful ("But an animation for make-up is not credible"), others applauded ("I like the fact of using virtual models in the promo. Models who never grow old. It's clever, since we now have the technology that allows it"). This is not the first time that Noonoouri has collaborated with Dior considering she had already appeared on the Instagram account of the haute couture brand during the presentation of the 2019 cruise collection in Paris.

Six months after its creation, the Instagram account of the avatar had already accrued more than 90,000 subscribers. Brand fans and other users can see her regularly wearing haute couture creations designed by Dior as well as Versace, Tom Ford, Vuitton, Giambattista Valli, Dolce & Gabbana, and Moschino. She was even part of haute couture parades with international human models such as Kendall Jenner.

HOW IS ARTIFICIAL INTELLIGENCE AI TRANSFORMING THE LUXURY EXPERIENCE?

AI refers to machine learning, which is a current application of intelligence accomplished by feeding machines human input data that will allow the machine to learn from itself. AI learning includes technologies such as neural networks (this is a computer system designed to function by classifying information in the same way as a human brain), deep learning (refers to a set of algorithms and the combination of different types of algorithms), and natural language processing (a software application to understand and analyze speech and language). It is important to note that the presence of AI is not new. It has existed in our lives for many years, but its use has evolved over time to become more useful and attuned to our needs, which is especially true for customer relationship needs and the improvement of the digital customer experience. There are many different forms of AI systems. By analyzing and processing many probabilities, an AI system can give users the most likely answer based on the information it is given. And the more the users provide data on the systems, the more they train them to develop artificial intelligence, and the more accurate the results.

Since the advent of AI in the 1950s, two major approaches have been adopted by researchers to design "smart" machines. The first approach, "making a mind," which can be described as symbolic AI, is designed to provide an AI system with reasoning mechanisms capable of manipulating the symbolic data that constitute the knowledge of a domain. This approach uses patterns and methods of logic. It gave rise to knowledge-based systems. A second approach, "modeling the brain," which can be described as connectionist AI, is designed to learn from the functioning of the cerebral cortex. The basic entity is a formal model of the neuron, a system being formed by the interconnection of a large number of such "neurons." This approach has given rise to current neuromimetic networks. Since the 1990s, a promising trend has been to develop hybrid models that combine these two approaches with complementary traits. In addition, "statistical models" are increasingly used for the great variability of the phenomena studied. A fundamental aspect of AI (and more generally, intelligence) is that of learning, and how it allows a system (or animal) to improve its performance (Nilsson, 1998). The design of effective methods of learning and adapting to new operating conditions is, therefore, an important area of AI activity. To characterize all AI activities, it is necessary to introduce other methodological domains, in particular:

- **AI can be used for problem-solving**. It is about designing effective strategies for exploring solutions that are often very vast. The study of games (e.g., chess, checkers) allows designing and testing problem-solving methods that are now found in many AI systems, as these systems address complex problems. For efficiency, these methods use heuristics, elements of information, and specific knowledge of the problem to be solved. AI has achieved great success in different areas, such as industrial production management, transportation planning, computer network management, or design.
- **AI can also be used for knowledge management and symbolic reasoning**. The recognition and interpretation of data are both an integral part of AI. These data can be very varied in nature and, consequently, require very different processes (e.g., symbolic information, time signals, images). Practical applications relate to the recognition of writing (e.g., optical reading of texts), image processing (e.g., remote sensing, biomedical, industry), diagnostics (e.g., medical, industrial, financial), monitoring, and the management of industrial processes.
- **AI is used for decision support**. The goal is to help a human decision-maker in the choices individuals have to make in the presence of various and uncertain information. Applications can be found in all areas: banking, financial, industrial, medical, or military.
- **AI is also part of action planning and robotics**. This is a question of precisely defining the sequence of elementary actions necessary to carry out a complex task, such as those that a mobile robot should achieve in a more or less well-known environment.
- **AI can help in the treatment of the natural language, written, and spoken**. Significant progress has been made in this complex area. Even if the problem is far from being solved, real applications exist in the translation of technical texts, the analysis, and indexing of written documents (e.g., search engines on the Internet), and the recognition of speech (e.g., voice dictation of texts, access to information by voice telematics).

Historically, artificial intelligence has been a logical continuation in the chronology of inno-vation since the invention of the first tools that increased the production capacities and cognitive skills of human beings. One can consider that one point of departure (as it applies to marketing) in the realm of artificial intelligence is marked by Alan Turing's work, specif-ically in his article 'Computing machinery and intelligence' (published in 1950), in which he posited a paradigm suggesting that a machine could think. He proposed a test, known now as the Turing test, to determine if a machine knows how to reason, and whether it can create autonomy. The actual notion of AI was then conceptualized and developed by John McCarthy at Stanford University and Marvin Minsky from MIT, amongst others. Different fields can be interested in AI. In fact, artificial intelligence is a field of computer science that groups together several very different technological building blocks, including algorithms. It is also an interface that adapts to humans and allows easy and intuitive communication with the machine. Artificial intelligence is, then, part of the cognitive sciences that deal with learning systems of various levels that aim to teach computers to see, hear, read, mem-orize, structure, reason, decide, and act. Today, the goal of AI is to replicate the four human cognitive abilities (perception, comprehension, action, and learning) that correspond to different groups of technologies (Figure 7.2).

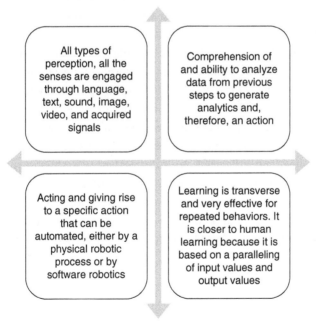

Figure 7.2   The four human cognitive abilities replicated by AI

So we come to the following question: How does artificial intelligence contribute to the crea-tion and improvement of the digital luxury experience? Today, AI is considered a key factor for improving the quality of the B2B and B2C customer experience. This was big news in 2016. The Gartner study not only revealed that surveys on the subject had tripled between 2015 and 2016, but the study also predicted it as the most strategic technological trend for 2017 (Gartner, 2016). To understand the real importance of AI and its impact in the luxury sector, we first should understand its meaning and its main features in this context.

Although legitimate, the question of whether artificial intelligence will replace the ancestral know-how of real individuals, which defines the reputation and uniqueness of luxury, may not be the right question. It is not a matter of artificial intelligence opposing the human element; rather, it is a matter of asking "How can the luxury industry integrate this technology when faced with the risk of disappearing into a world whose evolution we cannot stop?" In fact, artificial intelligence and luxury can go hand in hand. Artificial intelligence can and should become a partner of the exceptionalism of luxury brands. With its specificities, such as the ability to anticipate, authenticate, customize, and measure, the AI can help designers in the luxury fashion industry develop other creative processes. By capturing strong and weak signals within a large amount of information, artificial intelligence can enrich the phase of reflection upstream and downstream of the creation of a product. While this technology can accompany creativity and detect trends, it can also help the luxury brand understand what is happening around it to better anticipate the desires of its current customers and attract future ones.

It is not a question, here, of automating tasks, as the creator/designer remains the conductor; it is up to him/her to frame the artificial intelligence and make it an ally in order to widen his/her field of vision and create for tomorrow. By exploring the right data and analyzing it with meaning, AI can also become a great opportunity to deliver exceptional luxury brand experiences. Today, there are companies that use neuroscience tools to measure the emotions of consumers by detecting cues in their faces as well as the impressions and feelings associated with them. In the store, for example, this technology can enable staff to meet or even anticipate customer needs. It also allows luxury retailers to optimize the circuits in-store and the different spaces according to the emotions identified on the faces of the visitors. Thus, combining artificial intelligence with other technologies is a real opportunity for luxury businesses facing the creation of value and the enrichment of the proposition made to customers who want to live enjoyable and memorable experiences with the luxury brand.

TREND 7.3

GUERLAIN USES AI TO HELP ITS CUSTOMERS SELECT THEIR PERFUME

Choosing one's perfume is not always very easy with all the brands and scents on the market. Guerlain's idea is to use technology to offer a very efficient personalized customer experience to its clients. The luxury brand simplified the discovery and selection process with the use of artificial intelligence, including a voice assistant that will help customers select their perfume. Collaborating with Google, Guerlain set up a series of questions/answers that serve as a guide for the consumer in the choice of his/her perfume. This is an olfactory consultation based on 100 references of the brand. It is an artificial intelligence that directs individuals to the fragrance that suits them best. The user can use Google's voice assistant by mentioning he/she wants to talk to Guerlain. The user will then be prompted to start the consultation or listen to the perfumer Thierry Wasseur's podcast once the assistant connects to the house. During the consultation, questions are asked to identify the tones and notes that correspond to consumers' preferences.

The experience is largely based on a visualization exercise so that consumers can express their imagination. In fact, the consultation invites the user to close his/her eyes to imagine particular atmospheres and destinations. Then, the AI assistant offers users a range of perfumes that are likely to meet their expectations. Users can even get a summary of the propositions made to them by SMS as well as the location of the nearest brand shop.

Lastly, AI could also be considered as the guardian of memories in luxury houses that are busy gathering exceptional know-how. It is a fact: nowadays, it is difficult to recruit people who master the traditional skills. Handicrafts are learned on the ground, sometimes from generation to generation, and often in the secrecy of historic houses. It is not uncommon for this wealth to be held by a handful of insiders: it can easily be jeopardized by a generational change or a financial hazard, which poses a considerable risk of loss for the luxury houses and for our economies.

Artificial intelligence could then provide a solution to this problem and become a real transmission tool by decrypting the gestures, aggregating know-how, and by integrating the manufacturing processes, and then distributing products and services as and when needed. It is not a question of freezing the knowledge in time; rather, it is a question of whether luxury houses can capitalize on it. Thus, AI brings a knowledge base to the artisans without ever pretending to replace them, so that they can continue their work, their creativity, their uniqueness, and the evolution of their know-how. Well optimized and combined with other tools, this technology could help, tomorrow, to preserve the memory of an artisanal idiosyncrasy, and thus preserve the culture of a prestigious luxury house. As the idea of an exclusive object evolves into a premium, personalized, and multichannel experience, luxury companies from different sectors – from fashion to hospitality to beauty – can use AI to predict trends and sales, assist teams on the spot, and make the production process, as well as the in-store and online purchase experience, more efficient.

CHATBOTS IN THE DIGITAL LUXURY EXPERIENCE

A chatbot or conversational agent is a concrete application of artificial intelligence. These technologies are redefining the customer experience. For a very long time, customer service and support centers were departments that intervened only after the sale of a product or service to a customer, or when he/she had a question or a problem. Customer support, therefore, intervened, essentially, at the end of the customer journey. Nowadays, the chatbot is transforming these services by creating value during each customer exchange. A chatbot is a software robot that can interact with an individual or consumer through a series of automated conversations made largely in natural language. The chatbot originally used question and answer libraries; however, advances in artificial intelligence now allow it increasingly to analyze and understand messages with the characteristic learning capabilities of a machine. The first historical forms of chatbots were used as virtual agents, represented by an image or a human avatar, and were originally made available on websites. The term chatbot is now also used to designate chatbots offered on social networks, especially chatbots on Facebook Messenger, or those integrated within mobile applications. Applied to the field of intelligent assistants, chatbots can become voicebots that can respond to the logic of relational marketing, or have the function of pre-/post-sale customer support. They are also used to take orders directly, which is known as a transactional chatbot.

In the luxury sector, the use of chatbots was initially partly experimental because it presented a certain risk to the luxury brands due to the possible semantic wanderings and manipulations, or diversions also possible amongst Internet users. However, progress in the field has been rapid, and chatbots are now emerging in some contexts as a new support channel or customer contact that ensures availability and productivity gains. Chatbots are frequently used by brands to interact with their customers and for commercial purposes. A very innovative "Dialogue with the Artwork" initiative in the use of chatbots to enhance the museum visitor experience has highlighted the importance of this technology in improving the customer experience in the field of culture and art, which is inherently a highly experiential sector. In fact, in order to bring the visitors closer to art, BBDO Argentina and the Museum of Modern Art in Buenos Aires designed a chatbot that allows visitors to converse with works of art. Developers worked on different pieces in the museum to give them a voice and a personality. The goal was to facilitate the interaction between art and visitors. To develop these chatbots, the agency took into account the history of each work, while trying to bring out a personality consistent with the art work. This initiative revealed the playful side of chatbots and offered a more intimate experience with works of art than an audio guide by allowing visitors to start a discussion and try to obtain more personal information about why the artist did the work.

Nowadays, we can talk of the birth of a new generation of chatbots. In fact, first-generation chatbots were very limited in their ability to handle natural language, maintain a conversation, and answer ambiguous questions. But technology has improved a lot, and with the help of artificial intelligence, cognitive computing, and machine learning, these virtual agents are now able to understand and respond to a wide variety of questions. However, when implementing a chatbot for customer support, luxury companies should first evaluate all the options currently available on the market. For example, development platforms, such as the IBM Watson Chatbot Framework and the Microsoft Cortana Bot Framework (amongst others), allow luxury businesses to create a conversational agent easily and quickly. But, the chatbot is only the visible part of the virtual agent. In fact, in addition to trying to understand the purpose of a question by having a conversation using automatic natural language processing and automatic text generation, a knowledge base should also be created to give the chatbot the ability to respond in a relevant way to the identified request. This means that a well-thought-out and well-designed process and interface should be set up by luxury companies in order to build, maintain, and control the knowledge base.

Furthermore, real agents in stores need to be able to enrich their conversations, add information to the knowledge base, and use a dashboard to measure the use and effectiveness of the chatbots. When a virtual agent needs to answer a more specific question, the answer may require the integration of informational data with transactional ones. The platform should then provide an easy way to link knowledge base responses with data from separate online operational systems. In terms of customer behavior and data, the chatbot provides the e-commerce websites with access to new horizons to better understand and retain their customers. Tools such as Facebook Messenger, Google's Dialogflow, Microsoft's Azure Bot, Amazon Lex, and IBM Watson give luxury brands the ability to examine statistics on conversations, isolate certain data to analyze customer behaviors, and identify the most sought-after products and services via chatbot interactions and exchanges with users. All of this combined provides luxury businesses with a complete user experience in various areas:

- Recommendations on products related to customer purchases or research to personalize the experience;
- Shorten the purchase journey and finalize the order faster;
- Managing customer orders, including a change of information, making an appointment for delivery, etc.;
- Notifying the customer if the product is unavailable;
- Proposing products in relation to the filters used to align suggestions with the needs of the customer;
- Following up after the purchase.

As the relationship between e-commerce and chatbots is only at its beginning, we can expect further developments that will make the customer experience even more immersive, for example with voice assistants, like Apple's Siri, Microsoft Cortana, Google Assistant, or Amazon's Alexa – devices that create a real verbal dialogue with users. Other aspects not to be neglected by luxury houses when implementing a chatbot include its integration with existing security layers, the processing of personal data, and compliance with the General Data Protection Regulation (GDPR).

HOLOGRAMS AND THEIR ABILITY TO HUMANIZE THE DIGITAL LUXURY EXPERIENCE

The principle of holography was invented by Dennis Gábor in 1948. A hologram is a 3D image recorded on a two-dimensional photographic film allowing a 360-degree capture of the object. It is, therefore, a recording process for converting a 2D image into 3D. When we photograph an object in a conventional way, we record on a sensitive plate the brightness of the various points of this object. In other words, only the intensity of the light reflected by the object is taken into account. The hologram, however, is the result of the interference of two laser beams: one that is shone on a photographic plate, the other on the object to be rendered in 3D. The best-known usage of holography is in the entertainment and events sectors, but this process has been adopted in other contexts, particularly in the business sector. In cinema, holograms are most often used in sci-fi movies, such as *Star Wars* or *Avatar*, through processes that reveal a human form. One of the most popular applications is used to "resurrect" absent or deceased singers or actors by rendering them in 3D and animating their actions into a performance, for example, the singer Tupac Shakur or Michael Jackson. This process was also used for other artists, notably to create concerts with the virtual Japanese star Miku Hatsune. While some have fun in concert with holograms, others are working on the usage of the latter in business. Indeed, in a more "business" setting, holograms are used, for example, by some airlines to guide travelers more easily through the airport. Tensatour, an American company, is not a newcomer to this game. Indeed, it currently equips several airports with "welcome holograms" that explain to travelers the security constraints. Other companies are developing holograms for use in video conferences, to visualize, and manipulate 3D objects. Indeed, the future of video conferencing solutions will naturally lead to holography practices that will make the remote relationship experience less abstract, more tangible, and more visual.

Holograms are, then, a new challenge for marketing and digital retailers in the luxury sector. This technology can be especially useful in its application in luxury in-store experiences, for example, at a jeweler where rings, necklaces, and valuable watches are locked up. Thanks to holograms, there is the possibility of manipulating them virtually. Furthermore, holograms can also be used to customize an object: Do you have a watch model that you like? Using holographic technology, you can see what it looks like with different bracelets, for example. The next step in holographic technology was recently demonstrated by the University of Tokyo: holographic images that can be touched – at least, that is the goal.

If the images are made of light, like all holograms are, as we approach to touch them, an electronic tracking system (adapted from a Wii remote) ultrasound generator causes a tactile sensation. However, the process is not yet ready. It is not portable, and cannot produce very large holograms, but the technology looks promising.

TREND 7.4

CARTIER CREATES A HOLOGRAPHIC IN-STORE EXPERIENCE TO IMMERSE ITS CUSTOMERS

In order to enhance the in-store customer experience, Cartier created a hologram of a female arm that pierces the store window of its shop on Fifth Avenue in New York. The arm can be seen from the street and in its hand is an ornament of precious stones associated with the brand. Using holograms is also a way to make the customer want to enter into the store to buy a product while the same product is available online in a few clicks. Hologram technology allows luxury brands to showcase their products in a highly experiential context that includes storytelling and interaction with customers.

At a time when e-commerce and m-commerce (mobile commerce) seem to have taken over, the challenge for luxury brands is to continue to attract shoppers. To counteract the adverse effects presented by the convenience of online shopping and easy access to products, luxury brands such as Cartier are using holographic technology that guarantees the WOW effect, which perfectly addresses this issue by creating value for "offline" shopping, compared to online shopping. By using this technology, Cartier makes its products come to life under the customer's very eyes with animated 3D technology. In doing so, Cartier shows every facet of its displayed products. Therefore, holographic technology is a great opportunity for luxury brands to remain desirable and innovative.

To sum up, social virtual agents are able to interact with users using natural language in a personalized way with more or less relevant answers while integrating themselves into the luxury company's multichannel customer experience management. However, the use of a social virtual agent has some limits, including those related to artificial intelligence: risk of conflict between virtual agents and human collaborators in customer support services, risk of the temporary unavailability of the virtual agent, and resistance by some customers. Thus, websites with a virtual agent should contain a device that allows direct contact with a human assistant when the online agent is not able to give a satisfactory answer to the online customer. Also, virtual agents should be integrated into the multichannel business customer relationship strategy. Therefore, for luxury businesses, it is important to position the virtual agent as an entry point for the customer experience and to clearly define its role. This can consist of filtering contacts, giving first-level answers, and, when the question is beyond its competence, handing the issue over to a human adviser who has at his/her disposal all the information already exchanged. Therefore, the customer or prospect benefits from an immediate response and does not have to request another channel.

The role of the human agent is also valued since he/she can intervene as an expert and no longer has to deal with recurring requests. The way the human agent handled the client problem can then be analyzed to improve the virtual agent accordingly. It is, therefore, not realistic to think that the virtual agent can one day take the place of the human agent adviser. But, for luxury brands, a virtual agent can help strengthen teams and allow human advisers to focus on high-value customer experiences by responding to a client's requests or complex issues. When virtual agents are implemented on the luxury brand's website, there should also be a learning period, which should correspond to the private training of an agent, before it is fully operational. This learning is done, in part, with the staff of the customer relationship platforms into which it will be integrated. The challenge for the luxury company is properly distributing customer requests between automated virtual processing and human agent in order to offer the best customer experience while optimizing its resources.

HUMANOID ROBOTS IN THE CREATION OF EXCEPTIONAL LUXURY EXPERIENCES

A humanoid is a robot with its body shape built to resemble the human body. It is one of the ultimate achievements of robotics: it can move in environments designed for humans, use tools or devices designed for humans, and also communicate with them. In 1996, Honda launched the first complete and standalone humanoid robot, which was very good at human walking and able to climb stairs and manipulate objects with its hands. Since then, the humanoid robot has become a privileged research platform that brings together different disciplines and allows the emergence of a new field of research on "humanoid robotics." This is particularly so in Japan, which, in 1998, launched the national project "HRP" (Humanoid Robot Project) at the initiative of the Japanese Ministry of Economy, Trade and Industry. HRP was led by Professor Hirochika Inoue, one of the great founders of robotics in Japan. The project aimed to develop a robot that could work with humans, in a specific environment. This project brought together universities, research institutes, and industries. Therefore, a question that comes to mind is: How are humanoid robotics reinventing the customer experience?

Although a growing market in many sectors, humanoid robotics and cyborgs are in their fledgling stage. Able to welcome, accompany, and educate through an interface endowed with words and emotions, the robot offers a new customer experience.

In services, retail, or health, the business of humanoid robotics is still in its infancy. Yet, they are already reinventing the notion of user experience. Some humanoid robots can welcome, accompany, and inform visitors with empathy. This category of humanoid robots is the first generation of robots that have been able to recognize human emotions and adapt to them. It is an innovation that has given rise to a new, uncharted field of expertise: social robotics. It directly echoes two values: the collaboration between human and machine (as opposed to the replacement of one by the other) and the ability of the robot to integrate in the public space and interact with users (as opposed to the industrial robot confined to repetitive tasks in factories). Business benefits, therefore, apply to the humanoid robot as a point of digital interaction between the company's information system and the end user.

By capturing the reactions of visitors or customers, the robot collects and analyzes data – product quality, after-sales service, satisfaction questionnaire, input from internal teams, etc. There are several categories of robots, and their use depends on the role that the company wants to give it. For example, the Nao robot in Japan is used as a hostess in luxury stores. Nao, a humanoid robot, was conceived to be a cyborg partner in the digital customer experience. Developed by Aldebaran Robotics, the Nao Evolution programmable humanoid robot is the fifth-generation Nao robot with enhanced audio and visual capabilities, a dialogue engine, and an "emotion" engine. To date, Nao may be the most complete humanoid robot on the market in terms of functional, technical, and even empathic capabilities in regard to its interactions with humans. Nao is considered as a social robot that can be an integral part of the customer experience in stores, banks, supermarkets, events, and even at home. Japan has already used robots in events and as bank hostesses that can relay information in two languages: Chinese and Japanese. The human-controlled reception robot is available for events or lounges to welcome guests. It is also designed to entertain and accompany guests or visitors to different places. The robot can engage in conversation with guests and offer them food that it, itself, can serve. The built-in tablet can display products and give explanations as well as present small videos.

For luxury companies, the humanoid robot can offer services adapted to their customers, such as taxi booking, visitor identification and reception, multimedia content distribution, and satisfaction questionnaires. This service of convenience is then a place of exchange and communication where the luxury brand can interact with its customers in a different way. In retail, the robot is able to engage customers with the support of a touchpad, thus enabling a productive exchange of products, services, or special operations. A product catalog-type offers, for example, different paths (by technical criteria regarding popularity, price, etc.), thus providing a multitude of possibilities for fostering interactions with customers. Purchase tracking can be delegated to a seller or handled by the robot with a click-and-collect approach. Thus, the act of purchase is personalized and improved. For example, in product recommendations, purchase management, or payment programs, humanoid robotics can enhance the fluidity of the customer journey. Furthermore, humanoid robotics can allow luxury businesses the ability to offer unique and efficient customer experiences in the following ways:

- Creating new customer experiences: the humanoid robots would revive physical store traffic through the ultra-personalization of customer reception.
- Optimizing the customer journey by providing unpublished data on the physical flow and generating new tools for real-time analysis. The functionality of the simplest sensors, such as customer counting or trajectory tracking, as well as more advanced ones, like behavioral or emotional analysis, have important operational as well as employee and merchandising implications.
- Bringing fluidity to store procedures by significantly reducing friction points, such as the time spent at the checkout, or time and effort exerted searching for products, which could be solved with automated product picking.
- And most importantly, in-store, robots should be used by luxury houses to perform many low-value customer tasks. Humanoid robots could be the solution to time-consuming inventories carried out by human sellers.

SUMMARY

The most important challenge for luxury companies is the reorganization of their departments due to the arrival of artificial intelligence, chatbots, robots, virtual assistants, etc. What are the uses of AI and how can they reshape the customer experience offline and online? Which teams and job profiles will supervise this intelligence? How will these technologies transform existing processes and relationships with customers? What data will this AI generate? These questions are only a tiny fraction of the ones that luxury brand professionals who want to implement AI and other technologies to humanize the digital customer experience have to successfully explore. To sum up, this chapter underscores the idea that using technologies to humanize the customer experience holds great promise for enhancing customer relations in the future. It is no longer a matter of whether or not luxury brands should implement these new technologies; rather, the more pressing concern is, "How do luxury houses, brands, and industry professionals implement these technologies successfully?" in order to offer the ultimate luxury customer experience.

8

PROTOTYPED DIGITAL LUXURY EXPERIENCES

INTRODUCTION AND SCOPE

We are not yet fully appreciative of the extraordinary technological advancement of 3D printing and its implications for the fashion and luxury industry. In recent years, the usages of 3D printing in fashion and luxury have been multiplying: whether during the creation process, production, or in-store, this additive manufacturing technology allows fashion and luxury houses to expand the range of possibilities to meet the expectations of their customers. Thus, since the early 2010s, this technology has been progressively democratized to allow new creative digital experiences that offer consumers a new mass customization solution. In fact, 3D technology makes it possible to create a perfectly tailor-made reproduction of an item. It especially reveals new futuristic materials for creative designers and is considered to be an indicator, according to *The Economist* (2012), we are living in the age of the third industrial revolution. However, although there are some initiatives showing the rising use of 3D printing, luxury and fashion houses are lagging a little behind this phenomenon in relation to its importance, even if pioneering designers, like Iris Van Herpen or Catherine Wales, have seized with enthusiasm this remarkable invention.

If fashion and luxury are trailing behind, it is because 3D printing is rather unglamorous and technical. Additionally, the achievements of 3D printing are embedded within a traditional society of craftsmanship where the tradition is not only respected, but even constitutes one of the main arguments of luxury sales. Moreover, luxury businesses view 3D printing with caution because it also exposes the industry to the risk of easily made counterfeits; for example, it becomes very easy to copy branded bags, even if for the moment the 3D printer models sold to private individuals are too small or inefficient to create that replication exactly. Therefore, we can ask: How is 3D printing used in fashion and luxury today? What additional advantages does it offer when compared to traditional processes? In this chapter, I introduce prototyped digital luxury experiences and explain the way luxury companies can use 3D printing technology to offer highly customized and on-demand luxury experiences to their customers.

PROTOTYPING CUSTOMER EXPERIENCES VIA 3D PRINTING

3D printing is a rapid prototyping technology that allows companies to manufacture 3D objects using a 3D printer, which only requires a digital file that is often freely accessible (open source) and printing materials, which vary depending on the nature of the object to be printed (plastic, metal, resin, etc.). In fact, 3D printing is attracting more and more businesses as well as the interest of the public and end users, who are curious to explore all the possibilities offered by 3D printing, which allows them to create and personalize objects, such as smartphone cases, cups, figurines, jewelry, etc. Today's 3D printing technology (or rapid prototyping) is currently experiencing advances that make it more and more accessible and generate unlimited ideas, hopes, and fantasies. Therefore, in order to answer questions about the contributions of 3D printing to luxury, such as: What will be the impacts on the entire customer experience in the luxury sector? And, how does it transform the in-store luxury experience? Or is 3D printing a real opportunity for luxury retailers? We first need to understand how 3D printing works.

Technically speaking, 3D printing, also referred to as additive manufacturing, is a new technology that prints objects layer by layer unlike older manufacturing, such as mold injection or other processes that model an object by extraction, subtraction, or formation from a block of raw material by giving it a shape (heavy processes in tools and which require a qualified workforce). Early 3D printing technology appeared in the 1990s and consists of superimposing thin layers of powder of specific materials (metal, plastic, wood, steel, etc.) that we want the final object to be made of. A laser then heats the parts we want to solidify. The only step that remains is to remove the superfluous powder, after which the object becomes real, palpable, and functional. The manufacturing process is launched from a central application office CAO file (computer-generated 3D object). The idea is to reproduce the virtual object cross-section by cross-section using the printing system. We can then combine the digital context with a 3D printer to create something that operates in a similar way to a classic 2D printer, but with an added dimension. Thus, the 3D printer offers a digital representation of the object being printed. Besides, obtaining a 3D model can also be done by scanning an object using a 3D scanner that works according to the same principles as the traditional 2D scanner.

We can thus have a 3D digital model taken from an object from the real world. In its digital 3D file form, an object can be modified, shared, and enhanced by any user with access to the original file. Objects can accordingly evolve in an iterative way. There are three main technologies within 3D printing:

- **FDM (Fuse Deposition Modeling)**. This is an example of modeling that deposits molten material in order to create the object;
- **Stereolithography**. A UV light solidifies a layer of liquid plastic;
- **Laser selective fraction**. This is the connection of the material in the form of powder or by glue jet liquid by exposure to a laser.

Today, about 200 materials are available for printing: plastics (75% of impressions); resin, which is available in matt, gloss, and white or black; and metals, which are mainly titanium and stainless steel. Also, aluminum and cobalt-chromium as well as other metals are used, including gold, silver, and bronze, which are not manufactured directly with 3D printers, but rather need molds in which the precious metals would be injected. Ceramic and wood, as well as food materials can be used, for example, chocolate can also be used in 3D printing. Tech companies such as HP Labs (Hewlett Packard) are working on the development of a new material: glass, which could be a most promising material for 3D printing. For HP CEO Meg Whitman, glass is easy to recycle, it is environmentally friendly, and inexpensive. It is pleasant to the touch and already familiar to customers. Printing glass is a real challenge for current 3D printers and HP wants to explore all the possibilities with this material. The main goal of 3D printing is, then, to reduce the time and cost of production, but it can also be used to offer customers a new way of living their experiences. Soon, we will be able to create an object effortlessly with one click, in the same way that we can create websites today. We will create objects as a 3D file, send it to a 3D printing service that will deliver it to our home, or print it with a personal "home" 3D printer. This on-demand customization meets the customer's desire to obtain products at a reasonable cost, within a reasonable amount of time, and according to the distinct parameters set by the user.

Understandably, 3D printing was rapidly taken up by many companies and applied to their consumer goods. Consumers today want more choices on the final format of the product they buy. The emergence of many niche markets centered on on-demand products is the first step towards mass customization. Indeed, it is likely that in the future we will not have the same cup of coffee as our neighbor: we will have found one on Shapeways 3D printing service while our neighbor will have bought a different model on 3D hubs, another online 3D printing service, and so on. For these kinds of products, the standardization that is currently imposed by mass manufacturing will no longer be required.

TREND 8.1

CHANEL: ITS NEW MASCARA PAVES THE WAY FOR 3D PRINTING

Beyond new formulations, the cosmetics industry has never stopped innovating. From augmented reality to microbiology, and connected objects, the industry is pushing the limits of innovation ever further. Like many sectors, cosmetics show a growing interest in 3D printing. In recent years, 3D bio-printing has made a noticeable incursion into the beauty industry, particularly through L'Oréal and its partnerships with Organovo and Poeitis. In a key area where the container is just as crucial as the content, 3D printing finds another application in its role in packaging. That last nod was to the legendary Chanel house.

The famous French brand of haute couture and beauty products is preparing to launch its first mascara line entirely produced by additive manufacturing. This is the brand new Volume Revolution, a mascara with the first brush printed in 3D and marketed on a large scale. For the first time in the world, 3D printing will be the object of a massive industrialization by Chanel. Innovative to the tips of the eyelashes, this new cosmetic is the result of a 10-year partnership between Chanel Parfums Beauté and Erpro 3D Factory, a specialist in mass production 3D printing. The luxury house Chanel saw the potential of 3D printing before filing, in 2007, its first patent on the manufacturing of applicators of cosmetic products including a mascara brush in 3D printing. Highlighting the considerable advances in 3D printing now indicates a sign of industrialization. Chanel inaugurated, in June 2018, a production line consisting of six additive manufacturing machines. The brushes will be manufactured by laser sintering on a polyamide powder at a rate of 50,000 brushes in 24 hours, 250,000 brushes per week and up to 1 million per month.

All of them follow a process that is all the more rigorous in that the product is intended for the sensitive area of vision: analysis of the raw material, preparation of the powder, polymerization of the powder by laser beam, cooling of the brushes, and maintenance according to a specific process: rinsing, quality control, and mechanical tests. Everything has been put in place to meet Chanel's high-quality standards and requirements and to guarantee unquestionable performance and safety. In fact, the production line was developed in collaboration with Chanel and allows perfect reproducibility in the absence of a mold. It offers more freedom, flexibility, and responsiveness for mass production. Highlighting the precision of 3D printing and its ability to create complex geometries, the Volume Revolution brush has a specific shape with a hundredth of millimeter implantation of the pins for a homogeneous distribution of the material on the eyelashes. Microgravities have also been created to absorb the material and deliver the right amount without having to re-dip the brush during the application. In this highly competitive makeup segment, when traditional machines had reached the end of their innovation capacity, Chanel found a way to innovate on these products by fully exploiting the potential of 3D printing.

3D printing technology is a growing market; Gartner expects 3D printer market sales to exceed \$14.6 billion by 2019 (Gartner, 2015b). Stratasys represents the biggest player in this lucrative market. It is valued today at \$3 billion (representing 50% of the professional printer market and is considered the Google of 3D printing). The other competitor is 3D Systems, weighing in at a mere $500 million. Other players also offer printing services (totaling sales of $2 billion), such as Sculpteo and Shapeways. This technology is not only limited to industrial businesses, rather, the rapid democratization of individual 3D printers now allows personal manufacturing or personal fabrication, an industry that is booming. In fact, personal 3D printers allow consumers to satisfy their functional needs by printing various objects for various uses:

- **Everyday objects**. The website thingiverse.com now offers templates for free download. One can download and send them to the 3D printer, which takes care of the rest. A study by the Michigan Technological University (Goodrich, 2017) has shown that buying a 3D printer to print such objects is considered cost effective by the consumer.
- **Spare parts for broken objects**. Many everyday objects, especially plastic parts, can break. Most of the time, these parts cannot be found in the marketplace because the manufacturer has every interest in selling another whole new object rather than repairing an old one. Thus, by giving a second life to certain objects in our everyday life, 3D printing allows individuals to achieve substantial savings.

With individual 3D printing, it will now be possible to recreate objects and spare parts, personalized by no more than desire or by need and usage, and to fight against built-in obsolescence, as we enter the era of what might be called "the small series of the unique object." These machines, no bulkier than a microwave, have a remarkable power: that of transforming the status of the consumer from a basic passive actor to an inventive prosumer (producer + consumer) and creator. Personal 3D printing at home is, then, the next step towards the democratization of a technology that demonstrates a real enthusiasm for its mass adoption. Certain companies in different business sectors are already integrating 3D printing into their processes of design and production. For these companies, the use of 3D printing has three major advantages:

- Adaptation to the specific needs of the client;
- The manufacture of unavailable items (due to the obsolescence of the product);
- The manufacturing of small series.

With the improvement of the quality, the relative ease of use of this technology, and the wide choice of materials available, 3D printing is transforming and rethinking the way some industry players manufacture their products. It is very likely that most consumers will be able to have access to a 3D printer by 2025, whether by owning a 3D printer in their home, by using the services of an external 3D printing service provider, or by purchasing printed 3D products online.

TREND 8.2

GEMMYO MAKES LUXURY JEWELRY ACCESSIBLE THANKS TO 3D PRINTING

Gemmyo online jewelry stands out in many ways from a traditional jeweler. To lower prices, the French startup does not collaborate with any point of sale or has any stock: jewelry is made to order, thanks to 3D printing. Created in 2011, Gemmyo already displays 5,500 references in its online jewelry catalog. The startup allows its customers to personalize their piece by choosing the precious metal and the stone as well as adapting the size of the jewel to the measurements of the recipient. The secret of the young company is 3D printing. None of the jewelry presented on the website is real. All have been modeled in 3D and it is from computer images that customers make their choice. And as stated by its co-founder, Pauline Laigneau, it works: "We have a return rate of less than 0.5%, proof that the quality of the jewels we produce corresponds to what people expect."

In fact, with 3D printing, Gemmyo has put a rocket under the traditional luxury jewelry sector and is making it more accessible. Indeed, the most expensive thing in jewelry is the point of sale, usually located in such prestigious places as the Place Vendôme in Paris or Fifth Avenue in New York. Also, the storage of raw materials is very expensive and requires very costly security measures. By selling on the Web, Gemmyo does not need retail outlets, and with 3D printing, there is no need for stock. The company can then rely on 3D printers, which can produce about 50 pieces of jewelry per day. The 3D printer can simultaneously produce several pieces, however the necessary accuracy involves printing times that are rather long: from three to nine hours for the 3D printer to deliver its batch of molds. For the time being, 3D printers do not print precious metals directly: they generate a prototype that will be used for the microfusion of the final jewel. The accuracy of the process reaches 25 microns, which is more precise than that created by the human hand. A craftsman ensures the finish and sets the stones, then the piece can be sent to the customer. Such an operation allows the startup to display prices that are 30% to 40% lower than those of traditional luxury jewelers. Jewelry is a product that is very suitable for sale online. Such 3D printer services can be used by luxury houses to make some of their products more accessible to their customers, and allow them also to have firsthand contact with the brand.

The world of 3D printing is, therefore, positioned on all fronts to be a great tool for retailers. On the creative side as well as the production side, additive manufacturing meets the real needs of the 21st century. In an era where innovation and manufacturing are in a tight spot, 3D printing allows retailers to offer original and customizable experiences to their customers as well as fully or partially customized products that can create differentiation and enhance the competitive advantage of the company. Such technology will have a major role in the future (beyond customer personalization) in the way of creation, and regarding the costs and time of creation/manufacturing of products. For companies, especially in the luxury sector, 3D printing technology will enable them to relocate their manufacturing centers and some of their production directly in their points of sale. Luxury companies only need to learn how to handle software before acquiring machines that, over the years, will cost less and less, and thus contribute to offering new in-store luxury customer experiences. For instance, shoe printing is a popular use of 3D printing. In fact, amongst the particularities of 3D printing is the ability to personalize objects. It is this aspect that first encouraged retailers to offer a personalized customer experience. That is what Stan Smith endeavored to do in 2014, when the sneaker brand decided to open a pop-up store shaped like a giant shoebox. In addition to having a 100% corporate image, this original point of sale offered customers the opportunity to get their face printed in 3D on their shoes, instead of Stan Smith's face.

Apprehensive not to miss this new turn in technology, other retailers have also offered 3D printing services. Nevertheless, it is often offered online and is hindered by not having the necessary space to store machines. The experience is, nevertheless, equally rewarding since it allows consumers to express their tastes and to design their products individually, though this is not done directly in the store but rather on websites that provide them with 3D printing services. Beyond simplicity and customization, 3D printing is also a green consumption practice that is sustainable. In the fashion sector, 3D printing has also been introduced by brands to design customized shoes. Shoe brands offer to customize the heels of women's shoes, thanks to 3D printing that allows adaptation to customers' tastes. Here, then, is another way of conceiving fashion that manifests according not to brands' desires, but rather to customers' demands. Yet, the shoe industry is not the only one to benefit from this new technology; accessories is another sector that has used 3D printing to innovate. This technology, accessible online, allows customers to create their accessories in just two or three clicks. Thus, 3D printing improves the online customer experience and creates a strong relationship between the brand and its clients.

On the other side, in the cosmetic sector, Nail Artistik revolutionized nail art by introducing an additive technology that prints nail polish, adding the elements layer by layer to form the final design, onto the nails and by delighting passersby in shopping malls with the offer of a 3D manicure. The recent launch of Mink in the 3D cosmetics industry, an American startup created in 2014, allows users to choose any color from a website or in the real world, using a simple software already in existence, to print in color a blusher, an eye shadow, a lipstick, or any other type of makeup. Such 3D technology is currently focused on the pigmentation of an existing makeup base. For Mink, the 3D printing technology of the manufacturer Orleans Cosmetics consists of three technological innovations: the personalization of makeup for small series, the possibility of a laser marking on powders, or metallic packaging. Beyond factors of personalization and creativity, 3D printing is also a key solution to save time when it comes to creating an ephemeral point of sale. This was the case for Louis Vuitton, with its fully 3D printed pop-up store that debuted in Australia in 2016. This ambitious project was achieved in just two weeks. Louis Vuitton managed to create a 100% personalized space in the colors of its most recent collection, all tailor-made. It was a most remarkable achievement by the luxury brand, which definitely does not hesitate to innovate when it comes to promoting its collections.

3D PRINTING TO DESIGN ON-DEMAND CREATIVE LUXURY EXPERIENCES

The luxury sector is strongly related to the innovations of 3D printing. On the one hand, 3D printing technology allows luxury houses to add other practices to their traditional manufacturing techniques. Current 3D printing allows luxury companies to bring a form of personalization in a sector in which the uniqueness of the piece is important. In addition, luxury is more intended for small series rather than large ones and 3D printing meets this demand for production of small series with high added value.

This added value comes from the fact that parts can be made from one machine. This uniqueness in terms of tooling considerably reduces the production time and allows a great freedom in terms of creativity. Furthermore, haute couture designers have taken the lead and are now creating 3D printed pieces. The objective of haute couture designers is to unleash creativity as 3D printing technology is offering ever more innovative creations in terms of design or materials. For example, the designer Iris van Herpen is positioned today as an ambassador of 3D printing in the luxury and haute couture sector.

TREND 8.3

3D PRINTING AND HAUTE COUTURE: IRIS VAN HERPEN'S DRESS

Dutch fashion designer Iris van Herpen attracted public attention during the Fashion Week in Paris in 2018 with her "Bird," a silicone dress and 3D printed skeleton piece. For the designer, fashion should not forget how nature is itself artificial and technology is simpler than nature, which is complex. Softness characterizes this new collection from the designer. Entitled the "foliage dress," it was created by using a 3D printer that integrates Polyjet technology to print multiple materials simultaneously. The materials of the dress were made of a high-tech synthetic resin. In addition, the dress was printed directly onto transparent and lightweight tulle of 0.8 millimeters for "optimal softness." As the resin "hardens" under ultraviolet light, the designer has interchanged the material to create natural variations in color and transparency. The entire process took about 260 hours and 60 hours of manual work thereafter. The post-processing work was quite manageable because the structures printed in 3D tended to distort naturally. For the fashion designer, this design is a fusion of precisely controlled 3D digital modeling and the less predictable analog nature of distortion.

Thus, 3D printing can be regarded as a future modern movement in the fashion industry as it allows fashion designers to design unexpected creations. Thanks to a meticulous modeling, the constraints of matter, weight, and size are thought through from conception to realize new creations, which adapt perfectly to each wearer's shape. One more challenge is to expand the range of printable textiles in three dimensions and gain fluidity.

Additionally, 3D printing allows different brands in the luxury sector to create packaging or other wrapping products. Luxury brands can also adopt highly customizable communication tools. By positioning themselves with an innovative technology, they also succeed in revitalizing their image and offer innovative and engaging communication tools for the consumer.

TREND 8.4

LOCKHEED MARTIN FILES PATENT TO PRINT DIAMONDS

The American company Lockheed Martin, best known for its activities in the field of aeronautics or defense, presented in August 2016 a patent for the development of a 3D printer capable of producing synthetic diamond objects. The printer requires the combination of two materials: a ceramic powder and a so-called "pre-ceramic" polymer. The latter has the property of turning into a ceramic material when heated to a high temperature. The method described by Lockheed Martin begins with the deposition of a thin layer of ceramic powder on the printer tray followed by the extrusion of a transverse layer of the object from the polymeric material. The process is then repeated until the final form of the object is obtained. Finally, the mixture is baked at a high temperature to be solidified. Once the remaining powder residues are removed, the final diamond object is unveiled. However, the patent does not indicate whether it is the printer that will heat the object or a dedicated oven. Heating may require spending several hours, or even days, in high temperature ovens. This innovation could also eventually find applications in the field of jewelry. This patent would enable jewelry artisans to create highly customizable pieces and combine multiple materials into a single creation.

Luxury is often associated with the manufacture of high-end products crafted in a traditional way with ancestral know-how. This know-how was, nevertheless, at the time, advanced technology, just like additive manufacturing. Luxury houses can benefit from 3D printing technology and offer new products and new experiences to their customers through various means:

- **Reinforcing the feeling of exclusivity**. Many brands find in additive manufacturing the opportunity of limited series, capsule collections, or even a unique object.
- **Reducing manufacturing time**. For parts or finished product, manufacturing cycles are shorter, and customers have come to expect speed.
- **Embracing a responsible production**. Additive manufacturing techniques are practiced locally. In addition to reduced deadlines, they support local employment.
- **Reducing manufacturing costs**. The technique of addition of layers, rather than subtraction of material, avoids the loss of expensive materials (up to 80% of a metal used, for example, can be wasted through a traditional technique).

Therefore, we can ask the question: Why should 3D luxury companies consider 3D printing technology to offer new customer experiences online and in-store? The first reason that should motivate luxury brands to introduce additive manufacturing in the design of their experiential offerings is the prototyping allowed by this technology, which can be achieved in less than 48 hours: to control a shape, a model, to validate a concept and an idea, and then to produce the pieces, such as heel shapes, clasps, leather chains, and even soft, flexible embroidery. The second advantage of 3D printing for luxury businesses is the singularity and the tailor-made customer experience. In fact, one of the strengths of 3D printing is the resulting ability of consumers to produce unique parts, where many manufacturers only operate from large orders. It is therefore possible to create tailor-made pieces, depending on the morphology of a body, captured geometrically by a machine. The third reason is the technological solutions that 3D printing represents, such as printing titanium watch frames for the watchmaker Officine Panerai luxury brand, which has resulted in a weight reduction of 40%. This can also be associated with the use of other technologies in the aeronautic sector. Finally, the use of 3D printing responds to consumer engagement and consumers' ethical behaviors. Indeed, 3D printing is eco-friendly and consumes only the material strictly necessary to design the object; there is no waste (save for excess powder, which is reused), unlike the traditional subtractive manufacturing energy balance; and 3D printing has the added benefit of being manufactured locally, as noted above: no need to manufacture in Asia or in other developing countries. It also minimizes the risk of overproducing and overstocking an object as the manufacture is being done on demand, quickly.

However, 3D printing technology can present certain challenges for luxury businesses. First of all, the main challenge is to revolutionize traditional manufacturing as well as to propose a new direction: ultra-personalization. The risk, in terms of compromising intellectual property, remains high with the counterfeiting of models and files because there is a legal vacuum in this area. However, a legislative framework is in preparation for the future. The rules are identical to those of intellectual property law, which stipulates that a designer cannot be dispossessed of his/her copyright. As to the question of which materials we can print with, more than 200 materials are now exploitable. This is still not huge, but progress is rapid and we can now print on a base of materials such as polymers, polyamides, metal, steel, aluminum, silver, gold, and ceramic, although glass remains, at the moment, in the testing phase. We can then consider that 3D printing is a revolution similar to that of the digital/Internet. Luxury companies should be aware of the issues and future changes. This revolution is part of the design: namely, to think about the concept and the packaging differently. It is a revolution of creation and innovation. There is then a need for framing the design and shaping it in order not to miss the opportunity. Currently, 3D printing is a flourishing technology, replete with fabulous craftspersons who use 3D, and there are opportunities for opening up an extraordinary space for creators. Indeed, the 3D printing of luxury goods is already happening. We will create for ourselves or create for others, and develop a new technology that does not destroy the value of luxury: there is still a lot of learning to be done regarding this promising and revolutionary new technology.

SUMMARY

This chapter illustrates the challenges and advantages related to the use of 3D printing faced by luxury and fashion houses when creating tailor-made and unique on-demand customer experiences. As highlighted in this chapter, optimization of production processes, customization possibilities, cost optimization (storage with printing on-demand, production, as well as prototyping), creation of complex shapes, etc. are amongst the advantages of this innovation. The world of 3D printing opens new creative fields and facilitates potentially incredible advances in the luxury and fashion sector when compared to traditional techniques. Despite its current limitations, such as limited materials, environmental issues, costs and accessibility, 3D printing offers interesting predictions for different luxury and fashion businesses (accessories, jewelry, watchmaking, wearables, etc.).

Therefore, for luxury businesses, 3D printing is an area that they should observe closely as advances are being made quickly. In its report, Gartner (2017b) defines this fashion category under the term "3D-printed Wearables," and places the current era at the very beginning of the cycle for emerging technologies. This is a crucial period for the future of this technology in the fashion sector, which sees many digital players positioning themselves in the marketplace in a way that can assist the professionals in the luxury sector in the appropriation of this technology so that it is integrated in a natural way into their usual practices.

PART III

DIGITAL LUXURY EXPERIENCE: WHAT'S NEXT?

9

SWITCH TO THE EXPERIENTIAL MARKETING MIX (7ES) AND DESIGN THE ULTIMATE DIGITAL LUXURY EXPERIENCE

INTRODUCTION AND SCOPE

This chapter is based on the fundamental idea of the strategic framework of the new "experiential marketing mix." This framework (Figure 9.1) highlights controllable components of the mix luxury companies can use to implement effective experiential marketing and communication actions in order to create and share value with their customers. The components of the experiential marketing mix refer to the 7Es: Experience, Exchange, Extension, Emphasis, Empathy capital, Emotional touchpoints, and Emic/etic process. By implementing this new experiential framework, marketing managers can concentrate on the seven key decision domains related to the 7Es that constitute the experiential marketing mix, while designing luxury experience offers and forming their marketing plans. The 7Es are connected with each other and relate to decision-making, which means that a decision in one domain can affect strategic or marketing decisions in others. Luxury companies should build up a combination of the 7Es which can help them meet their organizational and strategic objectives, and guarantee a strong and sustainable competitive advantage generated by value creation and sharing, the highest level of customer satisfaction and loyalty, and a positive image offline and online. The 7Es of the experiential marketing mix are presented in the sections below.

Experiential marketing mix	Marketing mix
☐	☐
☐ Experience	☐ Product
☐ Exchange	☐ Price
☐ Extension	☐ Place
☐ Emphasis	☐ Promotion
☐ Empathy capital	☐ People
☐ Emotional touchpoints	☐ Physical
☐ Emic/etic process	☐ Process

Figure 9.1   The experiential marketing mix vs. the traditional marketing mix

Source: Adapted from Batat (2019a)

EXPERIENCE

Pine and Gilmore (1998) state that companies can achieve a competitive advantage and differentiate themselves within a highly competitive market by producing experiences instead of products. Experience should, then, be considered as a new category of offer that can be marketed to consumers. Also, luxury companies can produce experiences by taking a consumer-centric approach that focuses on cognitive, emotional, physical, intellectual, or even spiritual aspects. This section focuses on the offer of "Experience" itself as the first component of the "7Es" of the new experiential marketing mix that replaces the "P" of "Product," which is part of the traditional marketing mix based on the 7Ps. Following this perspective, new tools, such as the Experience Territory Matrix (ETM) as well as the EXQUAL tool to measure and improve the quality of customer experiences developed by Batat (2019a), can be used by luxury companies to create and design a suitable, satisfying, and profitable luxury digital experience.

EXPERIENCE TERRITORY MATRIX ETM

According to Batat (2019a), the Experience Territory Matrix (ETM) is a tool that helps luxury companies manage their portfolio based on experiences instead of products. The ETM is also a long-term strategic planning tool that helps luxury businesses consider opportunities by reviewing their portfolio of experiential offerings and the way they are perceived by their customers to decide where to invest in order to improve the quality of digital luxury experience, to renew the offer or services, and to develop new experiences to maintain customers. The ETM introduces four typologies of customer experiences that take into account a customer's perception of respect and the company's customer-centricity. These two bipolar constructs – consumer's perception of respect and company's customer-centricity – led to the identification of four "experiential territories," namely, enchantment, re-enchantment, disenchantment, and the enchantment-gap (Figure 9.2).

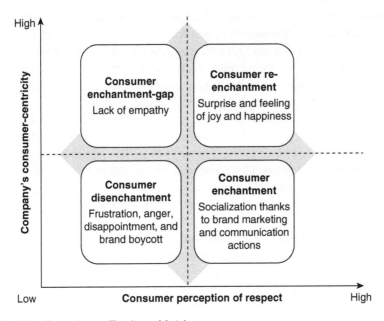

Figure 9.2   The Experience Territory Matrix

Source: Adapted from Batat (2019a)

- The construct of a consumer's perception of respect refers to a customer's feeling of being respected from his/her own perspective. This construct suggests that respect for customers is a major component that consumers take into consideration when evaluating their consumption experiences and reconsidering their relationships with the firm.
- The second construct, the company's customer-centricity, refers to the ability of firms to develop a solid management commitment, an organizational shift, schemes and process support, and revised financial metrics (e.g., Shah et al., 2006).

These two concepts help explain the paradoxes related to the subjectivity of customers and the way they perceive their consumption and shopping experiences within particular consumer cultures related to a specific territory:

- **Enchantment territory**. In the ETM, customer experience enchantment can be produced when a customer's perception of respect is high and the company's consumer-centricity is low. This means that the customer is enchanted in his/her relationships with other consumers although the company's customer-orientation is low. In fact, strong social interactions amongst customers in experiential settings when the company or the luxury brand is present can help the company to enchant its customers even though its customer-centricity is low, since customers may show satisfaction because they network, meet, and connect with new people, build social bonds, develop their social capital and social network, etc.
- **Re-enchantment territory**. As shown in the ETM, customer experience re-enchantment can be produced when the customer's perception of respect is high and the company's consumer-centricity is high too. This means that the customer is re-enchanted and positively surprised by the way the company treated him/her. In terms of feelings, customers might feel not only respected by the company, but also valued, considered, and unique.
- **Disenchantment territory**. Customer experience disenchantment can be produced when both the customer's perception of respect and the company's consumer-centricity are low. This means that the customer is frustrated, disappointed, and upset because of a feeling of being disrespected by the company, which does not employ a policy that is centered on its customers and their functional and emotional needs. This will produce a negative experience that leads the customer to look for other brands, products, and services offered by other luxury companies that provide them with respect and positive experiences.
- **Enchantment-gap territory**. The enchantment-gap experience is produced when a customer's perception of respect is low and the company's consumer-centricity is high. This means that the customer does not feel respected by the company, although the company's strategy is customer-oriented. This mismatch between the company's approach and the customer's perception can be explained by the lack of a deep understanding of the meanings customers attribute to their experiences.

EXQUAL TOOL

In order to measure the quality of customer experience from the perspectives of both the consumer and the company, Batat (2019a) proposed the conceptual framework "EXQUAL" to help luxury professionals and managers improve the quality of their customer experiences online and offline. Drawing on prior exhaustive research in service literature and the recent development of the SERVQUAL instrument, the EXQUAL, which combines four main measurement components (human, offering, environment, and value), is a tool that allows luxury companies to consider various elements to measure the quality of the perceived customer experience, as it is estimated through the four dimensions that are believed to represent customer experience quality.

EXCHANGE

Involving consumers in the co-creation of supply and consumption experiences is not an end in itself. A luxury company would engage in the co-creation process if the participation of the consumer is considered as a value that emerges from the "Exchange" between the customer and the company, which is the second component of the "7Es" of the experiential marketing mix, replacing the "P" of "Price" in the traditional marketing mix approach. Value-in-exchange can encompass different elements (e.g., self-fulfillment, confidence in skills, joy, fun, belonging, accomplishment, relational, self-respect, excitement, interpersonal) that are dependent upon the context in which the co-creation process is implemented, the objectives of the company, and the outcomes sought by customers. Thus, creating a value with consumers requires transparency, and therefore the sharing of information. Beyond products and services, luxury companies should offer their consumers a real experience of co-creation. Value is no longer unilaterally created by the company, but created together with the consumer.

Vargo and Lusch (2006, 2007) developed a new vision of consumers in services by introducing the concept of Service-Dominant Logic (SDL). They defined a new approach that underlines the shift in the marketing thinking from products towards a greater attention to services and facilities. Vargo and Lusch state that entire economies are service-based in which knowledge and specific skills are the fundamental sources for creating a sustainable competitive advantage by applying collaborative marketing tools. In fact, collaborative marketing is linked to the arrival of a new consumer with creative potential and his/her ability to co-create and co-produce offerings with the company. Collaborative marketing is applied to the fields of innovation, services, and design in which users/consumers are involved in improving products through their opinions, ideas, and suggestions. Luxury companies should, therefore, consider their customers as partners and economic actors capable of carrying the values of the enterprise or the brand, to communicate them, and to propose creative solutions to improve the quality of the experience, including products and services.

Collaborative marketing allows luxury companies to differentiate themselves from the competitors, and thus retain their customers by involving them and sharing values with them. In fact, collaborative marketing aims to engage customers in the creation process of the offer, which can take several forms. For example, consumers may be involved in product development (design, logo, packaging, etc.) or in the communication policy (promotion on social networks, participation in an advertisement, creation of a video, etc.). Consumers' participation depends on the degree of their creative potential and the level of involvement: consumers can vote for the design, name, or logo of a new product; animate a group of consumers around a brand; or co-create the product with the company. Today, collaborative marketing is booming thanks to the democratization of the use of social media and technologies that contribute to the development of creative exchanges between consumers and businesses. So, the exchange between a company and its consumers is rewarding for both of them as the consumers feel invested with an important mission and luxury companies can use the creative potential of their customers. From a company point-of-view, there are three main advantages in using collaborative marketing:

- To take advantage of the creative potential and ideas of customers;
- To know them better and retain them in the long term;
- Consumers who co-create can also talk about their actions and the new products they created.

Therefore, customers who are willing to collaborate can be involved at all stages of the offer development of the luxury brand: production and proposal of ideas, testing and validation of products and prototypes, communication and promotion, etc. The profile, knowledge, and status of the customer can guide the company in its choice to involve the customer upstream, downstream, or throughout the creation and production process, at the launch of a new product as well as during the different stages of the customer experience.

EXTENSION

To understand the fundamental triggers of the experience over a period of time, luxury houses need to design customer experience online and offline as a continuum that includes both extra- and intra-domestic experiences and explores the dynamic between the two consumption spheres to guarantee customer satisfaction and loyalty. Digital luxury experience offerings should be considered as an "Extension," another E of the experiential marketing mix. This approach influences luxury companies to broaden their vision by shifting the focus from the "P" of "Place" in the traditional marketing mix logic to a more extended consideration of customer experience that is dynamic, evolving, and goes beyond the physical environment.

In philosophy, Dewey developed the "experience continuum theory," which states that each experience includes aspects from experiences that have occurred in the past and influences in some manner the value and the quality of experiences that happen in the future. In applying the experience continuum theory to the experience of education, Dewey states that: "educational experience involves both continuity and interaction between the learner and what is learned" (1938: 10). Thus, Dewey's idea is that experience results from the integration of two principles:

- Continuity, which refers to almost all experiences (previous and current) that are accepted onward and affect upcoming experiences and choices;
- Interaction, which is defined as the neutral and inner circumstances of an experience.

Drawing on Dewey's research, luxury customer experience should at each stage build on what has been learned in the previous stages including the alternative and informal stages. In fact, experience and consumption do not directly relate because some experiences are not related to shopping or consumption (e.g., personal or family experiences that prevent or alter the development of future consumption experiences). The challenge of the experience continuum is to provide customers with quality consumption experiences involving all the senses that will result in advancing their learning, and their creative potential in their forthcoming experiences in order to create an experiential continuum. Therefore, the continuum of experience includes all cognitive (intellectual), affective (emotional), and behavioral changes during a lifecycle as new experiences adjust and change existing models. Furthermore, the experience continuum integrates the idea that any experience that is high in indirect service provision is also one that generates more opportunities for co-creation, up to auto-creation.

EMPHASIS

In the traditional marketing mix, communication is applied with a push logic to deliver messages to the audience. However, due to an increase in traditional and digital communication platforms, and the rise of experiential expectations, this is less efficient and luxury brands have had to compete with creative originality in terms of communication to get their message across. For this reason, it is important for luxury houses to shift the focus from a traditional communication policy focusing on brand content and media to a more holistic approach based on a brand culture emphasis that humanizes the luxury brand by bringing its personality to life, to create a strong relationship with its customers and thus differentiate the brand from its competitors.

A brand culture emphasis refers to the way luxury companies should use consumption culture elements to connect with their customers. Instead of using brand promotion, as in the "P" of "Promotion" that is part of the traditional marketing mix, the emphasis on brand cultural meaning provides a necessary complement to promotional strategies by including a focus on the meanings that are embedded and shaped by particular cultural settings and the meanings that the luxury brand shares with its customers. According to Batat (2019a), the transformation of branded content into cultural branding is a consequence of three main changes that have affected communication strategies and the content of messages to fit with the emerging consumption trends within a digital and experiential era:

- **The media context**. With the rise of the Internet and digitalization of societies, access to advertising is becoming easier and consumers are more and more involved. Thus, it becomes difficult to reach a large number of consumers with this multiplicity of media, which results in the fragmentation and the dispersion of audiences. Previously, there were only a few media sources (e.g., television, radio, cinema), which exposed a large number of people to the content of advertisers. The democratization of technologies gives new ideas to marketing and communication professionals, who occasionally ask their consumers to create their advertising.
- **The socioeconomic context**. In recent years, society, more specifically western society, has begun to feel that communication cannot ignore the ecology movement, inspired by a distrust of capitalism and the global economic crisis of 2008. This has led to the rise of new behaviors. Consumers today are expecting a more "responsible" communication content. The social and environmental responsibility of luxury companies is a crucial element that should not be neglected because today's consumers are very sensitive to social and ecological issues.
- **Historical context**. The evolution of communication can be divided into three stages: modernity, postmodernity, and alter-modernity. Modernity is a way of communicating that aims to valorize the brand as an agent of humanity's progress towards the satisfaction of its desires. In the postmodern era, communication and advertising were marked by self-deprecation, derision, and mockery; the brand made fun of itself. The current era refers to alter-modernity, which shows that communication is no longer conceived as a message centered on the brand, but as a service or content to the benefit of the consumer.

The shift from brand content to brand culture can be explained by the motivation of consumers to live experiences with the brands that are charged with meanings. Brand culture signifies that the cultural norms of brands affect brand significance and value in the marketplace. The brand culture concept captures the theoretical gap between brand identity as a strategic concept and consumer understandings of brand persona (e.g., Schroeder and Salzer-Mörling, 2006). From a cultural standpoint, luxury brands can be considered as communication items that the brand manager desires customers to buy into – a symbolic setting as expressed by the brand personality. Therefore, theoretically, brand management refers to delivering messages, which are expected to be connected to the brand owner's objective (Kapferer, 2008). Holt (2002), who examines brands in relation to the evolution of marketing practice and consumer culture in the current marketplace, argues that marketers struggle to incorporate their brands into different groups of popular culture. Brands that effectively achieve this cultural emplacement can, consequently, make consumers produce unique and distinct identities and, surprisingly, resist conformist business influences.

Brand culture is, then, a central element in building a strong brand since it is co-constructed by injecting cultural meanings embedded within different consumption experiences. Even if the luxury company is the starting point of the brand and defines its initial outlines, it cannot alone generate values, attitudes, and shared behaviors amongst consumers in their experiences with the brand. The brand community is an integral part of this cultural construction because brand culture can therefore go beyond the company. To be able to influence this culture, the brand manager should understand the mechanisms of the emergence of cultural meanings in consumption experiences. Holt (2004) states that the brand should thus be viewed as a cultural narrator that delivers identity value by addressing a collective meaning embedded within individuals' consumption experiences: "a brand becomes iconic when it delivers an identity myth: a simple story that responds to cultural tension by tapping into an imaginary world rather than the everyday lives of consumers. The aspirations expressed in this myth are the imaginary expressions of the identity desire of individuals" (2004: 8). To do so, luxury brand managers have to identify the mechanisms behind brand culture in a community and the characteristics of these cultural elements to design suitable and meaningful customer experiences.

EMPATHY CAPITAL

Empathy is the ability to take the perspective of others, to understand their reasoning and their emotional state. For a marketing manager, more specifically, it is the ability to take the customers' point-of-view and put him/herself in their place. "Empathy capital" is part of the experiential marketing mix framework, replacing the "P" of "People" in the traditional marketing mix. It helps luxury brands to design emotional and suitable digital customer experiences with employees who are able to empathize with customers, and efficiently respond to their needs. A good experiential marketing mix is then based on the idea that with a strong empathy capital, employees who are in contact with customers would think "customer first" at both emotional (how does he/she feel today) and cognitive levels (what does he/she need according to his/her feeling today). This can be achieved from the moment employees develop an adaptive empathy capital that helps them to use their social and interpersonal intelligence to identify the profile, moods, aspirations, and expectations of the client's experiential moment.

Most of the time, empathy is referred to as "I feel your pain," a shared emotional state that goes beyond "I know how you feel." Empathy is a multidimensional concept and involves both emotion and cognition. Applying empathy to the experiential marketing mix highlights the ideas underlined in Greenson's definition (1960), which suggests that a company's employees should have the ability to put themselves in their customers' shoes. Consequently, empathy can be studied as a broader concept, implying altruism, projection, intersubjectivity, compassion, or identification. Creating an empathic luxury experiential setting can be achieved either through a controlled process or instinctively that leads to behavioral outcomes. Empathy in customer experience is, then, the ability of salespeople to perceive and be sensitive to the emotional states of their customers, often combined with a motivation to worry about their well-being. The empathy of people (e.g., salespeople, waiters, front desk, and other company employees) who have direct relationships with customers refers to a complex mental state in which different perceptual, cognitive, motivational, and emotional processes interact with the "others." Empathy is deeply embedded in the lived customer experience, and it is this shared experience that allows people to recognize customers not only as clients, but as like-minded people who wish to be treated according to the logic: "I treat customers the way I would like to be treated."

Customer experience empathy includes two connected but different processes through which sellers (perceivers) relate to buyers (targets). The empathy experience framework assembles a set of processes that generate empathy that fit into three comprehensive categories:

- Experience sharing: vicarious sharing of customers'/targets' internal conditions;
- Mentalizing: clearly seeing (and possibly examining) customers'/targets' mental conditions and what underlies them;
- Prosocial concern: conveying a stimulus to advance customers'/targets' experiences (for instance, by decreasing their anxiety).

Therefore, empathy capital is important for luxury companies, and particularly for customer experience design because it allows marketers and brand managers to truly understand and decode the hidden needs and emotions of the customers they are designing the experience for. As such, luxury companies can design customer experiences that go beyond the three dimensions of an offering (product or service) – attractiveness, viability, and sustainability – by developing the empathy capital of their employees and training them to develop and practice their empathy potential. It is obvious that marketing professionals who demonstrate empathy provide better customer experiences with higher satisfaction. The best approach to train professionals in developing their empathy skills is to make sure that their professionalized empathy is customer-centric, focused on customer well-being, helpful, intentional, self-conscious, self-inspiring, and maintainable.

EMOTIONAL TOUCHPOINTS

Customer touchpoints are the points of contact between the company (products and services) and customers, who will interact with these service encounters and their experience might be affected in a positive or a negative way. Thus, touchpoints are an essential characteristic and one of the most important pillars of the customer experience design. However, in the actual definition and practices of experience touchpoints, emotions and the way they are generated and expressed by customers are not considered in the process and the focus is more on the tool or the platform of contact rather than the emotion generated by the tools. We know that a successful contact that emotionally engages the customer is a fundamental part of the success of the customer experience design. Therefore, the starting point for identifying customer experience touchpoints should focus more on emotions to define the touchpoint and not the other way around. Batat (2019a) proposed an approach to emotional touchpoints that could offer a very tangible input to the customer experience design base and shows how to support such customer emotional engagement in practice. "Emotional touchpoints" are a component of the "7Es" of the experiential marketing mix, replacing the "P" of "Physical evidence" which is part of the traditional marketing mix.

Emotional touchpoints go beyond the idea of customer journey touchpoints in which customers might find a brand online or in an advertisement, see evaluations and reviews, ask friends who have already had an experience with the brand, visit a company's website, shop at a retail store, or contact customer service before, during, and after their experience. In the journey touchpoints, luxury companies only focus on the individual transactions through which customers interact with parts of the business and its offerings in a very functional and optimized way. It is relatively easy to apply and control these touchpoints in order to ensure customers' satisfaction by connecting them with the company's services, products, salespeople, etc. Therefore, while customer touchpoints refer to the brand's points of customer contact from start to finish of the customer journey in a very functional way, emotional touchpoints primarily focus on the emotional impact of the moments where customers interact with different services and people. Thus, customer touchpoints, as described in prior works focusing on services and the customer journey, offer a narrow view since they focus only on those moments where a customer/user interacts in some way with the luxury company's services or products, such as arriving at the store, talking to a salesperson, or having a dinner at a restaurant, etc. The idea of using emotional touchpoints allows luxury companies to develop a deeper understanding of the emotions related to the experience by focusing more on the moments where the customer's memories are being activated. Were they touched in an emotional way (feelings) or a cognitive way (profound and long-term memories); this may happen independently or where there were profound moments in a customer's contact with the company (e.g., living a dinner experience or a hotel experience); or it may be a case of small, short-term interactions. All can have the same significance for the customer in terms of emotional and cognitive impact.

Emotional touchpoints were first used in the medical field, especially in nursing research, to improve the patient and family experience in hospitals and to support doctors, nurses, and other personnel to deliver compassionate, empathic, and dignified care (e.g., Dewar et al., 2009). Furthermore, evidence suggests that focusing on subjective experiences as customers define and perceive them is a successful approach to analyzing and understanding the changes in the touchpoints tools as well as marketing and communication practices. This allows for the development of innovative techniques and the creation of new tools and staff training to better interact with customers. Thus, establishing a contact and a conversation with customers through the use of emotional touchpoints is very helpful for luxury companies to guarantee customer satisfaction and loyalty, and thus create a durable competitive advantage.

Therefore, emotional touchpoints are one of the fundamental facets of customer experience design and an important component of the experiential marketing mix. They represent the connection between the service provider or the company's employees and the end user or customer. In this way, emotional touchpoints have to be first considered in terms of the emotions they generate and identification of the touchpoints that generate them and not the other way, as in the traditional logic of customer touchpoints. The emotional touchpoints approach is based on the use of empathic and ethnographic methods combined with other tools applied in the nursing and care field, such as a card-based toolkit (e.g., Bate and Robert, 2007; Dewar, 2013).

EMIC/ETIC PROCESS

Process, as applied in the 7Ps of the traditional marketing mix, refers to the idea that the value delivered to the customer follows a top-down (etic) logic in which meanings are created and delivered by the firm throughout the customer journey. Using an emic/etic approach fundamentally involves the observation of a single cultural group of consumers and offers structured and embedded observations about consumer behaviors that help the company in the design and the adaptation of the customer experience which matches different consumption cultures and subcultures. The "Emic/etic process" is a component of the experiential marketing mix that replaces the "P" of "Process" in the traditional marketing logic of the 7Ps. It extends the vision of process from a one-way, top-down process to inject consumer value into an iterative process that takes into account both consumer and company visions which are embedded within a particular cultural setting.

While emic and etic perspectives in understanding and organizing social behaviors were first applied in the cultural anthropology field, the use of these opposing approaches has developed since 1970 and become prevalent throughout several fields, specifically in studying consumer behavior, consumption cultures, and consumption meanings. However, as the use of emic and etic perspectives became more widespread, a number of definitions have been proposed that were either contradictory or confusing. Headland et al. state that "authors equate emic and etic with verbal versus nonverbal, or as subjective knowledge versus scientific knowledge, or as good versus bad, or as ideal behavior versus actual behavior, or as private versus public" (1990: 21).

In using emic and etic perspectives in the understanding of consumer behavior, attitudes, and cultural consumption schemes as well as using them to generate consumption experiences that are both intellectual and perceptual, these two thoughts underline opposing standpoints as they analyze behaviors by considering either the perspective of the insider (observed: consumer), or the outsider (observer: company). Therefore, the distinction between etic and emic can contrast the knowledge produced on behaviors of a community or social group (etic) and the knowledge produced by the members of the community themselves (emic). Assuming the subjectivity of customer experience, emic and etic viewpoints play an important role in defining the process that the luxury company can use to deliver meaningful luxury digital experiences. Therefore, the process by which to understand and design meaningful customer experiences should incorporate the two perspectives – emic and etic – because they are complementary, and valuable to the study of a specific consumption culture in which the experience is shaped and embedded (e.g., Patton, 2010). The use of both emic and etic processes is supposed to be an advantage instead of a constraint or a source of confusion when it comes to customer experience design. As the anthropologist Agar argues, "etic and emic, the universal and the historical particular, are not separate kinds of understanding when one person makes sense of another. They are both part of any understanding" (2011: 39). That said, differences between etic and emic processes exist and can be underscored by acknowledging the variables that can affect the understanding and guide the design of customer experiences. Amongst these variables, we can mention the following: the researcher's own system of values, the target's age, gender, sexual orientation, ethnicity, etc.

Therefore, for luxury companies, in order to design the ultimate luxury experience and offer their customers a satisfying, emotional as well as convenient customer experience online and offline, they should switch from a traditional vision of marketing based on the implementation of the 4Ps or 7Ps to a more holistic approach through setting up a digital strategy that incorporates a balanced experiential mix of the 7Es described in this chapter.

SUMMARY

This chapter provided a better understanding of the experiential approach to luxury marketing and management. For luxury companies, the understanding and the implementation of a successful experiential offering in the digital space and the physical place need to be integrated into the comprehensive framework of customer experience marketing provided by markers, drivers, and outcomes of the experience as well as its translation through the 7Es of a new framework, namely the experiential marketing mix, which extends the marketing, communication, and management practices. In this progression, the experiential marketing mix framework is particularly relevant since it provides luxury professionals as well as digital marketing actors with a structured and coherent approach to understanding customer experience, which is rather fuzzy, abstract, and difficult to grasp.

10

FROM BIG DATA TO IMMERSIVE SMART DATA: INSIGHTS INTO DIGITAL LUXURY EXPERIENCE

INTRODUCTION AND SCOPE

It is frequently thought that statistics tell us how things function and that there is no more exhaustive analysis than that of big data. The luxury industry is not spared from the massive development of big data. Beyond services, luxury brands are currently implementing connected objects and digitalized flagships. The challenge is, indeed, to know customers better in order to sell better without risking or forgetting the very principles of luxury (its exclusivity, uniqueness, rarity, etc.). At first sight, luxury and data seem antithetical, which may explain a certain delay of the sector in its consideration. For one thing, luxury plays on the intangible, the emotional, and the exclusive, while big data evoke transparency, technology, and mass information. Also, luxury, a breeding ground for creation, is historically a supply and innovation market that works intuitively, while big data are primarily aimed at analyzing existing demand. However, with digitalization, social networks, the importance of tourism, and exchange rates, luxury companies simply cannot ignore the use of data in their strategies and marketing actions.

Already, luxury businesses are increasingly taking into account these data to reinforce their knowledge of the consumers and the links they have with them, which is necessary to know better their economic environment and, more broadly, the current world and its opportunities. Thus, data become the most loyal allies of luxury brands. They can use data to imagine trends and predict and anticipate the expectations of their customers. However, big data are not enough to design the ultimate customer experience in the phygital environment because they do not allow the contextualization of the act of purchase or consumption and so re-embed the experience within a particular cultural setting. That is why contemporary luxury companies need alternatives to get access to relevant as well as profitable data.

Distinct from big data, which rely on direct aspects and statistical modeling, immersive smart data are mainly related to individuals' perceptions and definitions of their own world. This alternative method is complementary to big data and is well adapted to study and analyze customer experiences, as it allows contextualizing the act of purchase or consumption within a particular cultural setting. By using immersive creative tools that allow an exhaustive analysis of the luxury experience offline and online as well as a study of its subjective, paradoxical, symbolic, and emotional dimensions, luxury houses are able to innovate based on the anticipation of the tangible and intangible needs of their customers as well as to design suitable experiences and create a competitive advantage.

Chapter 10 introduces immersive smart data as an alternative to studying digital luxury experiences. In contrast to big data analytical methods, whose purpose is to measure variables related to the process of purchasing luxury goods at the point of sale, immersive smart data methods are more qualitative, immersive, and experiential and place human creativity at the heart of the analysis and interpretation processes. In fact, although big data have been a major trend in terms of consumer surveys, they are no longer relevant in the context of studying the digital luxury experience and its functional as well as emotional dimensions. Cessation of this trend heralds the beginning of a new era of "immersive smart data" where the data should be as accurate as possible and of the highest quality while allowing commercial actions with a Return on Investment (ROI). Immersive smart data are, therefore, the most appropriate tool that luxury companies can use for studying and implementing customer experience in the phygital environment. Moreover, immersive smart data are also a source of inspiration for luxury companies looking for new ideas and concepts to create unique experiences. The importance of using this new immersive approach can be explained by the evolution of the proliferation of massive data on consumer behavior, the change in regulation in terms of the collection, management, and storage of big data as well as the importance for luxury brands to have quality data which are profitable. This chapter will first start with an overview of the definition of big data, how they are used by companies to learn more about consumers, and what the limitations are in relation to the use of massive storage of data. Then, the second part will explore the new concept of immersive smart data, the tools, and the way luxury companies can use smart data to gain deeper insights on their customers, and thus deliver them with the adequate customer experience online and offline.

UNCOVERING THE DATA LANDSCAPE

This section explores the topics related to the rise and the use of big data by companies by answering the following questions: What do we mean by big data? How are big data used in marketing? What are their tools and functions? What is the place of human beings in the data analysis process? And finally, what are today's limitations regarding the exploration, collection, management, and storage of the massive amounts of data generated?

BIG DATA – WHAT IS IT?

The term big data first appeared in the 2000s and was introduced to companies following the release of McKinsey's report in 2011. The first big data users were GAFA (Google, Amazon, Facebook, and Apple) because of the amount of data generated from their activities on the Internet. Today, other big data players have joined GAFA, including exchange platforms and social networks such as LinkedIn, Twitter, Microsoft, and Yahoo. "Big data" does not have an accurate definition, and several meanings coexist. This can be explained by the confusion in the understanding and application of the concept. Thus, big data refer to the massive data production that companies face today and how they should deal with it to better understand the commercial and marketing challenges big data represent. The difference between traditional data produced by businesses through surveys and other CRM as well as billing databases is not only the amount of information to be processed, but also the type and manner in which these data are generated, organized, and stored. With big data, luxury companies have moved from relational data to organized databases aligned along two major axes: (1) variable, which refers to the classification criteria and corresponding information entry, and (2) online registration, which takes us towards a classification system in which the data are diverse, not classified according to a previously defined model, non-relational, and with an unstructured element (e.g., content of emails sent by customers, recorded phone conversations, conversations on forums and social networks, traceability of connections to websites). The data available today have three main characteristics:

- **Big**. Massive data stored and organized in internal and external databases;
- **Varied**. Diverse data including text, digital, video, photographs, etc.
- **Fast**. Instant data generated by rapid and prompt responses.

A definition of big data introduced recently by Pierre Delort, author of the book *Big Data*, published in 2015, highlights the main characteristics of big data according to 3Vs: volume, velocity, and variety.

- **Volume**. This refers to unstructured data, raw text from email exchanges or conversations on social networks, images, videos, voice recordings, traces of connection to websites, or signals transmitted by the connected objects. These massive formats make treatment more complex.

- **Velocity**. Data need to be collected and processed more and more rapidly to meet the growing decision-making needs of companies with faster and more real-time decision-making processes.
- **Variety**. The explosion of data is linked to the creation of content by users and machines, commented content online, social media exchanges, the Internet of Things (IoT), Radio-Frequency Identification (RFID) technologies, iBeacons, geolocation data, and so forth.

To these three variables, two other "Vs" can be added: the "value" of the data related to their relevance for commercial purposes, and their "veracity," which refers to the quality of the data that were subsequently added.

BIG DATA FOR MARKETING

The competitive context and massive data accessibility have pushed companies in different sectors, especially in luxury, to use big data for marketing purposes in order to optimize their targeting, decision-making, and advertising investments. Today, the majority of decisions in companies (e.g., sectors such as air transport, telephone operators, insurance companies, hotels, and banks) are based on data that are collected, analyzed, and considered as a reliable source of information that does not incur great risk-taking in relation to intuitions and the analysis of human beings. For example, in the airline sector, KLM Royal Dutch Airlines facilitates socialization between travelers by exploiting social big data. By using data from social networks and passenger profiles, KLM Airlines offers its travelers a social travel experience by providing them with the opportunity to view the profile of passengers seated alongside them based on their hobbies. Under the name of "Meet & Seat," the airline offers travelers the ability to access and share Facebook, Google+, or LinkedIn profile data about themselves and other customers several days before the departure of the flight. In doing so, travelers can now choose their seat based on their affinity to other users.

All business sectors are nowadays involved in the utilization of big data to conduct market research, consumer insights, as well as for marketing and commercial purposes using privileged access to customer data. Amongst the sectors using big data, the following are very active:

- Big data have had a large role in the digital advertising sector – one of the pioneers in using search keywords to detect and identify client "intentions" or from the IP addresses of websites and online pages visited. Thanks to Search Engine Marketing (SEM) and other programs (e.g., Google Adwords for visibility on the Internet), retargeting techniques, connected objects, and subsequently developed algorithms as well as digital advertising and the purchase of advertising space on the Internet have been improved.
- Distribution is another very critical activity sector in terms of using big data to better target customers in order to increase online and in-store sales (e.g., data related to

website navigation, data from loyalty cards, purchase invoices, iBeacons). With massive data analysis, traditional retail businesses or pure players, such as Amazon, can implement personalized actions and recommendations tailored to each customer profile.

Furthermore, with the digital revolution, several businesses, jobs, and departments were created following the explosion of big data and their application in marketing and in the different business sectors. Table 10.1 summarizes the new jobs that have emerged in the big data era.

Table 10.1   Big data professional roles

Function	Characteristics	Principal role
Chief Data Officer (CDO)	Director of data and guardian of ethics with an engineer profile. Leads a team specializing in data acquisition, analysis, and exploitation	Manages his/her team for the supply of interesting and consistent data specific to the company's interests
Business Intelligence Manager	From an engineering background, his/her job is to facilitate the decision-making of the CDO. This job requires a strong knowledge of English, computers, and data management	Uses new technologies to set up dashboards and reporting tools to integrate them into the IT system and make them accessible to users within the company
Data Scientist	Has an engineer profile with a triple skill in management, computer science, and statistics. He/she is responsible for the collection, processing, evaluation and analysis of big data in order to optimize the company's strategy	The role is to create algorithms for the company's business that produce useful information, particularly in order to offer customers the products they are looking for
Data Analyst	He/she is an engineer and uses statistical techniques and specialized computer tools to organize, synthesize, and translate the information companies need to facilitate decision-making	The role is to make the data "speak" and to extract concrete indicators at the service of the general management to exploit them for commercial purposes
Data Miner	He/she has skills in computer science, statistics, and business	The role is to identify the information amongst multiple data, to make them exploitable and useful for the company
Master Data Manager	A data manager that organizes the company information for optimal exploitation	The role is to check that the data are compliant and organized according to the defined management rules
Data Protection Officer	Responsible for the protection of personal data in the organization, jurisdiction, computer science, and communication	The role is to provide recommendations for upstream projects

BIG DATA AND THE ROLE OF HUMAN INTELLIGENCE

Big data have contributed to changing the analytical stance and the role of humans in the collection and processing of data. With big data, the interviewer has become an observer of data collected spontaneously and expressed freely on social networks and other devices without relying on traditional focus groups or face-to-face interviews. Moreover, in big data, the distinction between quantitative and qualitative insights is out of date, as is sampling, and the establishment of associations and correlations is no longer as important as before. In the big data logic, human innovation is absent from the creative and problem-solving processes, as shown in Figure 10.1.

Figure 10.1   Human creativity in big data

A complementary approach (Figure 10.2) should, then, be considered by luxury companies in order to fully optimize their data analysis and implement digital and experiential strategies where they can combine both the efficiency of the data collected as well as the human element of creativity and free thought.

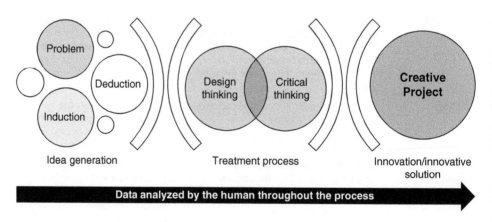

Figure 10.2   Human creativity through big data

In the context of big data, the starting point refers to existing massive data in unstructured databases that encompass information about the purchase behaviors of consumers, their reactions to promotions, the impact of advertisements, etc. This information is combined with other databases that include geographic information, weather, social media conversations, connected objects, and more, in order to generate new knowledge that makes sense and has commercial value. For example, Amazon has launched its personal assistant "Amazon Echo" to collect data on consumers by observing them in their consumption habits, especially in the field of fashion and clothing. In April 2017, Amazon unveiled its "Echo Look" product, a device that can take photos, make videos, and give feedback on the consumer's outfit. One can just give it the order: "Alexa, take a picture!" The device is voice activated, is connected to the owner's smartphone, and triggers a selfie. Its mobile app has a feature, Style Check, that can compare two outfits and decide which is best. The accessory was first on sale in the United States, for $200. To gain credibility in the world of fashion, Amazon has partnered with several fashion designers to refine its artificial intelligence dedicated to this connected object, which is considered not only as a clothing assistant and, also, a massive data collection mechanism for gaining insight into consumer behaviors in the field of fashion.

BIG DATA STORAGE AND PROCESSING TECHNOLOGIES

There are several technologies and algorithms that allow the collection and organization of massive data. Given the unstructured nature of big data information and the non-relational dimension of the data collected, new technologies have emerged to facilitate the collection, organization, and processing of this information in bulk derived from internal and external databases. Amongst these, there are two main technologies currently used by companies: NoSQL (No Structured Query Language) and Hadoop (inspired by Google's MapReduce, GoogleFS, and BigTable). These two technologies are, indeed, the pioneers in the field of big data, but they are not the only ones. Other similar or complementary technologies of storage or analysis of massive unstructured data exist, such as Storm, Hive, Pig, etc. Thus, the choice of a big data storage technology should be made according to the needs of the company and the quality of the storage. In terms of processing technologies for non-relational information from big data, there are five main technologies that companies are currently using: text-mining, graph-mining, machine-learning, data-visualization, and ontology. These technologies reveal new knowledge and have a common goal, which is the simplification of big data processing by providing companies with meaning and value.

- **Text-mining**. This method consists of counting occurrences (appearance of a term) as well as analyzing the meaning. This technology is founded on methods based on explicit rules (grammar) and data (dictionaries), or on learning or machine-learning.
- **Machine-learning**. This refers to design-learning systems that have the characteristic of being more and more efficient over time.

- **Graph-mining**. Allows the creation of relational graphs by isolating groups of information. This method is used by search engines on the Web to establish the "ranking" and to the detect communities and influencers on social networks.
- **Data-visualization**. Facilitates the reading and visualization of massive data via graphical formatting for real-time visualization of trends.
- **Ontology**. Refers to the update of "massively multifactorial" correlations, and thus confirms correlations, such as the impact of the weather on sales, or detects unexpected correlations.

BIG DATA AND DIGITAL LUXURY EXPERIENCE: THE LIMITS OF A TREND

Although big data produce interesting facts about the customer in the digital world and allow luxury companies to optimize the work of their teams and improve the ROI, they represent major gaps in the study of the customer experience and its tangible and intangible dimensions within the phygital era linking real and virtual spaces through a continuum that extends consumer experiences from offline to online, and vice versa. The enthusiasm of companies in all sectors of big data management activity, from tourism to luxury to education, has had an impact on marketing approaches. Big data have introduced changes in all strategic steps: market research and innovation, segmentation, communication, supply, design, retention policy, management of customer relations, staff training, recruitment, etc. Market research and consumer insights are an area that has been particularly disrupted by the introduction of big data in the study of consumer behaviors and profiles.

The impact of big data is mainly related to the change of logic in the way companies formerly conducted surveys. In fact, luxury companies have moved from the logic of new data production through consumer surveys to the logic of data recognition via the observation of trends revealed by the management of existing big data. Yet, American companies have begun to focus on data quality issues related to the "Big Data Bang" and have started producing new and complementary data in addition to the descriptive analysis of their big data. Despite the limitations of big data in terms of in-depth consumer insights related to experiences in the phygital environment, luxury companies are rather in favor of insights from big data, and the question of informational flood management is not relevant. In the luxury sector, the use of big data is not yet being questioned by companies due to obstacles related to data collection and analysis. These obstacles can include economic, financial, organizational, psychological, strategic, technological, and cultural elements (Figure 10.3).

Amongst the limitations of the use of big data, companies should consider the following:

- **Gaps related to the knowledge of customers and their tangible and intangible needs**. With the introduction of big data, consumers are no longer segmented by their actual

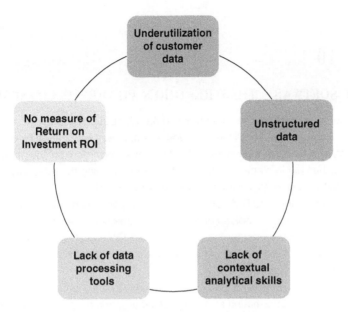

Figure 10.3   The main limitations of big data in the digital luxury experience

behaviors; rather, they are segmented by their browsing patterns and click rates. In addition, the completeness, relevance, and reliability of customer data, behaviors, and attitudes from big data management can also be questioned. Indeed, the data provided online by consumers might be consciously erroneous (the customer who filled in the wrong date of birth, place of residence, or email address due to suspicion with regard to the subsequent use of these data) or unconscious (error while entering information). On the other hand, consumers can use several connection devices (mobile phone, tablet, computer, etc.) to view information or purchase products. These devices are themselves used by several members of the family or shared by several people. This very random practice makes it difficult for companies to assign a cookie to a unique identifier – a key task to avoid losing customers in their multi-channel journey.

- **Limits related to the perception of intrusion**. The perception of intrusion linked to the use of retargeting techniques by companies can have a negative impact on the sharing of personal data. Consumers feel harassed and have more and more concerns about brands' use of their personal data, especially those from social networks, to offer targeted, personalized, and above all, repetitive advertisings. The loss of consumer confidence in the brand thus contributes to impoverishing, or even biasing the data collected on the targets. Consumers who no longer want to receive personalized information try to escape the possibilities of online spying using ethical and transparent browsers that do not allow the storage of their search history, IP address, geographical location, etc.

TREND 10.1

PRIVOWNY SOFTWARE THAT RESTORES POWER TO CONSUMERS

Privowny is a company that shares a vision based on values such as integrity and transparency to define a new approach to digitalization. Privowny empowers consumers by enabling them to control, protect, and manage their personal data from an environment they fully control. This startup company has put in place an ethical software questioning the relationship with companies which exploit the personal information of users for advertising and commercial purposes. On each page opened, the installed software establishes an accurate analysis of the site consulted by the user: how many cookies or so-called connection spies hosted by the site, what data were transmitted in the past by the user, etc. Even more useful, there is a tab that allows users to individually block cookies when surfing the Web without having the feeling of being tracked at the click of a mouse.

For users, this power should be in their control. In today's digital world, consumers are sharing more and more personal information and have little, if any, control over its use and the monetization of it. As consumer data usage and the cross-referencing of such data increase, privacy and consumer control become major concerns, but Privowny empowers consumers to create their own digital memory, manage their personal data, and market this information from a single platform that only they control.

- **Legal constraints related to the collection and use of customers' personal data**. The amount of information collected on the Internet and the development of more and more efficient algorithms have certainly enabled the monitoring of the consumer and the traceability of his/her behavior through geolocation or targeted marketing. However, these practices raise new issues in terms of the protection of personal data, and, therefore, regulations on the data collected and used by companies have come into force. In the French context, the use of personal data is regulated by the "Informatique et Libertés" law and the collection of indirect data on people, otherwise known as social networks (e.g., Facebook), is strictly prohibited. French regulations also limit the storage time of the data collected (e.g., connection data have a limited duration, unlike content data that are prohibited) and the type of information collected should be in line with the criteria defined by French law. The company collecting the data is also legally obliged to protect consumers even if it outsources data collection and retention. These regulations lead companies to invest in protection systems in addition to investing in big data while keeping in mind the limit related to the length of data retention, which exacerbates the situation in terms of comparison to data produced by companies through consenting consumer surveys in which information is stored and processed multiple times in a time-bound manner to derive value from changes in consumer behaviors, perceptions, and attitudes.

TREND 10.2

A NEW EUROPEAN REGULATION: GENERAL DATA PROTECTION REGULATION GDPR

Companies collecting consumer data must take into account the new General Data Protection Regulation (GDPR) law. This is new European privacy legislation implemented in 2017 and applicable from 2018. This new regulation redefines the legal framework for the collection, management, and use of personal data within the European Union. With the development of the Internet and new technologies, the previous legislation had very quickly been exceeded. However, the protection of privacy and personal data is a fundamental right, and it had been slightly undermined in recent years. GDPR will then mainly apply to economic players in all sectors, including the automotive sector. This obviously includes companies, but also businesses, administrations, associations, and local authorities. The GDPR aims to allow the consumer to control the use of his/her own personal data. If the company collects data in any way, it is crucial that it prepares carefully for this new legislation in order to avoid fines of up to 20 million euros. Although already partially defined by the 1995 regulation, the protection of personal data is reinforced by the GDPR. Companies are now required to obtain explicit consent to retrieve information about a person or a user.

The stakes of GDPR are too high to be ignored by luxury companies and they will urgently need to give priority to understanding their data: the nature, their storage location, the name of the person in charge, the level of security, and their use. An important problem for many brands in different sectors, especially luxury retailers given the rise of the omnichannel, is that customers can communicate through different touchpoints (Web, store, etc.), so the data can be stored in different systems and come in various forms. Retailers and other luxury businesses will need to harmonize all this information and understand what data are held, where, and how to protect them. Many luxury companies will also be required to appoint a data protection officer. Therefore, the GDPR marks a profound change in business habits regarding the collection, storage, and use of customer data. For luxury companies, the GDPR means that from May 2018, they will need to rethink their organization and their digital strategy in terms of data. To respect the GDPR regulation, luxury companies should apply the following procedures at both national and international levels:

- Obtain from clients their unequivocal consent regarding the processing of a consumer's personal data. Silence, pre-ticked boxes, or inactivity are not considered as consent.
- Delete personal data from their database in the case of a request. In the event of piracy of personal data, notify data breaches to the competent authorities within 72 hours.
- Appoint a data protection officer where the company processes a lot of sensitive data.
- Be aware that the definition of "personal data" is evolving. It now includes all identifying information, such as cookies and advertising identifiers.
- Understand that all companies in the European Union must comply. If data from EU residents are being stored, analyzed, or monitored, luxury companies operating in the EU market are subject to the laws of the GDPR.

- **Constraints related to the anonymity from big data**. The analysis of data from social networks is most often anonymous or attached to pseudonyms. In addition, the law obliges companies to process data anonymously and not to attach personal information (e.g., customer phone numbers and data to a mobile operator) to a well-defined profile. This anonymization of the data imposed by law, or stipulated by the consumer on social networks, makes the identification of the real profile of the consumer difficult, thus giving way to a rough analysis of behaviors.

TREND 10.3

FACEBOOK ACCUSED OF USING HIGHLY SENSITIVE DATA FOR COMMERCIAL PURPOSES

An Australian newspaper has recently revealed that Facebook has allegedly used highly sensitive data for commercial purposes. Although the founder of Facebook denies the existence of an internal document referring to tools developed by Facebook to analyze the moods of its users, the newspaper article refers to an Australian survey which reveals information about a software developed by Facebook that is used to collect emotional data in order to target 6 million users according to their current moods. According to the Australian newspaper, in an unpublished internal document, which Facebook would have produced on behalf of a large Australian bank, very sophisticated mood algorithms were developed in order to identify the moments of vulnerability in young people (e.g., lack of trust, uselessness, anxiety) through messages and photographs posted to target them with commercial messages.

- **Constraints related to the company's strategy and culture**. Big data are not only linked to the tools that companies have put in place to collect and analyze data, they are also seen as a strategy, which is part of the organizational culture that requires adjustments in the internal organization of the company. Big data are not a department; they represent the state of mind of the company and its project. However, the majority of companies set up the management of big data without asking any questions about their purpose or integration in the overall project of the company, which generates misunderstandings on the part of staff and confusion as to the previously central role of the insight department staff in the production of data via field surveys of consumers. Thus, the implementation of big data management, like any business project, requires a commitment from corporate management, and especially the commitment of all staff to the overall project, which is not the case today in the majority of companies. Indeed, the objectives of the different functions of the company, such as human resources, marketing, financial management, and supply chain as well as those of the general management, are divergent and sometimes contradictory. Another constraint related to the management of big data in the organization is related to the training of staff in terms of processing and valuing data from billing databases, CRM, social networks, etc. Big data staff should also be able to collaborate with the other departments and functions within the organization. The Chief Data Officer, who is a specialized (has statistical, mathematical and computer skills) and multidisciplinary (with analytical skills and basic knowledge of marketing, communication, etc.) professional, is unfortunately not often present in companies.

IMMERSIVE SMART DATA AS A MEANS OF UNDERSTANDING THE LUXURY EXPERIENCE IN THE PHYGITAL SETTING

Unlike consumer insights generated from big data, the unique purpose of which is to describe and measure variables related to purchasing and consumption behaviors, smart data are immersive, explanatory, and closer to the social reality of individuals. Immersive insights provide luxury companies with more relevant and in-depth understandings when it comes to analyzing and identifying the digital luxury experience and its tangible and intangible dimensions. Figure 10.4 shows a synthesis of the differentiation between descriptive data and exploratory data.

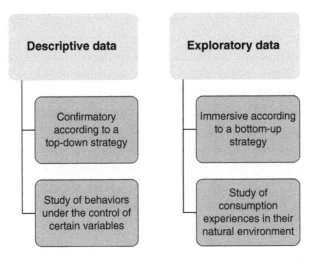

Figure 10.4 Descriptive data vs. exploratory data

The use of immersive data is necessary in order to identify the emotional and symbolic dimensions that are an integral part of the customer experience lived in a phygital environment. There are three methodological protocols that luxury companies can follow to thoroughly analyze data related to the digital customer experience: explanatory, descriptive, and exploratory. The choice of protocol depends on the objective defined upstream in the marketing strategy.

- **Explanatory data**. These help to understand the *why* of certain consumption behaviors and explain the motivations behind them.
- **Descriptive data**. These data represent the behaviors and consumption phenomena that we want to describe in depth.
- **Exploratory data**. This is a method that involves understanding new, emerging behaviors and the symbolic and experiential dimensions of consumption in settings influenced by macro-environmental variables (e.g., economic, technological, ecological, cultural).

The use of exploratory data is, therefore, a true source of innovation and differentiation for luxury companies wishing to create unique, memorable, and satisfying as well as functional and emotional consumption experiences. With exploratory data, luxury houses can learn more about current and potential customers as well as understand their expectations of buying and living experiences through a bottom-up approach, starting from the "client" and his/her own "perception" of luxury consumption in a particular technological and sociocultural setting.

TRANSFORMING BIG DATA INTO SMART DATA

The data generated through studies using an exploratory approach of the customer experience are necessary in order to collect quality data on the emotions of the customers during their purchase or consumption experiences, whether online and offline, by being closer to their social and personal realities. By allowing consumers to express their subjective opinions, their emotions, their functional, and symbolic needs as well as their experiences, exploratory methods help luxury brands to better understand the reality of the digital customer experience from the consumer's point-of-view according to his/her own definition of what a satisfactory digital luxury experience should be. Generated exploratory data have multiple advantages compared to big data. In fact, exploratory data allow luxury brands to make an analysis focused on a consumer-centric perspective, the starting point of which is the customer with all the dimensions of his/her behavior and consumption experience in a phygital environment (objective and subjective, rational and irrational, emotional and functional, tangible and intangible, etc.). Unlike the massive data or big data collected through internal and external databases, the exploratory data highlight issues that big data tend to quantify. Amongst the contributions of exploratory smart data to the analysis of the digital luxury experience, we can cite the following:

- Exploratory data identify the reasons for choice or behavior amongst consumers;
- They provide access to consumer subcultures and tribes;
- They allow marketers to study the meanings of consumption (consumers' symbolic needs, perceptions, etc.) and elements closely related to the digital customer experience;
- Unlike big data, exploratory data allow codes and consumption norms to be analyzed within a phygital setting;
- They also identify the typologies of the digital customer experience, its characteristics, and how it manifests and evolves;
- Exploratory data allow the identification of new customer experiences and translate them into offline and online innovations;
- Finally, exploratory data help luxury brands in the analysis of social dynamics and interactions in experiences that are often beyond the control of companies because they are expressed in a tacit manner.

By applying exploratory methods to data collection, the investigator does not need to recruit a large number of participants. The number of participants may vary from one to a few dozen people. The question of the representativeness and reliability of the results is no less important, however, and requires particular attention in the composition of the group studied. Also, the more the group represents the total population of consumers in its diversity, the more relevant the data will be.

WHY LUXURY HOUSES SHOULD USE IMMERSIVE SMART DATA

Immersive smart data have the advantage of allowing the crosschecking of big data and fast data by embedding digital behaviors and experiences within a well-defined cultural context in order to provide luxury companies with an in-depth analysis of consumer behaviors, and thus produce superior consumer insights. Immersive smart data are the most appropriate technique for studying consumption experiences in the phygital setting, that is, including both online and offline experiences. They are also a source of inspiration for luxury brands looking for new and innovative ideas and concepts (products/services) to create unique experiences that are tailored to customers' experiential and digital expectations. In doing so, luxury companies can retain actual customers and begin attracting new ones. The importance of using immersive smart data can be explained by the evolution of digital tools and data marketing, the proliferation of massive data on behaviors, and the emergence of new consumption trends in our contemporary societies.

Immersive smart data are the only complete tool that integrates mixed data in order to analyze in-depth the digital customer experience and its emotional, functional, and symbolic dimensions. Thus, immersive smart data provide answers to questions from luxury companies regarding three main areas:

- **Social and digital changes**. Immersive smart data enable luxury companies to better understand the challenges of transformations in terms of new behaviors generated by digital evolution as well as the importance of emotions and the consumer-centric approach in the analysis of the digital customer experience and its various dimensions.
- **The use of innovative methodological tools**. Immersive smart data use a wide range of qualitative and quantitative tools in gathering consumer insights. Indeed, the use of different methodological tools provides an in-depth analytical view of the digital luxury experience and its touchpoints. This facilitates the decision-making process regarding the improvement of the luxury experience, or the creation of a new experiential offering. Moreover, mixed smart data (instantaneous, quantitative, and qualitative) allow luxury companies to group together the maximum number of elements that can help the decision-makers better understand the types of digital experiences from a consumer perspective.
- **The paradoxical behaviors of customers**. Immersive smart data help decision-makers understand conflicting customer behaviors and the subjective dimensions that are part of the digital luxury experience. These paradoxical and symbolic elements play an important role in the consumption or rejection of certain luxury products and brands.

THE KEY TOOLS OF IMMERSIVE SMART DATA

The tools of immersive smart data can gather together several sources of information and are considered to be more efficient and better adapted to the study of the digital luxury experience as a whole. Therefore, luxury professionals can use immersive tools and also combine them with the big and fast data they have collected in order to obtain and contextualize an in-depth analysis of the customer experience. Figure 10.5 introduces a set of tools that luxury companies can use to generate immersive smart data. These tools are detailed in the next sections.

VISUAL SMART DATA

Visual smart data offer luxury companies the opportunity to identify and categorize the emotions of customers expressed during their digital experiences through the analysis of photographs selected by individuals and posted on social networks. These photographs represent objects and consumer practices that constitute the consumption universe of people. They may include videos, holiday photographs, or other consumer practices, montages, selfies, drawings, and the like posted online. The advantages of visual smart data include the following:

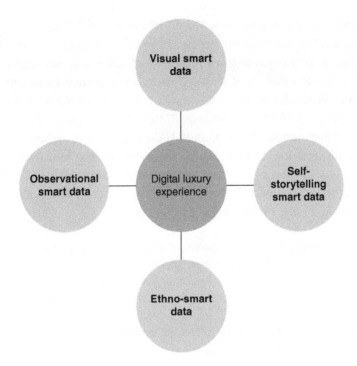

Figure 10.5   Tools to generate immersive smart data

- They allow the luxury company to conduct a visual analysis of the subjective photographs representing the people's universe of luxury consumption.
- The selection of photographs and visuals is done by the participants who choose and prioritize the elements they post.
- The visual allows luxury professionals to capture lived luxury experiences and analyze them through a back-and-forth exchange between the field and the photographs, thus leading the investigator to refine the results.

The use of visual smart data in the study of the digital experience allows luxury brands to better understand the symbolic and emotional dimensions. In order to get an in-depth analysis of the data and to have a cross-view (company/consumer) of the lived experiences, the visual smart data should also incorporate other qualitative techniques (e.g., participant observation, ethnography, focus groups) to question consumers about their own interpretations of visual data.

SELF-STORYTELLING SMART DATA

Self-storytelling smart data are a qualitative style of narrative that originated in the social sciences. These data can be used in marketing to understand the emotional and functional motivations behind the consumer experience. The life story describes the consumer's discourse about his or her own experience rooted in a phygital setting in which the customer is interacting with other customers, with the luxury brand's staff (salesperson, after-sales service, etc.), and with other social actors. Three main steps are necessary to analyze the self-storytelling smart data relating a consumer experience or digital purchase: (1) the identification of the problem to be studied; (2) the selection of participants who can tell us about their consumption practices; and (3) the collection of personal stories (at the level of the individual him/herself), which are collective (the individual in consumer groups or in luxury brand communities) and social (the individual in a sociocultural category of belonging or reference). In this step, the investigator should choose between two possible options according to the objective of the study:

- The focus on individuals and the deepening of their personal story by following a chronological or spatial logic of the customer experience;
- Collecting stories from other individuals and synthesizing all stories told by individuals to produce a shared story that is representative of the customer experience.

In self-storytelling smart data, all the practices, meanings, and consumption situations retained by the participant in the study are commented on in a subjective and detailed manner. These data are important for marketing and communication managers because they are produced and described by the participants, themselves, in terms of the perceived importance in their own lives. The hierarchy of events is not necessarily chronological; it may also reflect a classification according to the importance that these practices represent for the participant in the study.

ETHNO-SMART DATA

Ethno-smart data can be produced by using two complementary immersive approaches: the ethnography of the customer experience (applied offline) and the netnography of the customer experience (applied online). The use of ethnographic smart data is an exploratory, interactive, and immersive method that is part of the new qualitative methodologies, and is especially relevant for studying the customer experience in the phygital environment. The advantages of ethnographic smart data in the study of the digital customer experience are summarized in Table 10.2

Thus, ethnographic smart data help luxury brands in the process of identifying, categorizing, and analyzing in-depth digital customer experiences in different cultural settings in which the usages of digital technologies are dominant or emerging. In these cultural contexts, it is indeed essential to identify the typologies of usages of social media and other technologies within consumption experiences, and thus segment the consumer

Table 10.2   The benefits of ethno-smart data

Benefit 1	They help marketers understand the social interactions between different consumer profiles and market players, as well as the internal interactions within each digital customer experience
Benefit 2	They allow the analysis of the symbolic and emotional dimensions of the digital customer experience
Benefit 3	They help investigators to understand how consumers build and develop attitudes towards luxury brands in their own consumer experience
Benefit 4	They allow the use of visual and verbal data via behavioral recording in real consumption situations
Benefit 5	Collecting data in this setting allows the ethnographer to observe behaviors and react to participants in real time

market according to the maturity of users: early adopters, followers, and mainstream users. In order to produce relevant ethnographic data, immersion is the first essential step in accessing real-world data closer to customers to capture the full meaning of their luxury experiences according to the location (e.g., at home) and the nature of their shopping habits, whether the customer is shopping online or buying in a shop using digital technologies. The requirement to do an empirical study while being immersed in a real context is a ritual that gives meaning and contextualizes the interpretation of the data according to lived experiences.

Netnographic smart data are an online immersion technique on social networks and blogs whose main purpose is to analyze the discourses, images, and exchanges between consumers on the Internet. This method, developed by Robert Kozinets (2010, 2015), is based on the collection of qualitative and quantitative data on the Internet that are generated by online brand communities. Like ethnographic smart data, netnographic smart data focus on the study of online brand communities and their experiences of Internet consumption. The implementation of a netnographic device can incorporate several methodological tools: online interviews, participant observation on the Internet, or self-storytelling smart data. Overall, netnographic smart data production can be performed through participant or non-participant observations and follows five major steps. Figure 10.6 summarizes the five steps of netnographic smart data.

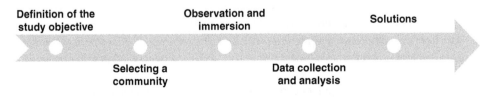

Figure 10.6   The five steps to collect netnographic smart data

The advantage of using the Internet to study online luxury shopping experiences is that it allows study participants to freely express their consumption practices without fear of judgment. Accordingly, market researchers can collect personal information through the absence of physical contact and, therefore, value judgment.

OBSERVATIONAL SMART DATA

Observation is a technique used to collect verbal and nonverbal data related to the consumption experiences observed in different consumer groups. Smart data derived from observation are an anthropological approach to data applied to understand social cultures and phenomena. The goal is to discover, through observation and interaction, the elements that form and organize the consumption experiences of individuals in their culture, in a store, hotel or restaurant, when buying online, etc. Observational smart data resulting from the participant observation of consumption experiences imply on the part of the investigator an active and prolonged immersion in the studied consumer universe (e.g., online car purchase, discussion on forums). Thanks to this deep immersion, the investigator may glean implicit, but observable information that may be inaccessible with other methods. Observational smart data resulting from observation and immersion allow luxury professionals to better understand certain internal operations, which remain difficult to access. The sources of smart data from observation include information from direct observation, comprehensive interviews, and the processing of personal documents.

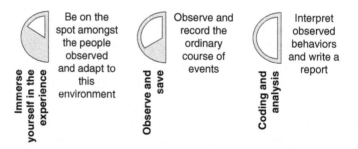

Figure 10.7   The observational smart data analysis process

- Data from direct observation in the field emerges by sharing the lives and activities of consumers with family, friends, at workplaces, on holiday, at home, in shops, etc.
- Data from the comprehensive interviews can be collected through occasional conversations, fieldwork, and formal/informal online and offline exchanges related to consumer practices.
- Data from the analysis of personal documents are collected through a diary, blogs, and social networks in which consumers express, in their own language, their point-of-view on their consumption practices and the brands they favor or reject.

In order to identify the different digital consumption experiences desired or experienced by consumers, the observer should follow three main steps. Figure 10.7 outlines the steps and the analytical process that investigators need to follow to collect observational data on consumption experiences.

SUMMARY

With big data, the investigator has become an observer of spontaneously collected data on social networks and other devices, thus limiting his/her analytical and creative skills. It is therefore vital for luxury companies to step back and make a paradigm shift to immersive smart data. The end of the flagship trend of big data heralds the beginning of a new era of "immersive smart data" in which the data should be of the highest quality, as accurate as possible and allow for commercial actions with an ROI. Unlike big data, which are generated, collected, and analyzed in an autonomous way, immersive smart data are, by their nature, exploratory and provide avenues for reflection in order to better understand the paradoxical behavior of luxury consumers within a particular luxury consumption setting. Regarding the aspect of embeddedness, immersive smart data tools allow luxury houses to better anticipate the motivations and attitudes of consumers with respect to their expectations for satisfying luxury experiences. In fact, immersive smart data offer a deeper consumer insight approach that complements the traditional approach of using big data to study the digital customer experience.

11

PHYGITAL LUXURY CONSUMPTION EXPERIENCES: A NEW PARADIGM

INTRODUCTION AND SCOPE

The customer experience is lived as a continuum between the physical place and the digital space, creating a new phygital (a portmanteau of physical and digital) environment. "Phygital" is a term that appeared in 2013 in the business sector and refers to a physical point of sale that integrates the data and methods of the digital ecosphere in order to improve turnover. By digitizing the point of sale, companies seek to optimize the effectiveness of their business strategy and attract new customers. The phygital context can be characterized by the installation of touch terminals offering different applications, including real-time price verification, or the perusal of an interactive catalog. Connected interactive terminals allow for more in-depth searches online. They can simplify custom 3D design or offer new options that are not yet available in stores. Therefore, the phygital sphere puts innovative tools and advanced technologies within the reach of the public. It also improves the marketing experience at the physical point of sale. So, the phygital experience is a major competitive opportunity for luxury companies in the years to come. Luxury brands should understand its components and typologies to create digital experiences that ensure a seamless and barrier-free continuum. In fact, the use of digital technologies and devices should be well thought out by luxury companies in order to facilitate the transition of customers from the physical context to the digital, and vice versa, without difficulty and with consistency and fluidity in the lived experience.

The digital luxury experience is, therefore, multiple and involves the use of various technological tools that are designed to meet specific objectives and are anchored in a defined phygital setting. The phygital customer experience will be a major challenge for luxury companies in the future to create unique luxury experiences that integrate gateways as well as physical (offline) and digital (online) channels between the real and digital worlds, and vice versa. Chapter 11 will explore the notion of the phygital experience in the luxury sector and show how companies can apply it and integrate new and innovative tools and devices to create a fluid continuum between the in-store experience and online platforms.

THE PHYGITAL LUXURY EXPERIENCE

Presently, new hybrid consumption experiences are blossoming, thanks to the ubiquity of digital technologies in our daily lives. According to Castelli (2016), the characteristics of these consumption experiences are neither exclusively physical nor fully digital; rather, they merge the characteristics of the digital and physical worlds, which give rise to a third context of consumption, bringing into proximity the digital and physical contexts: the phygital. The term phygital appeared in the marketing field in 2013 and was developed by the Australian marketing agency Momentum Worldwide, whose signature is "An Agency for the Phygital World." This term, which could have been an ephemeral buzzword, is now rooted in our vocabulary as it perfectly reflects a reality that no one disputes. It refers to the transformation of physical stores within the digital era: concepts are completely redesigned to offer a new customer experience and use digital tools as sales support. Phygital logic has given rise to a series of equally evocative terms from the marketing jargon, such as connected commerce or responsive retail, an interesting concept created by analogy with responsive design, which appeared in 2015. Phygital refers to the idea that today's e-commerce and retail stores should be flexible, attentive, and able to respond to the instantaneous needs of as well as interpret the paradoxes inherent in consumption experiences. Phygital is then the ultimate way to adapt to smart purchasing behavior and respond quickly in a multichannel way to the expectations of impatient and zapper consumers. It also helps companies develop successful relationships with their customers by offering better personalization that takes into account the symbolic meanings of consumption that emerge within their experiences.

The phygital environment is a context of consumption that integrates gateways set up by companies between different physical channels (offline and in-store) and digital channels (online) so that customers can switch from one to the other with ease, guaranteeing consistency in the experiential journey from the physical place to the digital space, and vice versa. For luxury businesses, then, it is essential to create effective, high-performance digital customer experiences that are firmly rooted in consumers' daily habits. This can be achieved by using different technologies one at a time, or all together simultaneously. Amongst these technologies, the following are good examples that illustrate the importance of the fusion of the physical and digital worlds:

- **The use of iBeacons**. This technology enables the digitalization of the physical customer experience at the point of sale. It looks like a small box and has a Bluetooth connection that allows luxury brands to interact with customers in the store, or provide them with contextual information through their smartphones. Introduced by Apple in 2013, iBeacon technology works on the principle of micro-location. It estimates the proximity of a smartphone to a given point, represented by a tag. Two conditions are necessary before the reception of the signals is possible: the possession of the application and the activation of the Bluetooth technology by the holder of the device. For example, the use of iBeacons is very important for enhancing the traveler experience. Airline companies can place the iBeacons in strategic locations throughout the airport to keep in proximity to travelers, including key points such as customs clearance, check-in, boarding, etc. In fact, this technology can be used to help passengers navigate airports using tags that trigger notifications that are automatically activated when passengers arrive at the security checking point, which invites them to open their boarding pass at the right time so that they are ready to present their passports and boarding passes to the controllers.

TREND 11.1

HOW BARNEYS NEW YORK IS USING THE IBEACONS TO ENHANCE IN-STORE CUSTOMER EXPERIENCES

Barneys New York is a luxury retailer renowned for having the most selective high-end items from the world's top designers, including women's and men's ready-to-wear, accessories, shoes, jewelry, cosmetics, fragrances, and gifts for the home. Barneys has just inaugurated its new high-tech flagship store in Chelsea, New York. The luxury retailer has placed iBeacons throughout the store to offer each customer an enriched and individualized shopping experience. The iBeacons entertain the visitor with multimedia content: videos, books, interviews with designers, etc. The iBeacons also accompany customers in their shopping. If a consumer makes a purchase, he/she benefits from a privileged treatment, such as avoiding the queue and paying directly in the department to a vendor equipped with an iPad with integrated Apple Pay that allows the sellers access to the customer's profile and purchase history on their tablets.

Furthermore, the inclusion of the iBeacons in the shopping experience can help Barneys solve several problems to encourage potential customers to buy online. One of the reasons why shopping centers have fallen in popularity is because the experience of visiting a shopping mall has largely lost its appeal. Because of the relative ease with which a person can make a purchase online using just a simple touch, customers are much less motivated to buy in-person. Barneys' use of the iBeacon technology is primarily to revive visits to the store by making it considerably more interactive. Customers are more likely to explore the store at a comfortable pace and seize any available shopping opportunities if they receive promotions, special treatment, and offers as they wander round. This approach has shown so much potential that whole streets have been transformed using iBeacons, creating interconnected and interactive buying experiences. This dynamic approach maximizes the value of iBeacons in order to attract bored customers back to the store. Also, this technology allows the store to offer most of the same services that were once the privilege of online shopping experiences. For example, many online retailers cross-sell by recommending items based on the customer's purchase history. A beacons-based mobile application is able to accomplish similar tasks by providing information about the store where similar products are sold at attractive prices. By attracting buyers to the digital services they are used to, iBeacons encourage luxury retail customers to return to the store as they expect to live a unique and customized shopping experience that is diverse in terms of products and increased interactivity with the vendors.

In fact, in some locations, such as luxury hotels, where the customer is welcomed as a unique guest, his/her habits and tastes are memorized (formerly recorded in a small notebook, now on a computer). The department stores do everything to make each customer unique. The iBeacon approach developed by Barneys allows the brand to position itself as one of the forerunners of these new customer journeys. For Barneys New York, the digital customer experience in its flagship store is as important as the design, products, and history of the venue. With the integration of iBeacons, customers can feel as if anything is possible when they walk around the store, especially since buyers of luxury goods require personalized premium experiences and service at all points of contact. By extending the use of technological solutions to its stores, Barneys has become the first luxury retailer to combine iBeacon technology and detailed customer information to deliver a premium experience focused on personalized content regardless of the channel used.

- **Quantified-self experience**. This is another example of the phygital experience that highlights self-quantified experiences. Consumers value self-quantified experiences when they use applications and connected objects to monitor, control, optimize, and improve their own behaviors. For example, a sports app such as Withings Health Mate™ focuses on measuring health through quantitative goals. It is a free application offering a quantified-self experience that focuses on two main areas: health monitoring and motivation retention. And the app can be used without the need to purchase Withings products. It allows the user to follow his/her activity (thanks to the built-in accelerometer on the phone), weight and body fat (manual inputs), heart rate (using the phone's camera), and blood pressure (manual entries). Moreover, the application pays particular attention to maintaining motivation. The user can invite friends and family to join his/her ranking and compete with them to be the one who walks the most each week. Regardless of whether they have a Withings product or not, thanks to the built-in step-tracking feature, the quantified-self application acts as an activity tracker. The user can add individuals who have the app on their smartphones. This feature is only available to the primary user of the account. When the user uses his/her activity tracker for a few days, the app will start sending him/her "insights," which is personalized advice and encouragement. This feature analyzes the daily activity of the user, which means when the user's activity is weaker than usual, the insights encourage him/her to continue to achieve his/her health goal.

TREND 11.2

APPLE WATCH HERMES OFFERS A QUANTIFIED-SELF SPORT EXPERIENCE TO ITS CUSTOMERS

A partnership based on a remarkable and avant-garde vision of the fusion of the digital and luxury worlds resulted in the latest Apple Watch Hermes collection, which mixes technological and ancestral know-how to offer modern, connected, and quantified-self experiences to users. This digital luxury connected watch is also a sensor of physical activity and can be easily transformed into a sports companion. Users can use the connected luxury watch for different purposes. For example, users can work out with their Apple Watch exercise app, which informs them of their progress during their exercise and alerts them when they reach their goals. Equipped with sensors to measure vital parameters, Apple Watch Hermes complements the range of Apple products dedicated to fitness, well-being, and health. It arises as the hardware counterpart of health, the application that makes the iPhone a digital health record. Furthermore, the watch incorporates a heart rate monitor, a GPS, and an accelerometer via the iPhone for monitoring sports and physical activities. Directly controlled on the screen of the watch, the application is easy to use. Like most smart watches, it is primarily aimed at endurance sports enthusiasts. Once the application is launched, it first asks the user to choose a physical activity from amongst a dozen options (running, walking, indoor cycling, rowing, etc.). Swimming is not part of the options, however, because the watch is not waterproof.

Apple Watch Hermes also has an incentive dimension. The activity application is easily transformed into a sports coach that helps the user adopt a behavior that is beneficial to his/her health. The objectives are developed according to the age, weight, and size of the user and progress along three levels of effort: moderate, sustained, or intense. Each level corresponds to a threshold of caloric expenditure. After each kilometer traveled or level of energy expenditure reached, it emits a small alert. It also notifies the user when he or she reaches the end of the course selected. These alerts can be relayed in audio, via Bluetooth headphones. When the objectives are fulfilled, the app awards trophies. More intrusively, it also provides advice in the form of alerts indicating, as necessary, that it is time to stand up (at least for one minute every hour), to walk, or run when the user has been inactive too long or did not fulfill his/her daily goals.

Furthermore, augmented and virtual reality, digital concierge services, and 3D printing experiences are other examples of phygital experiences (see Part II). A study conducted by Damala et al. in 2008 on physical and digital consumption experiences and consumer perception shows that some consumers adopt these devices because they find them new, exciting, and useful phygital experiences, while others reject them or consider them useless gadgets.

TREND 11.3

HOW DOES THE NET-A-PORTER MAGAZINE BUILD THE PHYGITAL SHOPPING/READING EXPERIENCE "SEE IT, SCAN IT, SHOP IT"?

Porter is a magazine published by Net-a-Porter, the world's leading digital luxury retailer. The print magazine allows consumers to search for items, scroll through information, and click to buy when browsing the magazine's print pages on matching images in the Net-a-Porter mobile app. The bimonthly magazine, published since 2014 and with a subscription price of $25 per year, is the Net-a-Porter website's answer to what high-end e-commerce content should look like in order to fit the profile of the luxury customer. According to *Porter* magazine editor Lucy Yeomans, this is a first for a traditional print magazine. With this phygital format, the customer can flip through the magazine and buy the products without delay because the products are available and the customer does not have to look elsewhere. The magazine today has a global circulation of more than 170,000 copies, representing a growth of 10% over 2015. In addition to the Net-a-Porter e-commerce site, *Porter* has helped spark interest in the products presented in the magazine and marked the positioning of Net-a-Porter as a service that caters to customers who have a high purchasing power.

How does it work? A page at the beginning of each issue of the print magazine tells readers how to buy. First, the reader must download the Net-a-Porter app. Then, select "Scan Porter magazine" from the menu and download it to the mobile phone. A "store" icon will appear, showing the brand, price, and purchase button for all items available at Net-a-Porter. Other sections on the app include services such as "find items," "see more," or "concierge," which reminds readers of Net-a-Porter's 24-hour concierge service. These headings allow readers to explore all items worn by a celebrity or model in the magazine, which include an average of 500 available items for purchase. In a reader survey of 2015, *Porter* found that articles were scanned 85,000 times with a connection rate of 78%. However, as readers browse the pages of the magazine with their mobile phones, the phygital reading experience can be a little boring, hence the need to adapt to the actual behavior of the reader, which requires a combination of the physical and digital contexts as well as immersive and in-depth studies of the phygital experience of reading the magazine. With the establishment of the phygital magazine, *Porter* counters the crisis in publishing and questions the idea of the death of print by disseminating editorial content that pushes the reader to purchase items.

For Rigby (2014), companies today have limited knowledge of what makes these phygital experiences useful to consumers because integrated technologies are new. Thus, in order to integrate new technologies and provide their customers with memorable and satisfying phygital experiences, luxury companies need to focus on identifying the elements of the phygital experience that can create value for their customers. More specifically, luxury companies should focus on three main issues: What are the values associated with phygital consumption experiences? What are the technological elements and tools that contribute to creating a valuable phygital experience that generates value for the company and its customers? And how does the value perceived by the consumer vary across the different stages of the phygital experience?

The experiential value is, therefore, a major component of luxury consumption in a phygital environment. It is perceived and shaped within the phygital setting by various individual, social, cultural, and technical factors. Personal characteristics, such as the empathy of luxury staff or the mood of the customers, play an important role in the perception of value. Additionally, social contexts (relationships, social networks) and cultural contexts (ideologies, social norms, practices, institutions) also have a significant influence on the formation of the experiential value. Thus, in a phygital environment, digital tools create distinct and unique experiences because of the socio-material characteristics of this context.

HOW CAN LUXURY HOUSES DESIGN CUSTOMER EXPERIENCE IN A PHYGITAL SETTING?

The implementation of an experiential digital strategy guaranteeing a continuum between the physical and digital contexts should take into consideration two main elements: immersion and functionality. In order to make users live digital and virtual experiences, immersive and interactive technological tools linking the luxury brand's physical environment and virtual context need to be considered, since they bring a realistic dimension to the online phygital customer experience. Thus, customers can experience virtual experiences that are almost identical to real-world experiences (in-store, hotel, etc.) because they can interact with virtual agents of the online brand as well as physical agents (staff, salespeople, etc.). Active participation of consumers is also essential for improving phygital experiences. Luxury brands should involve customers not only in the process of co-creating the product or service, but also in the marketing strategy and communication of the brand. Customers can then give their opinions on products and services and customize them according to their needs.

The importance of efficiency is vital in designing phygital experiences. Indeed, the phygital luxury experience has to offer a cognitive (convenience, time savings, assessment, personalization, etc.) and an emotional answer (hedonism, pleasure-seeking, online exchange, etc.) to consumers' requirements and expectations, which can emerge in the physical context and express themselves in the digital world. For instance, consumers might express a need for human assistance with appropriate skills to guide them in their purchase process (cognitive response) and they can also call for empathy skills (emotional response) when they encounter problems during their online purchase experiences. By applying an experiential digital strategy linking the physical and digital contexts, the luxury brand will be able to offer these customers the opportunity to experience browsing and buying on commercial websites through creative, innovative, and participatory content that generates a particular emotion, such as joy, admiration, surprise, etc. The emotion generated during this browsing experience is beneficial for the luxury brand which is attracting this target to its physical shops because the consumer has been seduced by his/her digital experience through the luxury brand's social networks, its commercial website, its application, and so on.

Thanks to the democratization of access to digital technologies and the proliferation of virtual reality tools, luxury companies are now able to offer users new experiences in browsing and buying online. However, luxury houses that set up a real phygital experience on their websites are rare. The websites exist primarily and sometimes exclusively for the purchase of the company's products and little else. At best, it enables an interaction via social networks provided by the luxury brands but fails to create digital experiences which are memorable and satisfying for their customers.

TREND 11.4

THE FRENCH LUXURY FASHION BRAND BALMAIN OFFERS AN INTROSPECTIVE PHYGITAL EXPERIENCE

When it comes to luxury brands and social media platforms, Balmain is ahead of the game. Unlike traditional marketing strategies, its ingenious digital marketing techniques have not only brought the brand back from irrelevance, but the company has also completely re-marketed and revitalized itself in an unbelievably cost-efficient manner. This was thanks to Balmain's newly appointed creative director, Olivier Rousteing, who is the creative force behind today's most talked-about Balmain fashion line. In Balmain's newly opened store located in Milan, Rousteing proposed incorporating technology and fashion by launching a one-of-a-kind phygital experience through the use of virtual reality (VR) that would plunge the customers into Olivier Rousteing's

(Continued)

(Continued)

head! All shoppers were invited to wear Oculus VR headsets to see into the mind of Rousteing by experiencing a creative and virtual world called "My City of Lights," which allows customers to discover all the feelings, risks, and doubts Rousteing goes through during the process of creating his new collection. Using this virtual experience, the art director wanted to create a journey through his creative process so that the user feels the emotions he has encountered in designing the Balmain collections. Rousteing's subsequent huge popularity combined with the reflection on his own taste through this entertainment marketing strategy turned Balmain into a success story.

This advanced virtual reality tour through an impossibly huge and spectacular world, from cavernous baroque halls to staircases, involved everyone in Balmain's commitment to inclusivity. It created a brilliant and memorable new form of communication between the Balmain brand and its customers. And to give it an immediate visibility and further significance, the brand planned the store opening to coincide with Salone del Mobile, the world's design trade fair. While many struggled with the shifting perception of fashion, Rousteing enjoyed the challenge and fell in love with the idea of being able to reach his audience on a more personal level. He confidently believed that technology is an inseparable part of fashion and wanted to connect his fans and followers through technology while maintaining the elegance and significance of Balmain's brand. And, with the rise of style bloggers and writers who eagerly await every fashion update, the whole story became far more digital and popular, elevating the Balmain brand to a higher status. For Balmain, the new technological tools will soon be inseparable from the world of fashion as the latter becomes more inclusive than ever, and there is no better way to include more people than technology and digital devices.

KEY SUCCESS FACTORS FOR PHYGITAL LUXURY EXPERIENCE OFFERINGS

Given the demand that luxury consumers demonstrate for digital and social interactions with brands, luxury companies have to invest in the implementation of high-quality, rewarding phygital experiences for their customers. A recent study conducted by Gartner found that over 90% of consumers have had one or more negative digital experience when using their mobile phones to search for information about a product or to reach customer service (Sorofman, 2014). To avoid the negative effects of poor digital experiences on customers in their multichannel journeys and to prevent them from switching to competitors, luxury businesses need to consider four key success factors in order to implement an effective global strategy centered on a highly qualitative and satisfying customer experience characterized by both the functional and emotional needs of luxury customers.

- **Key success factor #1: ensure the continuum between the physical experience and the digital journey**. In order to offer a successful phygital customer experience, the luxury brand needs to guarantee that digital tools complement existing customer journeys in the physical context (in-store experiences). Although the continuum between the physical and digital customer journey is a key element of consumer satisfaction, the majority of companies continue to inappropriately add digital elements to customer journeys that do not directly benefit the quality of the digital customer experience or are useless regarding the value proposed by the company and perceived by the customer. At best, these overlapping digital elements, tools, and devices do not immerse the customer and, at worst, they can make the digital customer experience unpleasant and disconnected from the journey and the real needs of customers. It is, therefore, not always relevant to introduce digital components to customer experiences that can rely on other forms of tools (e.g., buying a baguette in a bakery does not require answering an online survey, but can integrate the use of an application to place a special order in the shopping journey, which is a very important utility value in the journey that gives real satisfaction to the customer).

- **Key success factor #2: regularly collect immersive smart data to enhance the digital customer experience**. Data collection tools can improve the digital luxury experience by detecting weak points in the experiential journey offline and online. Luxury businesses need to be able to understand how customers feel and perceive a buying experience in order to offer them opportunities for improvement. Luxury companies should then focus more on the analysis of immersive smart data (see Chapter 10) in addition to the massive data generated from the processing of big data and their internal databases (e.g., CRM databases) and external databases (e.g., social networks).

- **Key success factor #3: focus on the consistency of multichannel content**. The coherence of the content broadcast on a multitude of platforms allows the customer to identify the luxury brand and its values. The multiplication of points of contact with the luxury brand might give the consumer the impression that the luxury brand offers inconsistent content, which varies according to the medium or point of contact through which the consumer has entered. Luxury houses should then optimize the phygital experiences of their customers and offer them a fluid experiential customer journey through various key points (e.g., the use of the same identifier that is already registered in the company's databases for in-store purchases and on the e-commerce website of the company to streamline the customer journey in the phygital sphere).

- **Key success factor #4: maintain a regular phygital experience through the visual and the sensory**. Providing a consistent digital experience also integrates visual and sensory dimensions into the use of digital tools, interfaces, and products. Consistency is required on many levels. Luxury companies should therefore design websites with an identical visual identity, sensory elements, and functional usages on different media, platforms, or devices. A strong and consistent visual identity of the luxury brand allows customers to easily immerse themselves in the brand universe and easily migrate from the physical sphere to the virtual space, and vice versa.

TOOLS FOR DESIGNING PHYGITAL LUXURY EXPERIENCES

There are three main tools that enable the creation of the customer experience in a phygital environment. All these tools (Web 3.0, interactive tools, and immersive technologies) can convey the luxury brand's values and create a strong emotional bond with the targets. Figure 11.1 illustrates the tools that luxury companies can use to create phygital experiences.

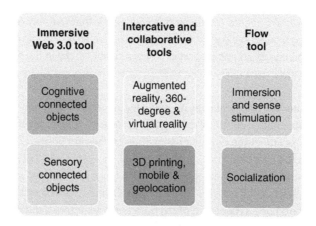

Figure 11.1   Tools for designing phygital luxury experiences

IMMERSIVE WEB 3.0

Luxury businesses can use the Web tools that are available to deliver memorable and satisfying customer online experiences. Web 3.0 is an Internet of connected objects in which aggregated data create meanings according to three essential elements: semantics, mobile objects, and connected objects. Web 3.0 marketing enables luxury businesses to use Internet-connected objects, database-enabled devices, intelligent sensors, and an instant responsiveness to the real world. In marketing 3.0, there are four main elements: data, objects (connected hardware), social interactions, and software. Connected objects represent a fast-growing market in all areas of activity: sports, well-being, home equipment, work, etc. There are two main trends amongst connected objects that luxury brands can consider in creating a phygital experience: cognitive connected objects and sensory connected objects.

- **Cognitive connected objects**. These objects collect data about their users, analyze them, and provide users with the results, as they want to know more about their own behavioral patterns, to control them, to share them, or to compare them with other users. Health and well-being are two sectors that are very attracted to this technology.

- **Sensory connected objects**. These objects are designed to detect the emotion that the user expresses when using the product or practicing a given activity. These objects have sensors for an emotional reading and offer options for adapting to the mood of the moment.

TREND 11.5

CONNECTED LUXURY TRAVEL EXPERIENCE BY LOUIS VUITTON

The luxury brand Louis Vuitton has successfully installed in-store its connected watch, called Tambour Horizon. It is designed with the comfort of luxury travel in mind. Since the 19th century, Louis Vuitton has always been on the side of innovation with one foot in the future and the other in tradition. Developed with Google, the imperative was to immerse the user in a Vuitton environment as soon as the watch is turned on.

The Louis Vuitton connected luxury watch, whose case and components are produced in Switzerland, as well as the processor, which is made in San Francisco (which makes it one of the few watches on the market produced through a Swiss–Californian collaboration), has all the classic functions included in this kind of model, such as call notifications and other messages as well as various applications. It stands out, however, thanks to some specific services, all of which revolve around the trip, including flight alerts, boarding pass displays, and remaining time to destination, etc. The idea is to connect and immerse the user within a luxury experience of travel by mainly referencing the content of the Vuitton City Guide for seven destinations: Paris, Los Angeles, London, New York, Tokyo, Beijing, and Shanghai, which are available through geolocation online services. On the display side, there are a multitude customization possibilities, with watch face options that include iconic motifs, such as that of the Monogram or Damier canvas, color bands with initials as well as subtle allusions to watch collections, such as multicolored flags and the Escale Time Zone. Vuitton launched, at the same time, an interchangeable strap, hidden behind the watch that is ultra-easy to use, thanks to its carbon hook, which fits all its watches, old or new.

INTERACTIVE AND COLLABORATIVE DIGITAL TOOLS

To create an online experience, it is important to involve the user/customer in the co-creation process of the product or service. Interactivity and co-creation should be at the heart of things to develop an effective and satisfying, functional and emotional phygital customer experience. There are several technologies that allow interactivity and collaboration with users/customers. From amongst these digital tools, luxury companies could use the following to adjust the customer experience to the phygital setting.

- **Augmented reality**. This is a technological tool that luxury companies can use to optimize the phygital experience by combining real and virtual existences. In an augmented reality, virtual objects are presented in realistic form through a 3D video.

TREND 11.6

RÉMY MARTIN COGNAC HOUSE USES CREATIVE AUGMENTED REALITY FOR STORYTELLING

The Rémy Martin French cognac house is testing a promotional campaign, using the Microsoft HoloLens mixed reality headset, to offer its customers an innovative and emotional phygital experience. The objective of the iconic luxury cognac company is to explain to its consumers why the brand is "rooted in the exceptional." In the proposed experience, the customer is invited to approach a 3D table covered with a topographical model accompanied by the voice of Baptiste Loiseau, the cellar master of Rémy Martin.

The HoloLens helmet projects elements from the vineyards of Grande Champagne and Petite Champagne. The use of mixed reality presents a special opportunity to tell a story and better reveal the roots of the brand, its essence, and exceptionalism. By extracting its customers almost literally from the real world, the brand allows them to discover its history and heritage while being seduced by the particular, exceptional territory of Rémy Martin. In fact, the technology used allows customers to interact with virtual content and holograms that appear embedded in the real world. Reality becomes mixed by bringing together people, places, and objects from the real world and the digital space. Moreover, Rémy Martin, which has been producing Fine Champagne Cognac for 70 years, has chosen an experiential and educational way to explain its DNA to its consumers.

- **3D printing**. This rapid prototyping technology allows luxury companies to manufacture three-dimensional objects using a 3D printer, a digital file (often accessible free of charge and open sourced), and the relevant materials, depending on the size and composition of the product/object to be printed (plastic, metal, resin, etc.). 3D printing is becoming increasingly attractive to more and more businesses as well as to the end user and anyone else who is curious to explore all the possibilities offered by this prototyping technology, as it allows consumers to create and personalize objects, such as smartphone cases, cups, figurines, jewelry, etc.

- **Mobile technologies**. These are nigh ubiquitous and most consumers are equipped with a smartphone. This has contributed to the spread of mobile technology and its incorporation into the phygital experience. In terms of functional interactivity, smartphones offer the opportunity for users to obtain product information through QR (Quick Response) codes that allow them to be in both worlds: real and virtual.
- **Geolocation**. This is another form of technology that luxury companies can use for effective targeting. As the term suggests, geolocation allows luxury brands to geographically locate and target the recipients of a marketing message on a smartphone-like mobile terminal or through their own websites.

TREND 11.7

THE DIGITALIZATION STRATEGY OF L'ORÉAL: TOWARDS A PHYGITAL CONTINUUM

To meet consumers' aspirations and needs at home and in points of sale in salons, L'Oréal, with 100 years of beauty experience, has identified these new technologies and is co-developing services focused on experimentation and innovation. It has also been able to bring creative and innovative services to the market ahead of others. The CMO of L'Oréal USA, Marie Gulin, recognized that digital contexts, especially mobile technologies, play an essential role in the way people choose their products and show their preferences for some brands over others. For instance, using mobile technology, customers were able to try out a hairstyle in front of the mirror anytime and anywhere in the world; at first an unattainable goal for beauty marketers, this then became a reality using mobile apps. To recreate the way in which the brand meets customers' needs, a fast-paced and smooth digital transformation had to take place. The following were amongst the ideas L'Oréal implemented:

- **Make it personal**: Mobiles helped consumers have a personal stylist, hairdresser, and makeup artist 24/7. A personalized digital experience needed to be offered to the customers. Hence, L'Oréal launched the Makeup Genius, a mobile app that helped consumers try on makeup virtually. The user's face is scanned, analyzed, and then the app displays how different products and shade mixes will give him/her different looks. Accordingly, consumers select the look that they want to achieve and get their products directly at just the press of a button.

(Continued)

(Continued)

- **Harnessing the power of data:** Because the purchase journey of almost all consumers starts online, close attention has to be paid to what they search for and watch. L'Oréal partnered with Google to find out what questions consumers had about contouring in order to launch the Maybelline Master Contour Makeup line and meet customers' needs. "How to Contour in a Quick Way" YouTube videos were produced, in which in three simple steps the art of contouring was demystified and advice was given about skin color and type. This initiative helped L'Oréal reach more than 9 million people through the data-driven approach.
- **Reimagine storytelling:** Speeding up its storytelling was a compelling and creative way for L'Oréal to spread its messages. A YouTube ad was created after the company launched the Root Cover Up Spray, where it revealed the value and usefulness of the product within the first six seconds of using it.

Finally, knowing that customers want products to be available "anytime and anywhere," e-commerce became a major focus for L'Oréal in hopes of increasing its share of sales. In addition to this, the company gathered data on social media and points of sale to analyze what factors influenced customers and accordingly improved its products and services to optimize sales. The information gathered helped L'Oréal reach end customers more effectively and made its products and services available to them, "anytime and anywhere."

THE FLOW TOOL

The concept of flow appeared in psychology research with the work of the pioneering psychologist Csikszentmihalyi, who introduced it for the first time in 1975. Csikszentmihalyi defined flow, or an ideal psychological state, as "an activation state" that is optimal and in which the subject is completely immersed in the activity. There are many elements related to the appearance and intensity of flow in an optimal experience linking the physical and digital environments. Figure 11.2 presents the elements of flow that luxury companies should use to enhance the immersion of their customers in the phygital experience.

The two American authors Hoffman and Novak, experts in online behavior, proposed in 1997 a definition of flow applied to an online navigation experience. For Hoffman and Novak, flow is a pleasant emotional state that appears during navigation, characterized by fluid communication, facilitated by interactivity, and accompanied by a loss of self-awareness and self-empowerment. In addition, flow can be facilitated by the characteristics and type of media used during the online experience. Thus, the consumer experience can be a satisfying cognitive and emotional phygital one, thanks to the rapid evolution of digital technologies and immersive tools that can reach out to the consumer as he/she browses on a commercial website.

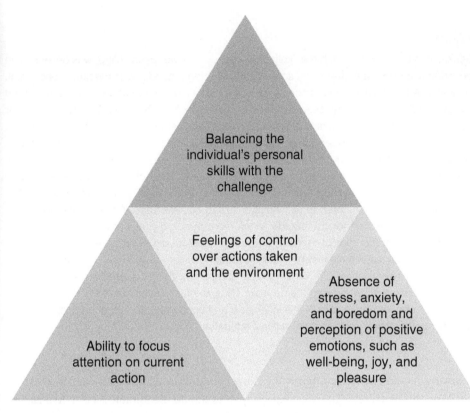

Figure 11.2   Elements of flow in the phygital luxury experience

TREND 11.8

DIOR EYES CREATES UNIQUE FLOW PHYGITAL EXPERIENCES

Dior Eyes is the world's first combination of virtual reality (VR) imaging and 360-degree sound recording technologies. Wearing a helmet, customers will be transported behind the scenes of the last ready-to-wear fashion show and witness the models being made up just before the show. This innovation allows customers to access a thrilling and wonderful moment that could previously only be witnessed in person at a Dior Fashion Show. This peep behind-the-scenes gives these users a feeling of privilege. The fashion house Dior is testing, within its flagships, the virtual reality headset allowing its customers to live a new experience in the store. Although this technology is becoming more and more popular, this is the first time a luxury brand has used it to extend the impact of its fashion show.

(Continued)

(Continued)

Designed in collaboration with the DigitasLBI agency, the Dior Eyes helmet was developed in three months. It offers a high-density screen, thus offering a good image resolution and a high pixel quality. A holophonic sound accompanies the visual experience as the user is immersed in a real virtual reality experience: a behind-the-scenes look at the latest Dior ready-to-wear fashion show. Furthermore, the digital device, the Dior Eyes helmet, is faithful to the DNA of the fashion house. It adopts a sober design, has elegant lines, and is branded. Since technology is now a popular medium amongst consumers, Dior has seized the opportunity for personal and technological interaction in order to create and maintain the bond between customers consuming the finished product and the artisans who are the "little hands" of the luxury house. The helmet will be available in stores to allow customers to observe Dior professional makeup artists at work in preparation for the parade. Much more than a digital innovation, the Dior Eyes helmet offers a real moment of emotion and a new in-store experience. This is an effective strategy, showing a fashion house that wants to respond to trends and modernize its communication. Thanks to its creation, Dior will be able to surprise its visitors/customers and extend the impact of its fashion show beyond the catwalk. Thus, the high-tech helmet serves to preserve the customer relationship, and with this innovative and unprecedented creation, Dior can mark its territory and position itself as an innovative educator.

Immersion is an essential component for luxury brands to create an ideal phygital experience. To do this, Batat (2019a) states that companies should incorporate six essential factors: atmospheric, functional, cognitive, human/social, symbolic, and identity (Table 11.1).

Table 11.1 Key factors of immersion in digital experience design

Atmospheric factors	These are linked to the site and include the technical elements related to the site's atmosphere and design (colors, sounds, type style, iconography, navigability, accessibility, speed of download, zoom quality, etc.)
Functional factors	These are related to the information needed to facilitate the purchase (information on the subjects, mode of delivery, price, functionality, etc.)
Human and social factors	These serve to establish links and make spaces for exchange between customers and the brand via virtual agents or between customers through discussion forums
Cognitive factors	These are related to the competence and expertise of the consumer in the use of the Internet. A user with high knowledge and a rich browsing experience will be more easily immersed in the virtual universe of the brand and will, therefore, live a satisfying digital experience that is both functional and emotional
Symbolic factors	These refer to the need of the individual to define a meaning to these online practices
Identity factors	These are linked to the identity quest process undertaken by the individual during his/her experiences of browsing and buying online on the different sites and platforms of the brand

SUMMARY

The phygital experience is part of hybrid luxury consumption practices that flourish thanks to the omnipresence of digital technologies. Thus, the characteristics of the phygital experience are not exclusively physical, nor fully digital. So, the question for luxury companies becomes, "What interest is there in luxury houses wishing to build on the customer experience in the phygital environment?" Creating a customer experience in a phygital environment is a winning strategy that allows companies in the luxury sector to ensure the reputation of their goods (products and services) while making them accessible to everyone on the Internet. By offering a rewarding phygital experience to its customers, the luxury company reinforces the feeling of quality and uniqueness of its products despite their dissemination and accessibility made possible by the Internet. This chapter emphasized the idea that luxury companies need to prioritize the phygital aspects of the customer experience in their strategies. It also pointed to the necessity to merge online and offline experiences in order to facilitate the buying and browsing processes, and thus assist and guide the customer/user throughout the consumption and/or purchase journey, from pre-purchase to after-sales service. The phygital component ultimately highlights luxury companies' need to innovate, rethink, and extend their stores to generate a memorable and efficient omnichannel experience; to gather and combine customer data to tailor the offer and service; to incorporate mobile devices to inform, instruct, and involve clients; and finally, to spread the luxury purchase experience across social networks and support users' connections with luxury brands.

CONCLUSION

This book is an analytical and practical guide that encompasses all aspects of the digital luxury experience. It is based on an up-to-date use of concepts and practices related to the digital transformation and the importance of the customer experience in the digital immersive and emotional era. The digital transformation brought about by the intensification of the use of digital technologies, the advent of a new consumer, the erosion of the borders between the real and the virtual worlds, and the ubiquity of smartphones are encouraging luxury brands to rethink their digital strategies and take a customer-centric approach that considers consumer experiences in a phygital environment characterized by a continuum of offline and online behaviors. These new behaviors have contributed to the emergence of new approaches in digital marketing in various luxury sectors (retail, hospitality, events, gastronomy, wellness and well-being, private banks, etc.) that compel companies to offer digital customer experiences which should fit with a consumer's needs at various levels: functional, emotional, hedonic, symbolic, relational, and experiential.

These digital luxury experiences contribute greatly to improving the quality of the online customer experience via the brand's site and social media as well as the real-world customer experience lived offline in shops, banks, hotels, restaurants, etc. However, with the evolution of digital technologies, connected objects, big data, and social networks, luxury companies are confronted with a huge problem concerning the creation of a digital luxury experience that is emotional, profitable, and effective. While the role of immersive and interactive technologies as a tool for creating the digital experience is confirmed every day, there are still many questions as to which elements are likely to make customers experience emotional digital experiences that are both meaningful and, above all, memorable, thus allowing the brand to build loyalty and create a sustainable competitive advantage. The digital luxury experience, therefore, must meet the needs of today's society, which has evolved considerably since the introduction of the Internet in the 1990s and the democratization of the use of digital technologies in everyday life. This book is intended for luxury professionals, startups, and engineers as well as marketing, communication, and digital practitioners who wonder about the future of e-commerce and the evolution of brands' websites and who would like to understand the potential of the digital experience for their company/brand while equipping themselves with practical guidelines for designing an effective and emotional customer experience with a continuum in the phygital environment.

REFERENCES

Abtan, O., Barton, C., Bonelli, F., Gurzki, H., Mei-Pochtler, A., Pianon, N., & Tsusaka, M. (2016). *Digital or die:* The choice for luxury brands. Retrieved October 20, 2017, from www.bcg.com/publications/2016/digital-or-die-choice-luxury-brands.aspx

Agar, M. (2011). Making sense of one other for another: Ethnography as translation. *Language & Communication, 31*(1), 38–47.

Andersen, P. H. (2005). Relationship marketing and brand involvement of professionals through web-enhanced brand communities: The case of Coloplast. *Industrial Marketing Management, 34*(3), 285–97.

Arnould, E. J., & Price, L. L. (1993). River magic: Extraordinary experience and the extended service encounter. *Journal of Consumer Research, 20*(1), 24–5.

Aron, A., & Aron, E. N. (1986). *Love as the expansion of self: Understanding attraction and satisfaction.* New York: Hemisphere.

Ault, S. (2014). Survey: YouTube stars more popular than mainstream celebs among U.S. teens. Retrieved October 20, 2017, from https://variety.com/2014/digital/news/survey-youtube-stars-more-popular-than-mainstream-celebs-among-u-s-teens-1201275245/

Azuma, R. T. (1997). A survey of augmented reality. *Presence: Teleoperators and Virtual Environments, 6*(4), 355–85.

Azuma, R., Baillot, Y., Behringer, R., Feiner, S., Julier, S., & MacIntyre, B. (2001). Recent advances in augmented reality. *IEEE Computer Graphics and Applications, 21*(6), 34–47.

Bagozzi, R. P., & Dholakia, U. M. (2006). Open source software user communities: A study of participation in Linux user groups. *Management Science, 52*(7), 1099–115.

Bain & Co. (2017). *Global personal luxury goods market returns to healthy growth, reaching a fresh high of $262 billion in 2017.* Retrieved October 25, 2017, from www.bain.com/about/media-center/press-releases/2017/press-release-2017-global-fall-luxury-market-study

Batat, W. (2019a). *Experiential marketing: Consumer behavior, customer experience, and the 7Es.* Abingdon: Routledge.

Batat, W. (2019b). *The new luxury experience: Creating the ultimate customer experience.* New York: Springer.

Bate, P., & Robert, G. (2007). Toward more user-centric OD. *The Journal of Applied Behavioral Science, 43*(1), 41–66.

Beauchemin, R. W. (2016). Augmenting education: Using augmented reality technologies to enhance teaching and learning. In D. Mentor (Ed.), *Handbook of research on mobile learning in contemporary classrooms.* pp. 160–80. Hershey, PA: IGI Global.

Bennett, A., & Royle, N. (1999). *An introduction to literature, criticism and theory.* Hemel Hempstead: Prentice-Hall.

Bitner, M. J. (1992). Servicescapes: The impact of physical surroundings on customers and employees. *Journal of Marketing, 56*(2), 57–71.

Bonnemaizon, A., & Batat, W. (2011). How competent are consumers? The case of the energy sector in France. *International Journal of Consumer Studies, 5*(34), 348–58.

Borowski, C. (2015, November 9). *What a great digital customer experience actually looks like.* Retrieved July 15, 2018, from https://hbr.org/2015/11/what-a-great-digital-customer-experience-actually-looks-like

Bourdieu, P. (1979). *La distinction: Critique sociale du jugement.* Paris: Éditions de Minuit.

Brewer, M. B. (1991). The social self: On being the same and different at the same time. *Personality and Social Psychology Bulletin, 17*(5), 475–82.

Brodie, R. J., Ilic, A., Juric, B., & Hollebeek, L. (2011). Consumer engagement in a virtual brand community: An exploratory analysis. *Journal of Service Research, 14*(3), 252–71.

Caillois, R. (1962). *Man, play, and games.* London: Thames and Hudson.

Campbell, J. (2008). *The hero with a thousand faces.* Novato, CA: New World Library.

Carmigniani, J., & Furht, B. (2011). Augmented reality: An overview. In B. Furht (Ed.), *Handbook of augmented reality.* pp. 3–46. New York: Springer.

Carù, A., & Cova, B. (2003). Revisiting consumption experience: A more humble but complete view of the concept. *Marketing Theory, 3*(2), 267–86.

Cassell, J., Sullivan, J., & Churchill, F. (2000). *Embodied conversational agents.* Cambridge, MA: MIT Press.

Castelli, A. T. (2016, February 22). The new revolution will be physical, not digital. Retrieved June 20, 2017, from http://adage.com/article/digitalnext/revolution-physical-digital/302734/

Catena, M., Remy, N., & Durand-Servoingt, B. (2015). Is luxury e-commerce nearing its tipping point? Retrieved February 25, 2018, from www.mckinsey.com/industries/consumer-packaged-goods/our-insights/is-luxury-ecommerce-nearing-its-tipping-point

Caudell, T. P., & Mizell, D. W. (1992). Augmented reality: An application of heads-up display technology to manual manufacturing processes. *Proceedings of the Twenty-Fifth Hawaii International Conference on System Sciences, 2,* 659–69.

Cavoukian, A., & Jonas, J. (2012, June 8). Privacy by design in the age of big data. Retrieved April 24, 2018, from https://jeffjonas.typepad.com/Privacy-by-Design-in-the-Era-of-Big-Data.pdf

Chaffey, D., & Ellis-Chadwick, F. (2012). *Digital marketing: Strategy, implementation and practice.* Harlow: Pearson.

Chang, H. H. (2010). Task-technology fit and user acceptance of online auction. *International Journal of Human-Computer Studies, 68*(1–2), 69–89.

Christensen, C. M. (1997). *The innovator's dilemma: When new technologies cause great firms to fail.* Boston: Harvard Business School Press.

Coll, S. (2013). Consumption as biopower: Governing bodies with loyalty cards. *Journal of Consumer Culture, 13*(3), 201–20.

Cova, B., & White, T. (2010). Counter-brand and alter-brand communities: The impact of Web 2.0 on tribal marketing approaches. *Journal of Marketing Management, 26*(3–4), 256–70.

Csikszentmihalyi, M. (1975). *Beyond boredom and anxiety.* San Francisco, CA: Jossey-Bass.

Csikszentmihalyi, M. (1990). Flow: The psychology of optimal experience. *Journal of Leisure Research, 24*(1), 93–4.

Da Silveira, G., Borenstein, D., & Fogliatto, F. S. (2001). Mass customization: Literature review and research directions. *International Journal of Production Economics, 72*(1), 1–13.

Dale, S. (2014). Gamification making work fun, or making fun of work? *Business Information Review, 31*(2), 82–90.

Dall'Olmo Riley, F., & Lacroix, C. (2003). Luxury branding on the Internet: Lost opportunity or impossibility? *Marketing Intelligence & Planning, 21*(2), 96–104.

Damala, A., Cubaud, P., Bationo, A., Houlier, P., & Marchal, I. (2008). Bridging the gap between the digital and the physical: Design and evaluation of a mobile augmented reality guide for the museum visit. In *Proceedings of the 3rd International Conference on Digital Interactive Media in Entertainment and Arts – DIMEA 08.* pp. 120–7.

Danziger, P. N. (2005). *Let them eat cake: Marketing luxury to the masses – as well as the classes.* New York: Kaplan Professional.

De Kerviler, G., & Audrezet, A. (2016). *Instagram and brand engagment: A preliminary study.* In *19th World Marketing Congress AMS*, Paris, France.

De Kerviler, G., & Demangeot, C. (2016). Authors of online reviews and their narrative voice – a qualitative study on Tripadvisor. In *45th EMAC Conference*, Oslo, Norway.

De Valck, K., Van Bruggen, G. H., & Wierenga, B. (2009). Virtual communities: A marketing perspective. *Decision Support Systems, 47*(3), 185–203.

Dehn, D. M., & Van Mulken, S. (2000). The impact of animated interface agents: A review of empirical research. *International Journal of Human-Computer Studies, 52*(1), 1–22.

Delort P. (2015). *Le big data.* Paris: PUF.

Denegri-Knott, J., & Molesworth, M. (2010). Concepts and practices of digital virtual consumption. *Consumption Markets & Culture, 13*(2), 109–32.

Deterding, S. (2012). Gamification: Designing for motivation. *Interactions, 19*(4), 14–17.

Deterding, S., Dixon, D., Khaled, R., & Nacke, L. (2014). Questionner les mises en forme ludiques du web: Gamification, ludification et ludicisation. *Sciences du Jeu, 2*, 15.

Dewar, B. (2013). Cultivating compassionate care. *Nursing Standard, 27*(34), 48–55.

Dewar, B., Mackay, R., Smith, S., Pullin, S., & Tocher, R. (2009). Use of emotional touchpoints as a method of tapping into the experience of receiving compassionate care in a hospital setting. *Journal of Research in Nursing, 15*(1), 29–41.

Dewey, J. (1938). *Experience and education.* Toronto: Collier-MacMillan.

DMR (2018, March 31). 20 important Foursquare stats. Retrieved March 15, 2018, from https://expandedramblings.com/index.php/by-the-numbers-interesting-foursquare-user-stats

Drell, L. (2014) The experience economy. The American Marketing Association. Retrieved October 4, 2017, from www.ama.org/publications/MarketingInsights/Pages/The-Experience-Economy

Dubois, B., & Laurent, G. (1996). Le luxe par delà les frontières: Une étude exploratoire dans douze pays. *Décisions Marketing, 9*, 35–43.

Dubois, B., Laurent, G., & Czellar, S. (2001). Consumer rapport to luxury: Analyzing complex and ambivalent attitudes. *Les Cahiers de Recherche du Groupe HEC, 736*, 1–56.

Feldon, D. F., & Kafai, Y. B. (2008). Mixed methods for mixed reality: Understanding users' avatar activities in virtual worlds. *Educational Technology Research and Development, 56*(5–6), 575–93.

Fields, B., Wilder, S., Bunch, J., & Newbold, R. (2008). *Millennial leaders: Success stories from today's most brilliant Generation Y leaders*. New York: Ingram Publishing Services.

Fitzsimmons, J. A. (1985). Consumer participation and productivity in service operations. *Interfaces, 15*(3), 60–7.

Gábor, D. (1992). Holography, 1948–1971. Nobel Lecture, December 11, 1971. In S. Lundqvist (Ed.), *Nobel Lectures, Physics 1971–1980*. Singapore: World Scientific Publishing.

Gartner. (2015a, November 10). Gartner says 6.4 billion connected "things" will be in use in 2016, up 30 percent from 2015. Retrieved September 8, 2016, from www.gartner.com/newsroom/id/3165317

Gartner. (2015b, September 29). 3D printer market sales will exceed $14.6 billion in 2019 – Pete Basiliere. Retrieved April 2018, from https://blogs.gartner.com/pete-basiliere/2015/09/29/3d-printer-market-sales-will-exceed-14-6-billion-in-2019/

Gartner. (2016, November 23). *Predicts 2017:* Artificial intelligence. Retrieved January 15, 2018, from www.gartner.com/doc/3519744/predicts—artificial-intelligence

Gartner. (2017a). Gartner says 8.4 billion connected "Things" will be in use in 2017, up 31 percent from 2016. Retrieved September 24, 2017, from www.gartner.com/en/newsroom/press-releases/2017-02-07-gartner-says-8-billion-connected-things-will-be-in-use-in-2017-up-31-percent-from-2016

Gartner. (2017b). The Gartner 2017 report on 3D printing. Retrieved August 20, 2018, from www.3dnatives.com/en/gartner-2017-3d-printing080820174/

Geerts, A., & Veg-Sala, N. (2011). How to manage the consistency of luxury brands with the internet communication? The importance of luxury brand values transfer. *The Global Journal of Business Research, 5*(5), 81–94.

Genvo, S. (2009). *Le jeu à son ère numérique: Comprendre et analyser les jeux vidéo*. Paris: L'Harmattan.

Geylani, T., Inman, J. J., & Hofstede, F. T. (2008). Image reinforcement or impairment: The effects of co-branding on attribute uncertainty. *Marketing Science, 27*(4), 730–44.

Goodrich, M. (2017). 3D printing: The greener choice. Retrieved October 15, 2018, from www.mtu.edu/news/stories/2013/october/3d-printing-greener-choice.html

Goulding, C. (2000). The museum environment and the visitor experience. *European Journal of Marketing, 34*(3/4), 261–78.

Greenson, R. R. (1960). Empathy and its vicissitudes. *The International Journal of Psychoanalysis, 41*, 418–24.

Hakulinen, L., Auvinen, T., & Korhonen, A. (2013, March 21–24). Empirical study on the effect of achievement badges in TRAKLA2 online learning environment. In *Learning and Teaching in Computing and Engineering (LaTiCE)*, Macau. pp. 47–54.

Hale, K. S., & Stanney, K. M. (2014). *Handbook of virtual environments: Design, implementation, and applications.* Boca Raton, FL: CRC Press.

Haller, M. (2006). *Emerging technologies of augmented reality: Interfaces and design.* Hershey, PA: IGI Global.

Hamari, J., & Koivisto, J. (2013). Social motivations to use gamification: An empirical study of gamifying exercise. In *ECIS 2013 – Proceedings of the 21st European Conference on Information Systems*, Association for Information Systems, Utrecht, The Netherlands.

Hamari, J., & Lehdonvirta, V. (2015). Game design as marketing: How game mechanics create demand for virtual goods. *International Journal of Business Science and Applied Management, 5*(1), 14–29.

Hamari, J., & Tuunanen, J. (2013). Player types: A meta-synthesis. *Transactions of the Digital Games Research Association, 1*(2), 29–53.

Headland, T. N., Pike, K. L., & Harris, M. (1990). *Emics and etics: The insider/outsider debate.* Newbury Park, CA: Sage.

Hewlett Packard. (2016). *Cyber risk report 2016.* Retrieved October 15, 2017, from www.thehaguesecuritydelta.com/media/com_hsd/report/57/document/4aa6-3786enw.pdf

Hoffman, D. L., & Novak, T. P. (1996). Marketing in hypermedia computer-mediated environments: Conceptual foundations. *Journal of Marketing, 60*(3), 50–68.

Hoffman, D. L., & Novak, T. P. (1997). A new marketing paradigm for electronic commerce. *The Information Society, 13*(1), 43–54.

Hoffman, D. L., & Novak, T. P. (2009). Flow online: Lessons learned and future prospects. *Journal of Interactive Marketing, 23*(1), 23–34.

Hoffman, D. L., & Novak, T. P. (2015). Emergent experience and the connected consumer in the smart home assemblage and the Internet of Things. Retrieved June 30, 2018, from http://ssrn.com/abstract=2648786

Hoffman, D. L., & Novak, T. P. (2018). Consumer and object experience in the Internet of Things: An assemblage theory approach. *Journal of Consumer Research, 44*(6), 1178–204.

Holbrook, M. B. (1994). The nature of customer value: An axiology of services in the consumption experience. In R. T. Rust & R. L. Oliver (Eds.), *Service quality: New directions in theory and practice*. pp. 21–71. Thousand Oaks, CA: Sage.

Holbrook, M. B. (1999). *Consumer value: A framework for analysis and research*. London: Routledge.

Holbrook, M. B., & Hirschman, E. C. (1982). The experiential aspects of consumption: Consumer fantasies, feelings, and fun. *Journal of Consumer Research, 9*(2), 132–40.

Holt, D. B. (2002). Why do brands cause trouble? A dialectical theory of consumer culture and branding. *Journal of Consumer Research, 29*(1), 70–90.

Holt, D. B. (2004). *How brands become icons: The principles of cultural branding*. Boston: Harvard Business School Press.

Holzwarth, M., Janiszewski, C., & Neumann, M. M. (2006). The influence of avatars on online consumer shopping behavior. *Journal of Marketing, 70*(4), 19–36.

Hostler, R. E., Yoon, V. Y., & Guimaraes, T. (2005). Assessing the impact of internet agent on end users' performance. *Decision Support Systems, 41*(1), 313–25.

Howard, J. A., & Sheth, J. N. (1969). *The theory of buyer behavior*. New York: Wiley.

Huang, S. I., & Lin, F. R. (2007). The design and evaluation of an intelligent sales agent for online persuasion and negotiation. *Electronic Commerce Research and Applications, 6*, 285–96.

Hunter, G. L., & Garnefeld, I. (2008). When does consumer empowerment lead to satisfied customers? Some mediating and moderating effects of the empowerment–satisfaction link. *Journal of Research for Consumers, 15*(1), 1–14.

Joachimsthaler, E., & Aaker, D. A. (1997). Building brands without mass media. *Harvard Business Review, 75*(1), 39–50.

Kapferer, J.-N. (2008). *The new strategic brand management: Creating and sustaining brand equity long term*. London: Kogan Page.

Kapferer, J-N., & Bastien, V. (2012). *The luxury strategy: Break the rules of marketing to build luxury brands*. 2nd edn. London: Kogan Page.

Kaplan, A. M., & Haenlein, M. (2010). Users of the world, unite! The challenges and opportunities of social media. *Business Horizons, 53*(1), 59–68.

Kasbi, Y. (2012). *Les serious games: Une révolution*. Paris: Edipro.

Kim, J., & Forsythe, S. (2007). Hedonic usage of product virtualization technologies in online apparel shopping. *International Journal of Retail & Distribution Management, 35*(6), 502–14.

Kleinginna, P. R., & Kleinginna, A. M. (1981). A categorized list of motivation definitions, with a suggestion for a consensual definition. *Motivation and Emotion, 5*(3), 263–91.

Kotler, P. (1986). *Principles of marketing*. Englewood Cliffs, NJ: Prentice-Hall.

Kotler, P., Kartajaya, H., & Setiawan, I. (2010). *Marketing 3.0: From products to customers to the human spirit*. Hoboken, NJ: John Wiley.

Kozinets, R. V. (1999). E-tribalized marketing? The strategic implications of virtual communities of consumption. *European Management Journal, 17*(3), 252–64.

Kozinets, R. V. (2010). *Netnography: Doing ethnographic research online*. London: Sage.

Kozinets, R. V. (2015). *Netnography: Redefined*. London: Sage.

Kozinets, R. V., De Valck, K., Wojnicki, A. C., & Wilner, S. J. (2010). Networked narratives: Understanding word-of-mouth marketing in online communities. *Journal of Marketing, 74*(2), 71–89.

Kretz, G., & De Valck, K. (2010). "Pixelize me!": Digital storytelling and the creation of archetypal myths through explicit and implicit self-brand association in fashion and luxury blogs. *Research in Consumer Behavior, 12*, 313–29.

Larbanet, C., & Ligier, B. (2010). *The internet use by the luxury industry: An interactive tool for a very demanding sector*. Saarbrucken: Lambert Academic Publishing.

Lemon, K. N., & Verhoef, P. C. (2016). Understanding customer experience throughout the customer journey. *Journal of Marketing, 80*(6), 69–96.

Levitt, T. (1969). *Innovation and marketing*. London: Pan.

Lim, S., & Reeves, B. (2010). Responses to interactive game characters controlled by a computer versus other players. *International Journal of Human-Computer Studies, 68*(1–2), 57–68.

Lipovetsky, G. (1983). *L'ere du vide. Essais sur l'individualisme contemporain*. Paris: Gallimard.

Manuri, F., & Sanna, A. (2016). A survey on applications of augmented reality. *Advances in Computer Science, 5*(1), 18–27.

Marwick, A. (2013). They're really profound women, they're entrepreneurs: Conceptions of authenticity in fashion blogging. In *7th International AIII Conference on Weblogs and Social Media*, Cambridge, Massachusetts, USA.

Mathwick, C., Malhotra, N. K., & Rigdon, E. (2002). The effect of dynamic retail experiences on experiential perceptions of value: An Internet and catalog comparison. *Journal of Retailing, 78*(1), 51–60.

Mathwick, C., Wiertz, C., & De Ruyter, K. (2008). Social capital production in a virtual P3 community. *Journal of Consumer Research, 34*(6), 832–49.

Mavrommati, I., & Kameas, A. (2003). The evolution of objects into hyper-objects: Will it be mostly harmless? *Personal and Ubiquitous Computing, 7*(3–4), 176–81.

McAlexander, J. H., Kim, S. K., & Roberts, S. D. (2003). Loyalty: The influences of satisfaction and brand community integration. *Journal of Marketing Theory and Practice, 11*(4), 1–17.

McAlexander, J. H., Schouten, J. W., & Koenig, H. F. (2002). Building brand community. *Journal of Marketing, 66*(1), 38–54.

McGoldrick, P. J., Kathleen, A., Keeling, F., & Beatty, S. (2008). A typology of roles for avatars in online retailing. *Journal of Marketing Management, 24*(3–4), 433–61.

McGonigal, J. (2011). *Reality is broken: Why games make us better and how they can change the world*. New York: Penguin Press.

McKinsey Global Institute. (2011). Big data: The next frontier for innovation, competition, and productivity. Retrieved May 2018, from www.mckinsey.com/business-functions/digital-mckinsey/our-insights/big-data-the-next-frontier-for-innovation

McLellan, H. (1996). Virtual realities. In D. H. Jonassen (Ed.), *Handbook of research for educational communications and technology*. pp. 457–87. New York: Macmillan.

Miller, D. (1991). Recent theories of social justice. *British Journal of Political Science, 21*(3), 371–91.

Mills, P. K., & Morris, J. H. (1986). Clients as "partial" employees of service organizations: Role development in client participation. *Academy of Management Review, 11*(10), 726–35.

Moulard, J. G., Garrity, C. P., & Rice, D. H. (2015). What makes a human brand authentic? Identifying the antecedents of celebrity authenticity. *Psychology & Marketing, 32*(2), 173–86.

Muniz, A. M., & O'Guinn, T. C. (2001). Brand community. *Journal of Consumer Research, 27*(4), 412–32.

Naylor, R. W., Lamberton, C. P., & West, P. M. (2012). Beyond the "like" button: The impact of mere virtual presence on brand evaluations and purchase intentions in social media settings. *Journal of Marketing, 76*(6), 105–20.

Ngai, E., Suk, F., & Lo, S. (2008). Development of an RFID-based sushi management system: The case of a conveyor-belt sushi restaurant. *International Journal of Production Economics, 112*(2), 630–45.

Nilsson, N. J. (1998). *Artificial intelligence: A new synthesis*. San Francisco, CA: Morgan Kaufmann.

Okonkwo, U. (2009). Sustaining the luxury brand on the Internet. *Journal of Brand Management, 16*(5–6), 302–10.

Okonkwo, U. (2010). *Luxury online: Styles, systems, strategies*. London: Palgrave Macmillan.

Olsson, T., Lagerstam, E., Kärkkäinen, T., & Väänänen-Vainio-Mattila, K. (2013). Expected user experience of mobile augmented reality services: A user study in the context of shopping centres. *Personal and Ubiquitous Computing, 17*(2), 287–304.

Ostergaard, P., Fitchett, J., & Jantzen, C. (2013). A critique of the ontology of consumer enchantment. *Journal of Consumer Behaviour, 12*(5), 337–44.

Pardun, C. J. (2013). *Advertising and society: An introduction*. Hoboken, NJ: Wiley-Blackwell.

Park, J., & Feinberg, R. (2010). E-formity: Consumer conformity behaviour in virtual communities. *Journal of Research in Interactive Marketing, 4*(3), 197–213.

Patton, M. Q. (2010). *Qualitative research and evaluation methods*. Thousand Oaks, CA: Sage.

Pine, B. J., II, & Gilmore, J. H. (1998). Welcome to the experience economy. *Harvard Business Review, 76*(4), 97–105.

Pine, B. J., & Gilmore, J. H. (1999). *The experience economy: Work is theatre and every business a stage*. Boston: Harvard Business School Press.

Pitkin, J. (2011). *The power of persuasion:* Effective use of influencer marketing. Retrieved June 20, 2017, from www.scribd.com/document/67287343/The-Power-of-Persuasion

Prahalad, C. K., & Ramaswamy, V. (2004a). *The future of competition: Co-creating unique value with customers*. Cambridge, MA: Harvard Business Review Press.

Prahalad, C. K., & Ramaswamy, V. (2004b). Co-creating unique value with customers. *Strategy & Leadership, 32*(3), 4–9.

Prensky, M. (2006). Listen to the natives. *Educational Leadership, 63*(4), 8–13.

Punj, G. (2012). Consumer decision making on the web: A theoretical analysis and research guidelines. *Psychology & Marketing, 29*(10), 791–803.

Punj, G., & Moore, R. (2009). Information search and consideration set formation in a web-based store environment. *Journal of Business Research, 62*(6), 644–50.

Qiu, L., & Benbasat, I. (2009). Evaluating anthropomorphic product recommendation agents: A social relationship perspective to designing information systems. *Journal of Management Information Systems, 25*(4), 145–81.

Ramaswamy, V. (2008). Co-creating value through customers' experiences: The Nike case. *Strategy & Leadership, 36*(5), 9–14.

Ratchford, B. T., Talukdar, D., & Lee, M. (2007). The impact of the Internet on consumers' use of information sources for automobiles: A re-inquiry. *Journal of Consumer Research, 34*(1), 111–19.

Reeves, B., & Read, J. L. (2009). *Total engagement: Using games and virtual worlds to change the way people work and businesses compete*. Boston: Harvard Business School Press.

Rheingold, H. (1993). *Virtual community: Homesteading on the electronic frontier*. Reading, MA: Addison-Wesley.

Rigby, D. K. (2014). Digital-physical mashups. *Harvard Business Review, 92*(9), 84–92.

Ritzer, G. (2004). *An introduction to McDonaldization. The McDonaldization of society*. Thousand Oaks, CA: Sage.

Ritzer, G. (2010). *Enchanting a disenchanted world: Revolutionizing the means of consumption*. 3rd edn. Thousand Oaks, CA: Sage.

Sarma, S., Brock, D. L., & Ashton, K. (2000). The networked physical world. Proposals for engineering the next generation of computing, commerce & automatic-identification. Retrieved November 2018, from https://pdfs.semanticscholar.org/88b4/a255082d91b-3c88261976c85a24f2f92c5c3.pdf

Schroeder, J. E., & Salzer-Mörling, M. (2006). *Brand culture*. London: Routledge.

Schumpeter, J. (1942). *Capitalism, socialism, and democracy*. New York: Harper & Brothers.

Schwartz, S. J. (2005). A new identity for identity research. *Journal of Adolescent Research, 20*(3), 293–308.

Semeraro, G., Andersen, V., Andersen, H., De Gemmis, M., & Lops, P. (2008). User profiling and virtual agents: A case study on e-commerce services. *Universal Access in the Information Society*, 7(3), 179–94.

Seno, D., & Lukas, B. A. (2007). The equity effect of product endorsement by celebrities: A conceptual framework from a co-branding perspective. *European Journal of Marketing*, 41(1–2), 121–34.

Seringhaus, F. H. R. (2005). Selling luxury brands online. *Journal of Internet Commerce*, 4(1), 1–25.

Shah, D., Rust, R. T., Parasuraman, A., Staelin, R., & Day, G. S. (2006). The path to customer centricity. *Journal of Service Research*, 9(2), 113–24.

Shang, R., Chen, Y., & Liao, H. (2006). The value of participation in virtual consumer communities on brand loyalty. *Internet Research*, 16(4), 398–418.

Sorofman, J. (2014). *Agenda overview for customer experience*, 2015. Retrieved June 20, 2017, from www.gartner.com/imagesrv/digital-marketing/pdfs/agenda-overview-for-customer.pdf

Spiggle, S., Nguyen, H. T., & Caravella, M. (2012). More than fit: Brand extension authenticity. *Journal of Marketing Research*, 49(6), 967–83.

Suh, K. S., Kim, H., & Suh, E. K. (2011). What if your avatar looks like you? Dual-congruity perspectives for avatar use. *MIS Quarterly*, 35(3), 711–29.

Sweeney, R. T. (2005). Reinventing library buildings and services for the millennial generation. *Library Administration & Management*, 19, 165–75.

Tăbușcă, A. (2014). Augmented reality – need, opportunity or fashion. *Romanian Economic Business Review*, 8(2), 307–15.

Tajfel, H., & Turner, J. C. (1979). An integrative theory of intergroup conflict. In W. G. Austin & S. Worchel (Eds.), *The social psychology of intergroup relations*. pp. 33–7. Monterey, CA: Brooks/Cole.

Tapscott, D. (1998). *Growing up digital: The rise of the Net generation*. New York: McGraw-Hill.

Taylor, T. L. (2002). Living digitally: Embodiment in virtual worlds. In R. Schroeder (Ed.), *The social life of avatars: Presence and interaction in shared virtual environments*. London: Springer.

The Economist (2012). The third industrial revolution. Retrieved September 15, 2018, from www.economist.com/leaders/2012/04/21/the-third-industrial-revolution

Thomas, M. J. (1997). Consumer market research: does it have validity? Some postmodern thoughts. *Marketing Intelligence & Planning*, 15(2), 54–9.

Tran, V., & Voyer, B. G. (2013). Teaching note: Chanel: should the icon of timeless fashion catch up with its time and sell its clothes online? *The Case Centre 12*, case 313-290-8

Turing, A. M. (1950). Computing machinery and intelligence. *Mind*, 59(36), 433–60.

Uluyol, Ç., & Şahin, S. (2016). Augmented reality: A new direction in education. In D. Choi, A. Dailey-Herbert, & J. Simmons Estes (Eds.), *Emerging tools and applications of virtual reality in education.* pp. 239–57. Hershey, PA: IGI Global.

Vargo, S. L., & Lusch, R. F. (2006). Service-dominant logic: What it is, what it is not, what it might be. In R. F. Lusch and S. L. Vargo (Eds.), *The service-dominant logic of marketing: Dialog, debate, and directions.* pp. 43–56. Armonk, NY: ME Sharpe.

Vargo, S. L., & Lusch, R. F. (2007). Service-dominant logic: Continuing the evolution. *Journal of the Academy of Marketing Science, 36*(1), 1–10.

Veblen, T. (1899). *The theory of the leisure class.* New York: Oxford University Press.

Venkatesh, A., Sherry, J. F., & Firat, A. F. (1993). Postmodernism and the marketing imaginary. *International Journal of Research in Marketing, 10*(3), 215–23.

Vigneron, F., & Johnson, L. W. (2004). Measuring perceptions of brand luxury. *Journal of Brand Management, 11*(6), 484–506.

Walther, B. K. (2005). Atomic actions – molecular experience. *Computers in Entertainment, 3*(3), 1–13.

Watkins, R. (2016). Conceptualising the ontology of digital consumption objects. In K. Diehl, C. Yoon, & M. N. Duluth (Eds.), *Advances in Consumer Research – North American Conference Proceedings*, Vol. *43*. pp. 275–76. Duluth, MN: Association for Consumer Research.

Whitson, J. R. (2013). Gaming the quantified self. *Surveillance & Society, 11*(1/2), 163–76.

Whitson, J. R., & Simon, B. (2014). Game studies meets surveillance studies at the edge of digital culture: An introduction to a special issue on surveillance, games and play. *Surveillance & Society, 12*(3), 309–19.

Zhou, F., Duh, H. B. L., & Billinghurst, M. (2008). *Trends in augmented reality tracking, interaction and display: A review of ten years of ISMAR.* In *Proceedings of the 7th IEEE/ACM International Symposium on Mixed and Augmented Reality*, Cambridge, UK. pp. 193–202.

Zichermann, G., & Cunningham, C. (2011). *Gamification by design: Implementing game mechanics in web and mobile apps.* Sebastopol, CA: O'Reilly Media.

INDEX

Note: Page numbers in *italic* type refer to figures and tables, page numbers in **bold** type refer to trend boxes.

Lightning Source UK Ltd.
Milton Keynes UK
UKHW032114070721
386794UK00002B/7